The American Foreign Policy Library

Edwin O. Reischauer, Editor

The United States and Burma

John F. Cady

Harvard University Press
Cambridge, Massachusetts, and London, England
1976

Library of Congress Cataloging in Publication Data

Cady, John Frank, 1901–
    The United States and Burma.
    (The American foreign policy library)
    Bibliography: p.
    Includes index.
    1. Burma—History. I. Title. II. Series.
DS528.5.C3   959.1   75–22256
ISBN 0–674–92320–0

Foreword by Edwin O. Reischauer

Burma has never loomed large in American eyes, nor is it likely to do so soon. Sandwiched between the vast populations of China and India, its thirty odd millions appear paltry by comparison. Even in the age of Western imperial conquest, it seemed no more than an appendix to British India. A vigorous American missionary movement failed to stir the same interest that a mixture of trade and missionaries aroused over China. Though only a generation ago the "Burma Road" as a back door to the war in the Pacific brought it brief fame abroad, since then its encircling mountains and still more its xenophobic aloofness have kept it free from both international frictions and wide attention.

Burma, however, is no inconsequential unit in a world fast being brought together by technology and economic interdependence. It is considerably more populous than Argentina or Canada and in geographic extent well over twice the size of the United Kingdom or West Germany. More important, it represents almost a classic example of many of the problems of the contemporary world.

In culture Burma is sharply distinct from all its neighbors, particularly its big ones in China and the Indian subcontinent, and it retains a strong sense of wariness and even hostility to all outsiders, both near and far. At the same time, it itself is an ethnic hodgepodge. The Burmans of the central plains are surrounded almost on all sides by various hill peoples who together make up around 30 percent of the population and have aspirations for greater independence that range from open revolt to quiet resentment. A mixture of concepts derived from modern industrialized countries together with a relatively low level of technical skills has produced the "Burmese Way to Socialism," which so far has proved merely a meandering trail to economic stagnation. The country's surface riches and potential for agricultural surpluses remain little developed and largely outside of world trade. Undoubtedly Burma will become more involved in time, though by what steps is not at all clear. In a sense, Burma is the traditional power vacuum that in the past has so often proven to be the low-pressure eye of the storm.

Burma is not a major segment of the world, but it is large enough to be significant, and it is certainly illustrative of many of the ills that beset our times. No one can say when or how or even if Burma in itself will prove important to Americans. But it is certainly a part of the world problems all men face, and as such deserves to be better known. We cannot afford to let it go on unnoticed, lying in the shadow of its two great neighbors and obscured by the screen of more spectacular events in nearby Southeast Asia.

Professor Cady has spent a lifetime of close contact with Burma, its history and culture, and its contemporary problems. Drawing on this long experience, he has written this comprehensive account of Burma's history and the culture and type of nation it has produced. This is a good starting point to learn more about this much too neglected portion of our world.

Contents

The United States and Burma

I The Setting and the People

Geography and Physical Features

The American public first became aware of the crucial strategic importance of Burma during World War II. The so-called Burma Road provided for several years the only available land route between the beleaguered National Chinese regime and the outside world. The Japanese armies invaded Burma in 1942 determined to close it off, and General Joseph Stilwell, commanding a largely Chinese army, fought for three years to reopen the link. The road had long been a commercial connection with Yunnan China, which imported oil seeds, salt, and cotton from Burma, but in wartime its strategic value overshadowed the commercial. The movement of men and materiel was helped, especially on the Burma side, by modern road and railway transportation facilities, which reached the Irrawaddy River route at Mandalay.

Topographical realities determine the strategic importance of Burma. The entire length of the Irrawaddy River is navigable to the Burmese city of Bhamo, near the China border. From the Burma side, the ancient Chinese entry route ran southeasterly from Bhamo and then north to the border cities of Namkham and Musé, located on the tributary Shweli River, which originates in China's Yunnan province. The commercial initiative in ancient Han times came from the China side, with caravans proceeding from the Yangtse valley to Kunming, thence to the important intermediary Nan Chao capital on Lake Tali, and finally across the formidable Mekong and Salween River gorges enroute to the upper waters of the Shweli. The route was repeatedly used for military purposes by Mongol, Ming, and Manchu armies from the later 1200s to the 1760s. Today, as throughout the long history of the region, Burma's central valley provides the only feasible ground communication link between China proper and the Bay of Bengal.

Even under the economically stagnant regime of General Ne Win's

"Way to Socialism," the country has not lost its strategic importance. Burma currently is a focal point of rivalry between expanding Soviet influence in southern Asia on both land and sea and China's continuing efforts to maintain its access to these same regions via the Burma corridor. China's political interests in Burma are hardly vital, but they are long-standing.

Burma's longtime association with neighboring India has been more important culturally than politically, and historic contacts have been mainly by sea. The mountainous boundary extends from coastal Chittagong northward, until it makes contact with the vast Himalayan range to the east of India's Brahmaputra Valley where it enters Tibet. The only feasible pass leading from Burma to India is via the rugged Chin Hills road leading to Manipur state. The mountains to the north of this opening reach at several points altitudes of more than two miles. Even more forbidding is Burma's watershed with Tibet and with adjacent portions of China's Yunnan Province.

In size comparable to Texas, the territory of Burma is politically divided into six constituent units: Burma proper, the Shan states, the Kachin state, the Chin Hills District, the Karen state, and Kayah, making up the Burma Union. The subordinate states are peripheral to the central valley region, which can be divided geographically into upper Burma, lower Burma, and the Tenasserim coastal region. The indigenous population is predominantly Mongoloid rather than Indian in ethnic origin. The country politically was never part of India except during the century of British rule.

Lower Burma proper contains three parallel watersheds. The Arakan Yoma range abuts the right bank of the lower Irrawaddy River. The less formidable Pegu Yoma run north and south above the delta between the Irrawaddy River and the smaller Sittang River. The eastern Yoma mark the edge of the Shan plateau east of the Sittang. To the west of the Arakan Yoma and along the Bay of Bengal coast lies the province of Arakan, which for many centuries constituted a political entity separate from Burma proper. Arakan's coasts are exposed to the full impact of the seasonal monsoon rains and the savage typhoons which are generated in the Bay of Bengal at the start of the rainy season in late May. Although occupied in part since ancient times by Tibetan (Pyu) people, Arakan was not conquered by the Burmans of Ava until the 1780s. Except for the port of Akyab in upper coastal Arakan, which became in early modern

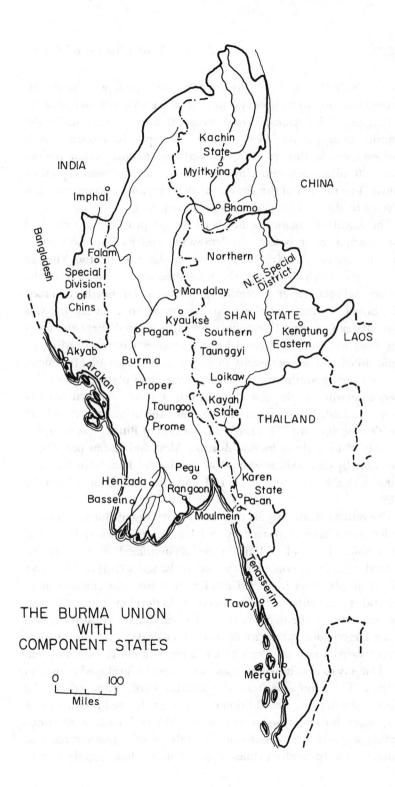

INDIA

CHINA

Bangladesh

Kachin
State
Myitkyina

Imphal

Bhamo

Falam

Northern

Special
Division
of
Chins

Mandalay

N.E. Special
District

SHAN   STATE

Kyauksè

Pagan

Southern

Kengtung

Eastern

LAOS

Akyab

Arakan

Burma

Taunggyi

Proper

Loikaw

Toungoo

Kayah
State

THAILAND

Prome

Pegu

Karen
State

Henzada

Rangoon

Bassein

Pa-an

Tenasserim

Moulmein

Tavoy

THE BURMA UNION
WITH
COMPONENT STATES

Mergui

0   100

Miles

times a valued source of surplus rice, the region was important
throughout most of its history only as a buffer area with neighboring
Chittagong. The Arakan Yoma range is also geographically significant for upper Burma because it intercepts the moisture-laden
monsoon winds, thus creating an oval-shaped rain-shadow region,
some 160 miles long, centering near the ancient Burman capital of
Pagan. The rainfall of the Irrawaddy delta region, by comparison, is
affected by the Arakan mountains only marginally.

The Kachin highlands of northern Burma provide the sources of
the principal river system, the Irrawaddy and its Chindwin tributary. Bordering the Kachin country on the east lie the Yunnan
mountains, which constitute the watershed separating it from the
narrow Salween River system, originating in far northern Tibet.
The broad Yunnan massif extends southward to make up the vast
Shan plateau region. The plateau averages around three thousand
feet elevation, and is bisected by the Salween River, threading its
rapids-filled course southward to empty at the port of Moulmein.

A narrowing southward extension of the Shan plateau mountains
veers somewhat to the east to constitute Burma's modern borders
with Thailand. The divide continues down the isthmian area behind
the Tenasserim coast. This peninsular region of Burma was occupied
in early historic times by non-Burman Mon and Karen peoples; it
was ruled by Cambodians after 1050, and by the Thai from the early
1300s until the late 1500s, while full Burman control dated from the
1760s.

The central Irrawaddy-Sittang valley heartland of Burma is under-
girded by an impervious tertiary rock base, much of which is covered
by a thick layer of sedimentation accumulated over centuries.
Coastal delta areas bordering the Bay of Bengal's Gulf of Martaban
receive ample water for wet-rice cultivation from the summer monsoon rains and controlled river channels. As developed under British
colonial control, the delta expanse of lower Burma constituted one
of the largest contiguous rice fields in the world. In the rain-shadow
areas located above the Pegu Yoma range, rice cultivation was confined largely to riverine borders and to variously developed irrigation
systems. Three important royal granaries were developed on the
edges of the dry zone. In addition to its present limited production of
rice, upper Burma grows quantities of millet and maize in the unir-
rigated sections, plus sessamum oil seeds, short staple cotton, and
ground nuts. In modern times, upper Burma's food supply had to

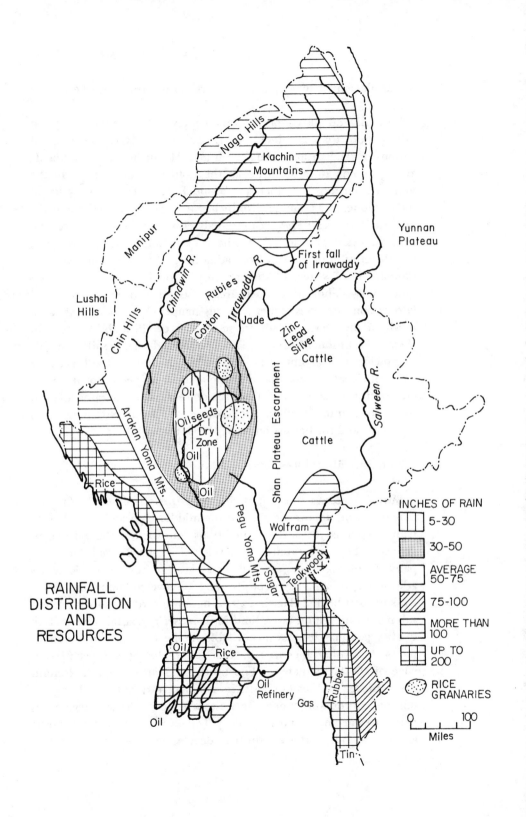

RAINFALL
DISTRIBUTION
AND
RESOURCES

Yunnan Plateau

Naga Hills
Kachin Mountains
Manipur
First fall of Irrawaddy
Lushai Hills
Chin Hills
Chindwin R.
Rubies
Irrawaddy R.
Cotton
Jade
Zinc Lead Silver
Cattle
Arakan Yoma Mts.
Oil
Oilseeds
Dry Zone
Oil
Cattle
Salween R.
Shan Plateau Escarpment
Rice
Oil
Wolfram
Pegu Yoma Mts.
Sugar
Teakwood
Oil
Rice
Oil Refinery
Gas
Rubber
Oil
Tin

INCHES OF RAIN

5-30

30-50

AVERAGE
50-75

75-100

MORE THAN
100

UP TO
200

RICE
GRANARIES

0   100
Miles

be supplemented by shipments of rice northward from the coastal areas.

Rainfall and soil resources vary widely. The summer monsoon brings more than 200 inches of rain to the fully exposed coastal regions of Arakan and Tenasserim and 115 inches in the delta. It averages some 40 to 80 inches in the Shan plateau (heavier in the southern portions) ; 33 inches at Mandalay at the northern edge of the dry zone, and a meager five inches at Pagan, at the center of the rain shadow area. The accumulated sedimentation in the central river valleys is productively fertile if extra water can be provided, but the erosion of top soil from adjacent highland regions, where a slash-and-burn system of shifting cultivation is followed, has been disastrously debilitating. Such areas also suffer from leaching and laterization processes under varying temperature conditions, as a result of the downward drainage of iron or silica soil content in chemical solution. Much of the leached upland surface soil is capable of growing little except coarse grass, while the laterized soils at lower levels of elevation can produce little apart from deep rooted timber growth. Burma experiences three seasons annually: the rains that fall from June into October, the cool season from November into February, and the hot season from March through May.

Non-Agricultural Resources

Burma possesses substantial resources in both oil and minerals. The oldest oil deposits located in the middle Irrawaddy valley were being exploited by surface operations long before the Europeans arrived. They were extensively developed by the Burmah Oil Company in colonial times, and currently are far from spent. Recently additional oil and gas deposits were discovered along the lower Arakan coast behind Bassein extending southward offshore along the submerged mountain range, and in Tenasserim coastal waters. High quality jade has long been available in the Kachin country far to the north, while rubies are still to be found along the upper western edge of the Shan plateau. The northern Shan states also contain silver, nickel, and lead deposits in commercial quantities. Tungsten mining is profitable along the western edge of the southern Shan plateau escarpment and in middle Tenasserim, where tin deposits are also found. Burma's industrial development potential is otherwise severely limited by the lack of high-grade coal and iron ore supplies.

Non-mineral resources include valuable timber stands along both slopes of the lower Salween River valley and in the Shan plateau areas adjacent to the Sittang River. Teakwood constitutes an estimated 20 percent of the total timber stand and has long been one of Burma's leading items of export. The principal saw mills are located near the months of the Salween and Sittang rivers, down which the log rafts are floated. The Arakan Yoma teak resources are less easily accessible. The most valuable animal resources are oxen and water buffalo, useful for plowing and land transportation. Many of the oxen are bred in the Shan states area and driven to markets in the central valley. Trained elephants handle most of the felled timber.

Modern transportation developed during colonial times of the late nineteenth century. Steamers on the Irrawaddy River proceeded upstream as far as Bhamo, near the entry of the China trade route. British-developed railway lines extended from the port of Rangoon in all directions. One branch ran eastward to Moulmein and thence southward down the Tenasserim coast. Another proceeded part-way up the Irrawaddy Valley. The main line ran northward up the Sittang valley to Mandalay, with two side spurs to the east penetrating the southern and northern Shan states respectively and a third going westward to the oil fields. A final railway projection proceeded west of the upper Irrawaddy and northward as far as the capital of the Kachin state. Since World War II air transportation radiates in all directions from the central airport near Rangoon.

The Principal Peoples of Burma

The 70 percent Burmese-speaking majority of the country's twenty-seven million total population, concentrated largely in the central valley area, are descendants of peoples who once lived in the eastern regions of Tibet. The first Tibeto-Burman immigrants, known as the Pyu people, were present in lower Burma as early as the third or fourth century A.D. The Burmans proper migrated to the central valley in the ninth century, coming by way of the independent Lo Lo-ruled state (also Tibetan) of Nan Chao, with its capital at Lake Tali in western Yunnan province of China. The newly arrived Burmans conquered the surviving Pyu peoples in the

north, along with the Mon creators of the several central area
granaries. Around 1050 A.D., the Pagan Burmans also took over
the Mon territories in the south. Later migrations of Tibeto-Burman
peoples included the Kachin and Lisu tribesmen who still inhabit
the mountains of upper Burma and adjacent China border areas.
The variegated Chin tribesmen occupying the India border hills are
also Mongoloid, but are less easy to classify ethnically.

Most of the 330,000 Kachin tribesmen who were enumerated in
the 1931 census spoke the Jingpaw language, but seven or eight other
Kachin languages were identified. Many of the more accessible valley
areas in the Kachin country were already occupied by Burman and
Shan cultivators before the Kachins arrived. These older resident
groups probably today constitute a majority of the population of the
Kachin state. Those Kachins who elected to move into the valleys
adjacent to the Shans and Burmans were assimilated culturally, but
most of the tribesmen preferred the cooler and less constricted mountain elevations. The Kachins live by hillside cultivation, by opium
poppy production, and by banditry. Because present-day Burma is
so short of consumer goods, Kachin opium is currently finding its
way to world markets via northern Thailand and Loas, where such
needed goods are available. Indigenous governmental institutions
among the Kachins were rudimentary, with petty chieftains of
patrilineal lines functioning as local leaders. The hill population
has been perennially subordinate, politically and economically, to
the more productive valley dwellers, but social assimilation has been
proceeding at a slow pace. The educated minority of Kachins of the
current century have been Christian rather than Buddhist, and the
Kachin population as a whole, since 1962, has been in rebellion
against Rangoon.

The Shan peoples of northern Burma and the eastern plateau
region are kinsmen of the northern Tai. Their exercise of economic
and political control over the vast area of the plateau is attributable
to their wide tolerance of minority tribal rights and to their own
superior political and ethnic cohesion and long occupancy of the
more productive areas. The Shans moved into eastern Burma several
centuries after the main Burman invasion in the ninth century.
Many Shans had previously been subjects of the Nan Chao kingdom
of the Lo Lo, which was finally destroyed by Kublai Khan's armies in
1253. The Shans developed their own writing system in late Pagan
times (twelfth and thirteenth centuries), using the Burmese script.

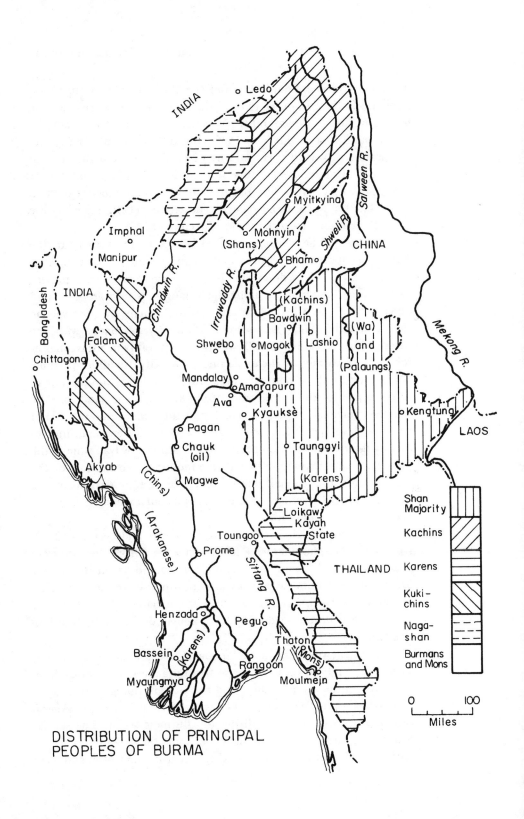

INDIA

o Ledo

Imphal

Manipur

Bangladesh

INDIA

Chittagong

Falam o

Akyab

(Chins)

(Arakanese)

Chindwin R.

Irrawaddy R.

o Myitkyina

Mohnyin
(Shans)

o Bham o

(Kachins)

Bawdwin

Shwebo   o Mogok

Mandalay o

Amarapura

Ava

o Kyauksè

o Pagan

Chauk
(oil)

Magwe

Shweli R.

CHINA

(Wa)
and
(Palaungs)

Lashio

Salween R.

Mekong R.

o Kengtung

LAOS

Taunggyi

(Karens)

Loikaw
Kayah
State

Toungoo o

o Prome

Sittang R.

THAILAND

Henzada o

Pegu o

Bassein   (Karens)

Myaungmya o

Thaton

(Mons)

o Rangoon

Moulmein

Shan
Majority

Kachins

Karens

Kuki-
chins

Naga-
shan

Burmans
and Mons

0   100

Miles

DISTRIBUTION OF PRINCIPAL
PEOPLES OF BURMA

They also learned Buddhism from the Burmans and Mons. Relatively uncivilized Shan tribesmen (the Mohnyins) later crossed into northern Burma proper and threatened the older centers of population around Ava in the early 1500s. Burma's Shans can today communicate orally with their cousins in north Thailand, but not in writing. They numbered around one million at the time of the 1931 census, but they may be approaching double that number at present. They, like the Kachins, have been generally in rebellion against the Rangoon authorities since the Ne Win coup of 1962.

The most numerous ethnic minority group in Burma are the Karens, composed of two principal language communities, the Pwo and Sgaw, plus a half dozen smaller groupings. Karens were present in the lower Shan plateau, along the Sittang-Salween watershed, and down into Tenasserim before the Tibeto-Burmans ever arrived on the Irrawaddy. The Pwos were traditionally associated with the Mons in the coastal region of lower Burma, possibly in a slave-master relationship. Many of them became nominally Buddhist in time. The Sgaws lived in mountain areas further inland, fanning out in recent centuries along both sides of the Sittang Valley and into the western portions of the Irrawaddy delta, where several Karen colonies developed. The less aggressive Bwe Karens continue to occupy their traditional homeland in the Karenni-Kayah state of the present Burma Union, located in the mountains to the east of the mid-Sittang valley. A half dozen other related Karen groups reside in the southern portions of the Shan plateau extending eastward across the Thailand border.

Partly because of their characteristic timidity and deep-seated distrust of the Burman majority, few Karens apart from the Pwo were ever attracted to Buddhism. The Christianized elements, largely Sgaw, currently number possibly a half million of the three million Karen total. Christian groups provide virtually all of the more progressive educated leadership. The remainder are largely primitive animists.

The several distinct Karen languages are all monosyllabic but vary widely in both vocabulary and tonal practices. They range from five tones in the south to three and two only in the Shan state area. The Pwo and the Sgaw languages were reduced to writing by American Baptist missionaries, utilizing the Burmese script. The several Karen languages appear to have been modified considerably by borrowings in both vocabulary and syntax from their Mon and Shan neighbors. Karen groups differed among themselves, but all shared their distrust of Burman neighbors. The Karens opposed British withdrawal after World War II, and elements among them have rebelled at various times since 1949.

The once ruling Mon inhabitants of lower Burma, who entered the region from the north several centuries B.C., have been virtually absorbed by the Burmans over the last two hundred years. Early Mon settlers in the interior of Burma developed the original irrigation facilities at Kyauksè and Minbu, but the center of their power was in coastal Burma to the east of the Irrawaddy delta. They established early seaborne contacts, both commercial and cultural, with India. The Burma Mons were long associated politically and culturally with the extensive kindred settlements in the Chao Phraya valley of modern Thailand, centering at Lopburi in the south and Lamphun, near Chiengmai, in the north. This three-sided Mon confederacy was disrupted by the conquering Cambodians in the eleventh century, leaving the Burma Mons with alternative capitals at Pegu and Thaton to face the rival Pagan Burmans. Once conquered by Pagan, the Mons became the tutors of the politically dominant Burmans in literature, religion, architecture, and government. Mon-speaking peoples can still be found along Burma's far northeastern borders among the Palaung, Lawa, and Wa tribesmen, who apparently ran aground in these areas along ago enroute southward from the original Mon homeland in south China.

Burma's prewar population also included more than a million immigrant Indians (mainly lower caste Tamils, Telegus, Oriyas, and Bengalis). They were brought over under British colonial auspices for economic development reasons. Approximately half of Burma's Indian population fled to India during the course of the Japanese conquest, and many of those who returned after the war have recently been obliged to leave. The present Indian population of Burma is less than half the prewar figure. With the exception of immigrants to Akyab from the Chittagong Muslim region of Bangladesh, Burma's Indian residents are mainly Hindus. All of them assimilate very slowly, and Indians generally have been made particularly unwelcome in independent Burma.

By contrast, the Chinese minority in Burma has more than doubled since the end of World War II. They numbered around 200,000 in 1941 and are now estimated at a half million. They are more easily assimilated ethnically than are the Indians, despite

striking cultural differences with the Burmans. Lower Burma's
Chinese residents usually arrived via Malaysia, from ancestral homes
along the south China coast. Along the northern Shan state borders
many Chinese settlers and several thousand political refugees have
moved across the line into Burma since the end of the war and the
advent of the People's Republic of China in 1950. 20,000 Eurasians
complete the confused medley of Burma's population. None of the
minority groups are in a position to challenge the majority Burman
group, who set the character of the nation.

Social and Cultural Traditions

Burma is still a country of villages, some 50,000 of them. Urban
areas have multiplied in population since World War II, due to
wartime disruption of cultivation routines and postwar disorders
throughout much of the countryside, but the population in general
continues rural in character. Villagers customarily live in bamboo
houses elevated on stilts and covered with thatch roofs. Government-
approved village headmen are assisted in the performance of their
manifold duties by influential elders possessing prestige (*pon*). The
elders formulate local policies and see to the enforcement of law.
Village discipline was traditionally maintained in precolonial times
by excluding offending individuals from access to communally
regulated land and other local facilities.

Clusters of adjacent villages usually maintain a Buddhist monastery, which is supported by the daily alms of the householders and
functions as a place of worship and center for elementary educational
training for the village youth. The head monk is accorded "great
glory" and prestige (hence his designation as *pongyi*). He maintains
discipline within the pagoda precincts, and supervises the operation
of the elementary schools (*kyaung*), as well as the more serious training of the neophyte *Ko-yin* candidates for the monkhood. Approximately half of Burman youth traditionally attained a reasonable degree of literacy and elementary acquaintance with the Buddhist
scriptures in the monastery schools, but the percentage was much
lower among the excluded girls. Burmese women nevertheless enjoy
full equality in property ownership and tend to dominate domestic
affairs. The wife actually controls the family purse-strings, supervises
buying and selling (including the operation of bazaar stalls), assists
in planting and harvesting routines, and runs the household gen-

erally. Women could, of course, hope to be born as men in the next transmigration, while making the best of their current existence in a very practical fashion.

Pagoda festivals, which are scheduled during the off-season for cultivators (after the rice planting and prior to the harvest), constitute the peak of the year's social activities. Popular dramatic performances (called *pwes*) depict traditional episodes from the Hindu classics (Rama and Sita legends) with many local adaptations. The performances sometimes continue throughout the night. The principal entertainers are the clown actors posted on the edge of the stage, who maintain a humorously spontaneous repartee with both actors and audience. Movies vie in popularity with pwes in recent decades.

Burmese music is based on a five-tone scale, with no semitones, while the orchestras include stringed instruments, xylophones, and drums. Burman craftsmanship is particularly adept at producing art objects in wood and ivory carving and conventionally decorated lacquerware. Pagoda trustees and wealthy donors still expend substantial sums in pagoda construction and maintenance; major shrines such as Rangoon's Shwe Dagon have been covered with multiple layers of gold leaf.

Burmans are a self-respecting people, assertive rather than docile, capable of intense anger and violence when provoked, but generally good-humored and relaxed. The typical Burman possesses a lively sense of humor, is fond of sports and gambling, and is not easily taken in or deceived.

Religion

Buddhism functions at several clearly identifiable levels. The upper two are more strictly Buddhist; the lower two are largely indigenous in character. After the collapse of Burma's monarchical system in the 1880s, the disciplinary structure of the Buddhist hierarchy progressively disintegrated. Among the scripturally trained pongyis and *Sayadaws* (royal teachers) who serve as heads of pagoda establishments, Buddhism is concerned with the theoretical search for Nibbana (or Nirvana), or an escape from the endless wheel of existences through union with the ultimate reality. Relatively few aspire to such objectives. The great majority of Buddhists remains on the secondary level, which focuses on the more feasible goal of

accumulating merit (*kutho*) in the present as a means of enhancing
one's prospects in future rebirths. Here the Indian principle of
Karma (the Law of Deeds) is operative. Wealthy merit seekers contribute to the needs of the monks and to pagoda construction and
maintenance, but all Buddhists are exhorted to conquer material
and physical desire and to follow the eightfold path of righteous living. In postwar times, the definition of meritorious activity has been
expanded, somewhat paradoxically, to include contributions to
material economic development in the national interest. Under the
Theravada system of Buddhist practice, all persons seeking merit
must acquire it on their own, with no possibility of any vicarious
contribution by outsiders, as is permissible within the Mahayana
(Greater Vehicle) Buddhist pattern of China. Nearly all of the
Burman and Shan populations are Buddhist; some 75 to 80 percent
of the population.

The third level of Burmese religion includes methods of protecting life, health, and material interests generally through prescribed
rituals addressed to the spirit world. Religious activities frequently
involve the use of magical talismans, the observance of calendrical
rites on appropriate occasions, and are often connected with astrological considerations and numerology. Spirits associated with villages or residence locations, or with natural sites such as lakes,
streams, mountains, or gnarled trees must be placated from time to
time. Burman traditions also identify a special pantheon of 37 per-
sonalized vagrant *nat* spirits. The most important of them allegedly
occupy shrines on the higher slopes of Mount Popa, an isolated
volcanic peak located in central Burma near Pagan. The several
persons whose spirits became vagrant share in common the experience of violent deaths, with the apparent result that they somehow
missed out on the normal cycle of transmigration. They include, for
example, a slain brother-sister couple, whose particular shrine on
Mount Popa became the object of annual pilgrimage. Some spirits
were adjudged to be vindictive and predatory, such as certain frustrated women who had died in childbirth and who thereafter undertook to make good their loss by taking away the spirits of newborn
babies. Thus heavy infant mortality, intestinal disorders, and other
tragic personal experiences contribute much to popular concern to
propitiate the special spirit pantheon.

A fourth and final level of Burmese religion reflects the long surviving faith in the millennial tradition, involving catastrophic or

arbitrary interventions of a cosmic character. In the context of this belief, one can only adjust to events rather than undertake to control them.

Taken in their entirety, Burmese religious practices cover virtually all the vicissitudes of life. The traditional ritual forms tend to persist within the differing theoretical assumptions. Thus Christian Karen cultivators continue to observe the traditional spirit-directed planting and harvesting rites, just as Americans still celebrate Thanksgiving on Thursday, in the Scandinavian tradition. Religion in Burma is something more than a Buddhist veneer over an animist substratum, as is sometimes asserted. The disparate plural aspects of the faith can be identified theoretically, while recognizing at the same time that, in practice, they are closely amalgamated to deal with various aspects of the human experience from its joyful or tragic moments to its bewildering and mysterious aspects.

Until monarchy was eliminated in 1886, kingly authority was substantially buttressed by religious sanctions. Ritual expressions of divinity were borrowed from Indian lore, such as the royal palace-replica of Mount Meru, the mythical abode of the gods, the sacred scepter and crown, and the ministrations of Brahman priests at court. It was also assumed that elevation to kingship involved the operation of Karma derived from the incumbent's deeds in a previous incarnation. Burmese kings frequently posed as avatars of Vishnu, or as emerging Buddhas. But governments generally were distrusted, often being characterized as one of the four scourges to be endured, along with flood, fire, and malevolent persons. Orthodox Burmese Buddhism rejected the Emergent Buddha (Bodhisattva) tradition. Even so, most Burmese villagers today still look forward to the appearance of the righteous king, who will exercise authority and justice according to the Buddhist ethic of right conduct.

Secular Aspects of National Identity

Within Burmese tradition, democratic sanctions for governmental authority are largely meaningless. Government's claims that it is really concerned about improving material standards of living or even the revival of the Buddhist faith have been heavily discounted. General Ne Win's "Burmese Way to Socialism," for example, involving direct governmental intervention in the economic spheres, tends in reality to hamper rather than to assist the average Burman to earn a decent livelihood. The Marxian ideology, involving the struggle of the workers and peasants against capitalist exploiters, is even more meaningless in the Burmese context. Its application currently involves the impoverishment of the entire nation for the benefit of a ruling military caste and its associates.

The Burmese concept of national identity includes positive as well as negative elements. Burmans had developed, prior to the British-Indian conquest in the nineteenth century, a proud military tradition. Historically, they had thoroughly conquered their Shan neighbors to the north and east and the Mons to the south. In the latter half of the 1500s and the 1700s, Burman armies overran Siam and Laos, culminating in the complete destruction of Ayuthia in 1767. Except for the incursions of Kublai Khan's armies in the 1280s, the armies of Burma have successfully repelled all Chinese invasions via Yunnan. Burmese forces were preparing to invade British Bengal in the middle 1820s prior to the outbreak of the disastrous Anglo-Burman war in 1825. The Burman nation traditionally was capable, under vigorous leadership and over a limited period of time, of demonstrating terrific power. Invaded peoples experienced repeatedly their uninhibited capacity for violence. A century of colonial domination, imposed by Indian troops and later enforced by British-trained Karen and Kachin regiments, virtually destroyed Burma's militant identity. But the population's deep-seated assumption of prideful superiority still persists and will continue to seek expression.

The military dictatorship under which the Burmese people have suffered since 1962 is related to the problem of national integrity. General Ne Win's takeover in 1962 was motivated in large measure by Burman concern that the subordinate portions of the Burma Union, particularly the Shan, the Kachin, and the Karen states, and possibly even the Mons and Arakanese, might actually break away under the permissive policies pursued by Premier Nu's government. The integrity of the union and Burman determination to maintain control were allegedly at stake. The anti-foreign exclusiveness demonstrated by the Ne Win government was designed in part to rid the country of western and Indian interference. It also reflected widespread popular concern that the country must not again, as had happened in the early forties and as Indochina has experienced in more recent times, become a theater of world conflict. When the Burmans themselves, including elements of the army, become sufficiently tired of exploitative dictatorship, when world turmoil begins to subside, and when rebellious minorities can be reconciled with eventual Burman control, a turn for the better can be envisioned. Burma possesses adequate endowments in natural resources, manpower, and intelligence to assume its appropriate role in the world community.

The Scanty American Awareness

As a longtime integral part of British India, Burma was little known to Americans prior to World War II. It was a source of elephants, teakwood, and rice, with mining resources which had attracted Herbert Hoover's engineering services prior to World War I. Missionary Baptist groups had heard about Adoniram and Ann Judson, and many had read about Dr. Gordon Seagrave, the "Burma Surgeon." Judson College had become after 1920 part of the newly developed Rangoon University, with an attractive campus built with Rockefeller Foundation assistance.

After 1939 the Burma Road got into the press. Students of the Burma military campaign learned something about Joseph Stilwell as commander of the Chinese forces, fighting first to defend Burma and then to reopen access from northeast India to Kunming and Chungking. An American airforce unit participated actively in the expulsion of the invading Japanese from India in 1944–1945, and carried on an airlift over the Burma "hump" to Chungking. "Merrill's Marauders" were immortalized to the readers of Charlton Ogburn's moving monograph.

Postwar Burma was nevertheless regarded in Washington as a British-Indian responsibility and a matter of little or no concern to the United States. Judson College was absorbed into Rangoon University, and American missionaries returning after the war were less than welcome among the Buddhist Burman majority. This was especially true after a portion of the Karen Christian community became involved in the rebellion of 1948–1951. Official American concern did not develop until after the communists triumphed in China in 1949, and in consequence Yunnan refugees began to flee into the easternmost Shan states. The misconceived secretive promotion of C.I.A.-sponsored airlift aid from Taiwan to Nationalist

Chinese groups along the Burma border eventually poisoned American relations with Burma by 1953, creating an atomsphere of distrust which virtually nullified thereafter American influence in Rangoon. American economic advisers operating independently during the middle fifties on Burma's invitation, were expelled by the Ne Win government in 1958. All missionary personnel were obliged to leave by the middle of the 1960s. The concentrations of Kuomintang refugees, located in Burma's easternmost state of Kengtung near the Thailand border, became a main source of expanding opium and heroin production after 1953.

Under Ne Win's dictatorial control, Burma reverted to its traditional anti-foreign posture, while the self-appointed revolutionary council embarked on its own "Way" to a socialist welfare state. Organizationally, Ne Win's government was patterned on Eastern European practices; ideologically it borrowed from the People's Republic of China. To most Americans Burma has remained an enigma. It is of current interest primarily as an area of Asian rivalry between Soviet and Chinese communist influence. Here as elsewhere in eastern Asia, it is important that interested Americans learn to understand the emerging nation as it struggles with formidable problems of governmental patterns, economic development, and international relations.

II Origin and Consolidation of Pagan

Early Population and Cultural Orientation

History is concerned with salient events of the past and the accomplishments of national leadership, but also with the long-term emergence of identity concepts and political traditions. National character develops from shared experiences, from a common awareness which finds articulate expression in literature and art, in religious symbolism, and in governmental institutions. One of the relevant questions that emerges with respect to Burma is why the illiterate Tibeto-Burman tribesmen who reached the Irrawaddy valley around 840 A.D. eventually put their characteristic stamp on the country, rather than the more intelligent Mons, who preceded them by more than half a millennium, or the Shans, who arrived some 300 years after the Burmans.

One causal factor was that Burma's Mon inhabitants constituted only one fragment of the larger ethnic group which settled mainly to the east of Burma in the Chao Phraya valley of Siam. The main body branched into the Dvaravati Mons who developed cultural centers at Nakorn Pathom and Lopburi in the south, and the Haripunjaya Mons (near modern Chiengmai) who occupied the northern extensions of the valley. The two groups succumbed in the early eleventh century to the conquering Cambodians, and the lower Burma Mons were spared the same fate only by the timely intervention of the Pagan Burmans in 1050.

The ensuing 240 years of Burma's Pagan empire produced a succession of able leaders, who were not only conquerors and statesmen, but also patrons of learning, religion, and architecture. Pagan Burma borrowed much from the Indianized culture of the conquered Mons, but also learned Theravada Buddhism from Ceylon and borrowed from Vishnu traditions of India. Under vigorous leadership, Pagan became in time a creative expression of the Burman spirit. Its revered cultural reputation long survived the em-

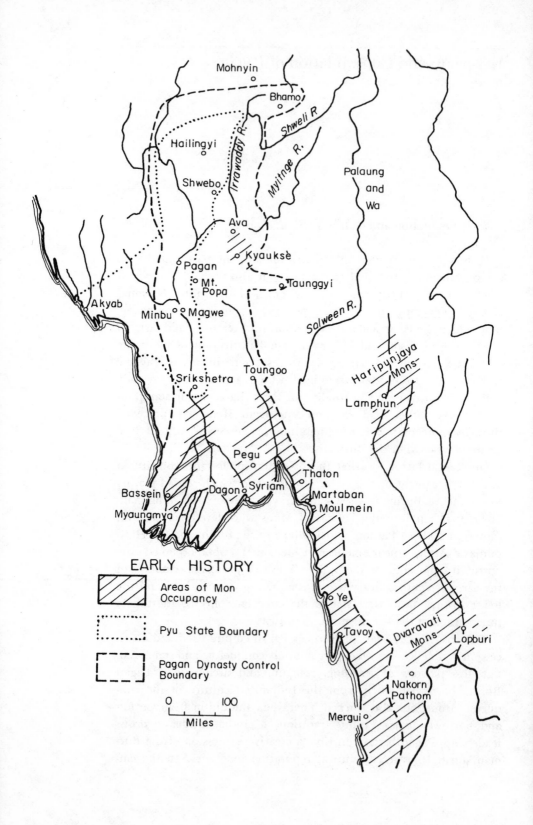

EARLY HISTORY

Areas of Mon
Occupancy

Pyu State Boundary

Pagan Dynasty Control
Boundary

0   100
Miles

pire's political collapse in 1287 by the armies of Kublai Khan. Even the successor Shan military chieftains who established themselves at Ava, following the final departure of the Chinese forces around 1300, themselves chose to rule central Burma as the presumed descendants of the Pagan dynasty. The monument-studded landscape of ancient Pagan offers concrete evidence of an imposing national performance.

The story must start with the Mons. The original Mon settlers who took up residence in lower Burma entered via the Sittang River corridor possibly during the third century B.C. Their numbers were augmented from time to time by the migration of ethnic kinsmen from both Haripunjaya and Dvaravati, sometimes undertaken for political reasons. A loosely joined Ramanyadesa confederacy, including all three Mon principalities, came into being during the tenth century. Burma's Mons were closer to the overseas commercial and cultural contacts with India than were the other two centers and were probably more directly influenced by Hindu cults, including Siva worship. They were also vulnerable to attacks from up-country by later arriving Tibeto-Burman tribesmen and from the sea by pirates, predominantly Malays. At an early time in their history, a substantial body of Indianized lower Burma Mons moved up the Sittang valley to develop the Kyauksè irrigation center located south of modern Mandalay. Kyauksè long continued as a center of Mon occupancy and cultural influence. The Mons also probably developed the initial stages of the less extensive Minbu-Magwe irrigated facilities some 300 miles from Kyauksè down the Irrawaddy valley. Generally speaking, however, the areas of firm Mon occupancy in Burma lay along the eastern borders of the Irrawaddy delta, extending over to the mouth of the Salween River and thence part-way down the coast. The substantial presence of south Indian Telegus in Mon Burma influenced later Burman arrivals to dub the Mons themselves as *Talaings*. Mon occupancy of the coastal areas of lower Burma was shared by the generally subservient Pwo Karens. Important capitals of the Burma Mons were developed at neighboring centers of Thaton and Pegu.

Subsequent to the Mon migrations, the Pyu invaders from Tibet moved down the right bank of the Irrawaddy valley from an entry point around Bhamo. The Pyu failed to dislodge the Mons from Kyauksè and from the Sittang valley generally, but they did overrun

the Minbu-Magwe granary and extended their control down the
Irrawaddy valley to the northern edges of the delta. The building
of the Pyu capital Srikshetra (City of Splendor), located near
modern Prome, is usually dated at 628 A.D. It established cultural
and commercial connections overland with Akyab port on the
Arakan coast and with adjacent Bengal. Traces of Pyu language
usage have been identified among the indigenous Arkanese in
modern times. During several centuries of their residency in lower
Burma, the Pyu developed close cultural connections with Bengal
in particular, centering around Mahayana Buddhism. Hindu
Vishnu worship was also prominently in evidence at Srikshetra. This
admitted Bengali association does not explain the puzzling fact that
the writing system which the Pyu adopted was based on Karanese, a
language spoken only in south India's Mysore state. It may be sur-
mised that south Indian scholars were long resident in the Mon
section of Burma.

Srikshetra's ruins indicate a city of imposing dimensions. A col-
lapsing gateway and three imposing cylindrical stupas 150 feet tall
survive as evidence of the city's dependence on north Indian patterns
of construction. Chinese sources indicate that the Pyu state constituted the southernmost extension of the overland trading system
from Yunnan to the Bay of Bengal which developed in late Han
times and was revived under T'ang emperors in the eighth century.
Pyu settlers were probably the first to occupy the site of the later
Burman capital of Pagan, where they constructed a number of cylindrical pagodas in the Indian style, the most impressive being the still
well-preserved Bupaya. Tantric aspects of Bengali Buddhism were
prevalent among the Pyu, and the same rituals were followed by the
Burman successors of the Pyu after 850.

Sometime in the late 700s, the Pyu were obliged to withdraw from
Srikshetra northward. They may have been threatened by maraud-
ing tribesmen who moved westward from the Shan plateau above
the Pegu Yomas to intercept the Irrawaddy line of communication
at Minbu. The Pyu later established a new capital far to the north,
called Halingyi, where they continued for a time their active participation in the revived trade with T'ang China. A Chinese record
from the time describes the Pyu people as being artistically talented
and strongly Buddhist in religion.

But the new Pyu capital in the north did not long survive. Halingyi was overrun in 832 by the armies of Nan Chao, then ruled by a Tibetan Lo Lo elite. Pyu leaders were taken to the Nan Chao capital of Tali as captured slaves, and the group ceased thereafter to play a significant role in Burma's history. Successive Nan Chao tributary missions sent to the T'ang capital of China included Pyu dancers and musical entertainers, and Pyu soldiers constituted a part of the Nan Chao army which seized Hanoi temporarily in 863. Within Burma, Pyu descendants continued to reside at Pagan as well as in Arakan. Kyanzittha, the leading general who served the illustrious King Aniruddha, the eleventh-century founder of the Pagan empire, was apparently of Pyu ancestry.

It was only some twenty years after the collapse of Pyu Halingyi that Burman tribesmen coming by way of Nan Chao entered the middle Irrawaddy valley from the adjacent Shan plateau to capture control of the Mon irrigation centers at Kyauksè. They later moved southward to occupy the Minbu-Magwe granary complex and then northwest up the Chindwin River valley. The more highly civilized Kyauksè Mons, although emasculated politically, became the teachers of the Burmans. Near the end of the 800s, the Burmans made the older Pyu city of Pagan their capital despite its location at the center of the dry zone, perhaps because it lay near Mount Popa, the shrine of the potent pantheon of vagrant spirits. Pagan did not exert major political or cultural influence for a century and a half, while its inhabitants were consolidating their domination of the central valley of upper Burma. They were obliged repeatedly to ward off incursions of Nan Chao armies from the north.

Burmans gradually assimilated the older resident population but were slow to adopt their civilization. They developed in time a Burmese language script and a numeral system, both adapted from Mon patterns. They also took over Mahayana Buddhist practices and the Vishnu cult of their predecessors, along with the indigenous Naga snake symbol, as lord of the soil and the waters. The more precise Theravada Buddhist religious system did not become dominant in Burma until the latter half of the eleventh century, and Burmese writing did not come into official use until a century after that. Even so, the older practices persisted in tolerant association with the new, while the traditional semi-feudal social and governmental patterns gave way to centralized administration adapted from Mon practices. Pagan's rulers repeatedly aspired to become avatars of Vishnu, emerging Buddhas, and even Chakravartin universal rulers, following the Indra-Hindu pattern, even though such aspirations were not strictly orthodox.

The Development of Pagan Supremacy

The emergence of Pagan's authority as the dominant political power throughout the country in the mid-eleventh century was associated with circumstances attending the breakup of the three-sided Mon confederacy of Ramanyadesa. Confronted by the rising power of a unified Cambodia, Dvaravati and Haripunjaya fell to quarreling around 1000, with refugees from the latter state fleeing to the Mon center of Thaton in Burma. Shortly thereafter, Dvaravati was invaded by Malayan armies, which captured the capital at Lopburi and then moved eastward to take Angkor in 1011. By the middle of the century the Cambodian usurper, Suryavarman I, had incorporated all of Dvaravati into his expanding Cambodian domain.

Meanwhile, Thaton's position was weakened by differences with nearby Pegu Mons and by attacks of aggressive Malayan pirates who harassed Thaton as well as other coastal points. Faced by a formidable Cambodian invasion via Tenasserim in 1050, Thaton's King Makuta elected to reach an accommodation with the Saivite invaders, while the partisan Buddhist faction at Pegu decided to resist. In response to Pegu's appeal for assistance, Pagan's King Aniruddha, who had come to power in 1044, moved his Burman armies southward down the Irrawaddy into the western Irrawaddy delta. With the eventual cooperation of the Peguans, Pagan's youthful army commander Kyanzittha captured Thaton in 1057, aided by Haripunjaya refugees from inside the city. He enslaved the Cambodian garrison and transported the captured King Makuta and entourage to the vicinity of Pagan itself. Pegu became a vassal state of the growing Pagan empire.

The story of the rise of Pagan under Aniruddha as presented in the Burmese historical Chronicles gives a religious interpretation which has little discernible relevance to the actual events. The Chronicles were related primarily to Burma's subsequent identification as champion of the purified Buddhist faith in contrast with the adulterated Mahayanist system borrowed from Bengal and hostile Hinduized influences centering at Thaton and in Cambodia.

According to the Chronicles, Pagan forces attacked Thaton after the Mon ruler had refused to provide Aniruddha with requested copies of the Pali *Tripitika* scriptures. Actually the only Pali scriptures available in Thaton at the time were the abbreviated Jataka Commentaries. Pagan acquired the full Buddhist canon a decade later (1065) from Ceylon.

Buddhism sorely needed a champion at the time. The faith had virtually disappeared from India's Deccan by the eleventh century, and it was being smothered in Bengal by a resurgent Hinduism and by Islamic army incursions moving down the Ganges valley. Muslim armies reached Benares in 1033 and Bihar in 1039. The Tamil Cholas from south India had attacked and conquered the neighboring Buddhist island of Ceylon in 1017. They were not expelled until 1070, and then partly as a result of Burmese assistance sent by Pagan. Thus political trends tended to reinforce the assumed, if not entirely accurate, posture of Pagan Burma as champion of the true Theravada faith.

The Reign of Aniruddha, 1044–1077

The thirty-three-year reign of King Aniruddha was one of the most noteworthy of Burma's long history. The ruler's very title underscored his aggressive temperament, for Aniruddha in Sanskrit meant "self-willed" or "ungovernable." His efforts to organize and defend his expanded realm were prodigious. The long Cambodian frontier extending from the mouth of the Salween River southward to Tavoy was guarded by more than two score fortresses built during the 1060s. The extreme northern frontier of Pagan Burma proper bordered on territories under Nan Chao control, the boundary extending from below Bhamo westward to the borders of Manipur state in India. In this area Aniruddha allied with Kadu peoples (probably Pyu descendants) to hold back the Nan Chao. Along the western escarpment of the Shan plateau another two score fortified towns were founded extending northward from the Toungoo region in the lower Sittang valley to some distance above Kyauksè in the north. Pagan's suzerain control extended eastward across the south Shan states as far as the Inle Lake area. Aniruddha apparently made no attempt to conquer the upper Chindwin valley or the region of Arakan.

Burma's substantial commitment of assistance to Buddhist Ceylon lasted fifteen years. Material assistance included contributions of valuable sandalwood and camphor, which enabled the Ceylon ruler to sustain the allegiance of his wearying and mutinous troops until attacks from India subsided. In response to Ceylon's request, Aniruddha later dispatched learned *bhikku* monk scholars to assist in restoring the orthodox initiatary rites of the Sinhalese monkhood. Ceylon responded by contributing the full text of the Pali *Tripitika* scriptures and by sending an alleged Buddha tooth relic, which Aniruddha duly enshrined in the foundation of the new Shwezigon Pagoda at Pagan, a structure completed near the end of the eleventh century. Relations between the two allied Buddhist states remained close during the ensuing century.

Burma's assumed role as the champion of Theravada Buddhism (of the Teachers) actually served to enhance the status of the highly literate Mon portion of the population. The bhikkus sent to Ceylon were Mons. Only Mon scholars were competent to evaluate the *Tripitika* scriptures and the Jataka Commentaries, along with numerous other sacred symbols acquired from Ceylon and Thaton. The conquering Pagan armies stripped Thaton of skilled builders and craftsmen, painters, sculptors, perfume specialists, animal trainers, and even expert cooks. Such persons were later afforded opportunity for creative expression within the rising Pagan capital. It required approximately a full century for Burman technicians and scholars to match the performance of the more civilized Mons. Compared with eleventh-century Mon literature, with its polished poetic forms and its superior insight and clarity, the early Burmese writing at the time was rudimentary, factual, and prosaic. Pali Buddhist literature familiar to Mon scholars was extravagantly flamboyant in style. Thus in early Pagan, the civilizing pattern was Mon, whereas much of the energy and creative urge behind the cultural flowering at the capital was Burman. Gordon Luce (*Early Pagan,* I, 43) comments that Pagan's "newly discovered soul . . . strained the energies, inspired art and architecture, breathed through the writing, and even guided . . . the government." Aniruddha and his Burman associates emerge in Luce's account both as outstanding national leaders and as international statesmen. They were the fashioners of an imperial domain and the inspired instigators of a Buddhist revival which established the permanent sense of identity of the Burman people.

The Reign of Kyanzittha, 1084–1113

Near the end of his long reign, Aniruddha quarreled with his able half-Arakanese military leader, Kyanzittha, presumably over his amorous relations with a gift princess at court. The estranged general retired to his home near Kyauksè, still Mon-inhabited, where he bided his time.

Following Aniruddha's death in 1077, political conditions deteriorated rapidly under the rule of his spoiled Mon-educated son, King Sawlu. The Chronicles condemn Sawlu as a scapegrace and victim of his own folly, but he did contribute materially to art and architecture. Sawlu quarreled with the governor of Pegu, who eventually initiated a rebellion against the king. Kyanzittha's assistance against the rebels was enlisted by palace ministers, but too late to save the capital from the attacking Pegu forces. Sawlu himself was captured and executed in 1084. Kyanzittha's forces retreated northward, managed to rally support from the Kyauksè and Shwebo areas, and eventually restored Burman control over Pagan itself. As a means of pacifying the distraught countryside of lower Burma, Kyanzittha assumed the title of Thiluin Man (King of the Mons) and negotiated a compromise agreement with the grandson of Makuta, Prince Asaw, who had meanwhile seized the royal regalia at Pagan and fled to Mount Popa. Asaw and Kyanzittha were associated in their opposition to both the Aniruddha line and the Peguans. The resulting agreement, which was later enshrined in the famous Myazedi inscription, provided that the crown should bypass the claims of Kyanzittha's male progeny and go to the descendants of the youthful Asaw to whom the king gave his own daughter in marriage.

Peace with the Mons was thus restored, and the door was also opened wide to their full participation in the ensuing flowering of Pagan culture. A learned Mon monk, Shin Arahan, became the close associate of King Kyanzittha after 1084. Kyanzittha himself was literate in Mon and apparently acquainted with both Sanskrit and Pali. The inscriptions of his reign in these two languages ignore Aniruddha entirely. The new regime was more permissive than the previous ones had been, less closely identified with the Theravada orthodoxy, but still identified politically with both the Dvaravati and Ceylon traditions. Kyanzittha based his kingship status on Hindu sanctions, coupled with fulfilment of alleged prophecy and his own emergence as an avatar of Vishnu. Inscriptions of the reign associated his ancestry with the legendary Asoka Buddhist missionaries of ancient times, and even with the alleged Pyu founder of Srikshetra. The imposing Shwezigon pagoda containing Ceylon's Buddha tooth gift, which Kyanzittha completed, included shrines to the 37 vagrant nat spirits along with much Hindu symbolism. Thus Pagan continued to treasure its identity as the champion of the true Buddhist faith, but not at the cost of persecuting rival traditions.

Culture and Religion under Kyanzittha

The creative achievements of Pagan Burma under King Kyanzittha and his Mon-oriented lineal descendants were attributable in part to the liberal and tolerant policy which he initiated. The varied religious and governmental sanctions employed at his court included the essentially indigenous Naga snake cult (Lord of the Soil and the Waters) and other spirit (nat) propitiation practices. The influence of Hindu India was represented in a limited way by a few figures of the Brahma and the elephant-headed son of Śiva, Gonesha, but more importantly in the Indra-centered coronation ceremonies and the presence at the court of Brahman astrologers and magicians. The earlier Bengali Bodhisattva (Emerging Buddha) tradition also survived together with remnants of Mahayanist Tantric cult practices. In competition with such rival cults the consciously propagated Theravada Buddhist faith attained ascendency only gradually and in adulterated form. G. E. Harvey's interpretation of Pagan's religious policy (*History*, 33) is particularly relevant: "Men will not come [to the Theravada shrines] for the sake of the new faith. Let them come for their old gods, and gradually they will be won over."

Indigenous and borrowed patterns were frequently combined in eclectic fashion. The Naga cult ritual, for example, required that foundations for gateways and wall fortifications be strengthened with the protective presence of the spirits of selected victims sacrificed on the spot, a custom known as *myosade*. Also placed in foundation excavations were precious metal offerings (gold, silver, and copper leaf), cloth-wrapped cooked rice and fresh milk, male and female symbols, and precious gems, all properly blessed. Important ceremonies were performed only on propitious days selected by Indian astrologers. In the construction of sacred palace foundations Vishnu cult practices were much in evidence, a practice carried over from earlier Mon and Pyu traditions. The court regalia including coronation items (crown, sword, musical instruments) were placed under the custody of court Brahmans. In times of warfare tattooing was practiced to attain invulnerability, and the assistance of cooperating spirits was enlisted along with the use of favorable omens and magical talismans. Astrological and magical considerations also helped determine the location of capital cities, and children were named in accordance with astrological calculations connected with the day of the week when they were born.

King Kyanzittha himself assumed the dual status of an avatar of Vishnu and an Emergent Buddha (Bodhisattva), the performer of impressive works of merit. He was less anti-Indian than Aniruddha had been, and particularly lax against Ceylon's Chola enemies in south India. His favorite wife was a Bengali Mahayanist Buddhist. He completed the pyramidal Shwezigon pagoda, then fashioned the inspired Ananda temple at Pagan, and contributed substantially to the repair of the sacred Bodhgaya monuments in India. He achieved popular esteem by making a holiday out of religious ceremonial giving by featuring music, dancing, and the presence of sacred elephants and birds. The Bodhisattva images at Pagan dating from his time were far from otherworldly and austere, being relaxed, smiling, and profusely decorated with necklaces, wristlets, and anklets. Temple paintings and wall decorations reflected the Buddhist legend not as rigid dogma but as a way of life, not omitting dubiously-orthodox Tantric practices and demon activities. Even so the less exacting Mahayanist tradition was steadily fading, partly because the Muslim conquest of Bengal, completed near the end of the twelfth century, eliminated an important inspirational source and generally weakened Burma's Sanskrit cultural link. The Theravada Buddhism of Ceylon gained increasing importance following the virtual elimination of the faith from India proper. Burma's long-term future lay with the Theravada tradition, but by no means exclusively so.

The numerous and frequently impressive Mon-type temple premises and decorations became the important agencies of creative expression and educational change in Kyanzittha's Pagan. The impressive Shwezigon pagoda style, with its truncated pyramidal design of solid masonry topped by a broad-based bell-shaped stupa gave way to the cave-like patterns of the Mons. The inner shrine of the Mon temple was usually approached by a darkened low-roofed corridor, flanked by small window openings. The massive central core of the building, against which the Buddha image stood, helped support the ceiling of the encircling vault. Interior walls and ceilings were covered by plaques and images in carved relief depicting many aspects of the life story and tradition of the Buddha. These decorations were often accompanied by explanatory glosses in Pali and Mon languages, adapted mainly from the Jataka scripture Commentaries.

The most impressive temple built by Kyanzittha, the Ananda, quadrupled the cave-like effect by developing elaborate entry corridors approaching the central-core stupa from four directions. Each darkened entryway led to the high-ceilinged interior vault, where a twenty-foot tall Buddha stood on an altar with his back against the central core. These four major images were lighted by apertures built into the masonry above. Shorter and narrower passageways paralleled the four main entryways at ground level, all of them terminating in niches containing small Buddha figures. The 1,500 terra-cotta plaques which lined the interior walls of the Ananda featured graphically many episodes in Buddha's story, with appended descriptive legends in the Mon language. Above the four major entrances, exterior staircases led upward to the very base of the magnificently fashioned central stupa, each series of steps flanked by three smaller lotus-bud shaped tower gateways, all of them covered with burnished gold leaf. The Ananda and other temples at Pagan have been well preserved partly by reason of the scanty rainfall (five inches annually) at the site. Exteriors are still today impressively attractive, while the interior wall decorations portray a wealth of religious symbolism and literary texts artistically done. Other Mon-patterned temples at Pagan comparable to the Ananda include the Kubyaukgyi structure, where the famous Myazedi inscription was eventually placed.

The major temples at Pagan and elsewhere served as educational institutions. Lectures for students were provided regularly by the learned *theras* (teachers) connected with such shrines, and instruction was available for all visitors on Sabbaths and fast days. Monks in charge of village monasteries performed a similar teaching function for local youth. Both temple settings and instructional content were intensely devotional in character. Virtually all of the religious texts in Kyanzittha's time were couched in the Mon and Pali languages, with bare references to archaic Pyu and only slight indications of the development of a Burmese writing system. Wealthy donors also provided libraries where the Pali scriptures were studied and reproduced. Thus Burman military conquerors were influenced culturally for more than a century by Mon art forms and literature.

By far the most valuable historical document found in the early Mon-type temples was Burma's Rosetta Stone, the so-called Myazedi Inscription of 1113. It was placed in the Kubyaukgyi (Great Variegated Temple) by Prince Rajakumar, Kyanzittha's son by the Bengali queen, who had been passed over in the royal succession agreement of 1084. The inscription told the story of Kyanzittha's decree supporting the succession of the Makuta line heir, using four languages: Mon, Pali, Burmese, and Pyu. It is one of the earliest recordings of written Burmese, still unperfected, and one of the last examples of archaic Pyu. All except the Pyu used adaptations of the same south Indian script probably borrowed from the Dvaravati Mons. The Pali account in particular was a literary gem presented in verse and in free translation, possibly the work of Rajakumar himself.

The accompanying inscriptions reflect no personal ill will or jealousy on the part of the rejected prince. The temple as a whole was an act of Buddhist devotion, housing a gold figure of the Buddha which the prince-scholar was presenting to his dying father. Other Mon inscriptions within the Kubyaukgyi pagoda reflect the sponsor's great interest in historical events and his refreshing sense of humor. They cover the historical origins of the Theravada tradition, with minimal emphasis on learned theological aspects of the story. Rajakumar did not lack parental respect and sympathy for the poor and the orphaned, but he also loved a good tale for its own sake and saw literary possibilities in the emerging Burmese written language. When Kyanzittha died in 1113, he was succeeded, as previously planned, by Cansu I (Alaungsithu), his own grandson, and Makuta's great-grandson.

Governmental and Social Aspects of Pagan Burma

Kyanzittha's compromise with the dissident Mon faction in 1084 accomplished much for establishment of internal peace. One serious external threat developed after 1100 from the north, which necessitated strengthening defense facilities, including development of a standing army, the construction of stronger walls and fortified gateways. When the actual Nan Chao invasion took place in 1106, the attack was halted at the site of future Mandalay, but not without difficulty. On this occasion Kyanzittha sent a special embassy to the Chinese Sung center at Kai-Feng asking for assistance in restraining the Nan Chao forces, but to no effect. The northern Sungs were threatened elsewhere. The only other international event of any consequence was Pagan's cooling off in its political relations with Ceylon, although not to the point of disturbing intimate cultural connections.

The components of the society of Pagan Burma below the court level can best be reconstructed by examining the descriptions of numerous "slave villages," which were given to monastic institutions as works of merit by wealthy donors. Slave villagers so donated apparently lived and worked very much as did their free neighbors, since monastic rule was lightly imposed. The Buddhist *Sangha* monks could have whatever produce and services were required for the functioning of the monastery or temple shrine, but were not allowed to make a profit. In the end it was the government's revenues rather than the slave villagers themselves that suffered from religious donations. Later rulers of Pagan took action to check such accumulations of wealth in land and slaves for religious purposes, because the government was losing much needed funds. Royal commissioners were eventually assigned the task of recording and authenticating approved grants to religious orders. The many hundreds of temple pagoda premises which clutter the twenty-five square-mile environs of Pagan afford convincing evidence that merit-seeking donations reached the point of diminishing returns if measured on other than religious grounds. A group of heretical *Arana* forest-dweller monks later pursued an aggressive land-acquisition policy, presumably in contravention of royal control.

Burma's kings themselves developed in time special claims to the products and services of the inhabitants of major irrigation regions, such as Kyauksè, Minbu-Magwe, and later the Shwebo area. In early modern times, such populations were accorded special *ahmudan* status, as compared with the less prestigious *athi* majority of the population, who paid direct household taxes. Not all slaves were menials. Monasteries as well as the court commanded the services of special servant-slaves trained as legal experts, as artist-craftsmen, as stone-cutters and builders, as musician entertainers, and as *ahmudan* army officers. Bankrupt debtors who took refuge in slave status could later purchase freedom by paying their owners a *viss* of copper. War captives in Burma as elsewhere in southeast Asia became automatically royal slaves.

Subjects of the king, whether *ahmudan* or *athi,* were customarily ruled locally by hereditary township headmen (*myothugyis*). Because they constituted a major link between the village population and the central government, *myothugyi* status had to be authenticated by the royal court. Headmen mediated local civil disputes, exercised primary police jurisdiction, and handled minor criminal offenses. Eventually they were required to keep census records of households within their respective jurisdictions and to supervise delivery of taxes and services due the court. Villagers usually maintained discipline by denying offenders access to family-owned cultivable land. Within the countryside, work cattle were the principal evidence of movable wealth, while a measure of salt provided the basic unit of value. During most of the century following Kyanzittha's accession Burma enjoyed internal peace and prosperity, conditions which alone could have financed the construction of the many monuments which graced the capital.

Successors to Kyanzittha

Pagan attained its cultural flowering under the long reign of Kyanzittha's grandson, Cansu I (Alaungsithu), 1113–1160. The title translated means "Future Buddha, Victorious Hero." Cansu was not only builder and ruler, but also a scholar in Sanskrit, Pali, and Mon, an ardent champion of the Therevada faith, and a distinguished poet. He planned and executed the construction of the impressive Thatpinnyu temple and also the smaller Shwegu shrine, which became the Burmese variants of the Ananda Mon pattern. Discarded were the darkened cave-like corridors; wide open doors replaced the tiny windows. The elevated foundational structure which housed the central Buddha figure was open to light and air and approachable by a single frontal staircase penetrating a series of elaborately decorated gateways. Traditional Mon standards here encountered Burman preferences for well-ventilated devotional symbolism omitting the plethora of detailed texts. But in the literary field, the ardently Buddhist ruler remained more Mon than Burman, since the Burmese language had not yet achieved mature stature. G. H. Luce has translated with appropriate eloquence

(*Early Pagan* I, 85–89) the hundred-verse poem in Pali, composed
by the king or his counsellor, which extols the Buddhist faith. The
poem calls for virtue, wisdom, and calm, for the rejection of pomp
and splendor, greed and hatred, which breed delusion and desire
and would keep both men and spirits bound to the endless and
burdensome seas of change. The Burmese Chronicles praise Cansu
I, obviously with good reason, as a saintly king who cared for the
needs of his people and performed impressively meritful deeds.

Although Cansu's control of upper Burma frontiers to the north
remained firm, his later years witnessed a deterioration of royal
authority elsewhere. This was especially true in the distant Tenasserim coast area and somewhat less so along the Arakan frontier.
Lower Burman forces, with or without royal authorization, attempted to take advantage of Cambodia's difficulties in its long war
with coastal Champa (Chams actually captured Angkor in 1177)
to seize control of the lower isthmian portage routes. Both Burmese
and Ceylon Chronicles indicate that friction developed over
Burma's seemingly gratuitous efforts to deny Ceylon access to the
Cambodian domain from the Bay of Bengal for both commerce and
diplomatic contact. Both accounts appear to exaggerate their varying interpretations of the episode. Governmental stability deteriorated rapidly following Cansu's death in 1160 under the faltering rule of his son and successor, Imtaw Syan. The new incumbent
apparently clawed his way to power over the bodies of royal relatives. As had been the case following Aniruddha's death a century
earlier, an able ruler proved to be an overindulgent father.

Hostile Burmese Chronicles, prepared later, characterized Imtaw
Syan as a usurper and tyrant, a murderer of relatives, including his
own Indian wife. His murder in 1165 was reportedly accomplished
by eight Indian assassins, who gained access to the palace disguised
as court Brahmans. All eight allegedly committed suicide following
the gruesome deed. The episode resulted in nearly a decade of confused factional strife, which ended with the eventual accession of a
prince-descendant of the older Aniruddha Burman line, Narapa-
tsithu, who took the royal title of Cansu II in 1174. The Burman
faction thus triumphed over the Mons as did orthodox Theravada
standards over a more liberal religious orientation, and pro-Ceylon
policies over anti-Ceylon. The outcome also involved the abrupt
substitution of the Burmese for the Mon language both at court and
in literary expression, and the eventual Burmanization of the entire

cultural atmosphere of the capital. Emerging Burmese literature was less poetic, more factual and historic, less concerned with king and court, more aware of the common man, the cultivator and slave, and the earthy factors of hill and plain. Pagan's architects, artists, and scholars continued for some time to maintain a high standard of performance, but the tone was now Burman rather than Mon. The last example of Ananda-plan architecture was the Dhammayan-gyi temple, dedicated in the 1160s to the dead Imtaw Syan by a sister-donor, princess Ajawlat.

The longer Sinhalese version of Burma-Ceylon crisis of 1164–1165 accused the Burmese of flagrant provocations. Charges included thieving interference with Ceylon's isthmian trade with Malaya, Pagan's refusal to authorize gifts or sale of elephants to Ceylon, and Burman imprisonment of Sinhalese governmental representatives, including a princess-bride enroute to Cambodia with gifts. Ceylon's forceful restoration of trading contacts with Cambodian "Lanka" in 1165 is fully credible, but the accompanying boastful account of a massive invasion of Burma via Bassein is much less so. The Ceylon Court Chronicles indicate that the invading Ceylonese armies actually captured Pagan and slaughtered the offending ruler Imtaw Syan. What can be credited is that the pro-Ceylon faction at Pagan gained the ascendency during the course of the conflict. Cansu II's successor government after 1174 allied itself by marriage ties with Ceylon and resumed close cultural relations on the Theravada pattern. Sinhalese consorts, priests, and diplomatic representatives became prominent both at court and at Buddhist temples in Pagan. The Mon language survived at the capital only among Pali scholars. It persisted longer in Mon-inhabited areas of lower Burma from Pegu to Tavoy as well as on the Siam side of the watershed from Haripunjaya southward into the isthmus.

G. H. Luce's summary of the differences in temperament between Mon and Burman cultural traits (*Early Pagan,* chapter VI) deserves explicit citation. Old Burman literature, he comments, was "less sensitive, simpler, rougher, and more vigorous. . . . Old Mon is full of poetry. Old Burman is empty of it." Burman architecture attained "a note of grandeur, which Old Mon architecture, with all its mystery and beauty, hardly attained." The prosaic matter-of-fact Burman "hated gloom and loved brightness and clarity. He wanted height, strength, and grandeur." Open doorways therefore replaced the perforated windows; dark corridors and vaulted shrines gave way to multiple-storied temple structures surrounding the solid masonry of the central core. Burman builders also corrected structural weaknesses in the older Mon temples and made the new ones more enduring. Whereas the Mons undertook to bring the otherworldly Buddha-awareness down to human experience, the Burman pattern endeavored to lift the human spirit within the context of a distant and more inspiring perspective.

It can be suggested, however, that Mon genius itself helped substantially to suggest the pattern for the allegedly Burman characteristics of the imposing Thatpinnyu temple and of Cansu II's own Gawdawpalin. It is also apparent that the arbitrary elimination of Mon influence after 1174 eventually brought Burman architecture back to the uninspired step-pyramidal pattern of the early Shwezigon pagoda, with its single exterior staircase, its lack of interiors, and its square exterior passageways encircling the massive pile of masonry at successive levels, topped by a circular stupa. The pretentious Mingalazedi temple of the mid-1200s thus resembled structurally the earlier Shwezigon, being significant only for its wealth of terra-cotta plaques lining the walls of the square passageways. Pagan's last builder in the grand style, King Natonmya, died in 1231. It was during his reign that the capital was swept by a disastrous fire. One contributing factor to the decline of building activity was the depletion of royal resources, due in part to the decline of tax revenues owing to clerical accumulation of wealth in land and slave villages. The vigorous genius of Pagan, whether Mon or Burman, was substantially exhausted by the latter half of the 1200s. It had nevertheless contributed an enduring legacy, both political and cultural, to the Burmese nation.

III From Pagan to Toungoo, 1287 to 1752

The Fall of Pagan

Important events associated with the Asian expansion of imperial Mongol power overtook Pagan during the reign of the boastful and despotic Narathihapate (Cansu IV), 1252–1287. The first development directly affecting Burma was the Mongol capture of the border state of Nan Chao in 1253. The episode did not appear to be particularly threatening at the time, because Mongol forces were more interested in subduing the Chinese southern Sung state than in venturing beyond Yunnan into Burma. The elimination of the long-hostile Lo Lo government of Nan Chao, and the march of Kublai Khan's forces down the Red River valley to Hanoi (captured in 1257) relieved Pagan of immediate danger and encouraged a measure of bravado on the part of Cansu IV. More abrasive contacts developed after 1271, when Kublai assumed the Chinese dynastic title of Yuan, "The Beginning." Pagan's ruler rejected Kublai's summons to become tributary to China, transmitted by the Mongol-appointed governor posted at Tali, the former Nan Chao capital. When a similar summons was transmitted by an imperial Chinese envoy a few years later, Cansu had him executed and then proceeded to invade border states subservient to Peking. Armed strife developed beyond Burma's northern frontier in 1277. Marco Polo's second-hand account of the ensuing battle of Ngasaunggyan told how dismounted Mongol archers panicked the large Burmese elephant corps. Prisoner mahouts were forced to recapture several hundred beasts, that were then incorporated in the Khan's army. Following the collapse of Sung resistance in Yunnan in 1279, Kublai turned attention to the upstart Burmese. In 1283 his armies captured the Burmese fortress above Bhamo, a move which opened the country to invasion and precipitated widespread rebellion against the unpopular Cansu IV.

The ensuing disintegration of Pagan's authority affected all regions of the empire. Shan tribesmen from the border plateau regions to the east of the upper Irrawaddy intruded in a westerly direction across the river and over into the Chindwin valley. Tagaung in the north became the capital of the newly created Chinese governor-province of Chieng-mien. The Thai cousins of Burma's Shans had earlier penetrated the upper Chao Phraya valley. In 1219 (some say 1232), a semi-autonomous Thai governor assumed control at Cambodia's Sukhotai outpost, located south and east of the older Mon center of Haripunjaya-Lamphun. The second son of this governor, who earned the title of Rama Khamheng (Rama the Brave), asserted Sukhotai's complete independence in 1270. He later initiated a conquering expedition southward along the right bank of the river, through the old Dvaravati country down into Malaya.

In 1281, one of Rama Khamheng's captains of the guard, a military adventurer and native of Thaton named Wareru, eloped with a royal princess of Sukhotai, fled to lower Burma and seized control of Martaban at the mouth of the Salween River. He later joined the Mon rebels of Pegu to destroy the authority of Pagan in lower Burma. In 1287, Wareru murdered his Peguan rival and proclaimed himself king of the Mons.

Pagan itself fell to the Mongols in 1287. The refugee ruler, Cansu IV, had agreed to become the puppet tributary ruler to China, only to be killed by one of his sons while returning to the capital. This act provided the excuse for the Mongol army to fight its way southward to occupy Pagan while the ensuing princely feuding ran its gruesome course. The invaders withdrew in 1289, after installing the only surviving son of Cansu, prince Kyawswa, as governor of the additional proposed Chinese province of Meinchung. Two years later the Mongol authorities abandoned the second province idea and confirmed the harried Kyawswa as their tributary king at Pagan.

Central Burma disintegrated politically during the 1290s. The discredited king was challenged by a trio of Shan brother *myo-thugyis* (provincial chieftains) from the Kyauksè area, who obtained in 1293 royal acknowledgment of their de facto control of the key granary. When strife threatened in 1297, Kyawswa dispatched his eldest son on a tributory mission to Peking to obtain further authentication of his authority. Following an abortive internal revolt in Pagan in 1298, the Shan brothers seized control, imprisoning the king and his sons. When faced with the threat of overt Chinese invasion in 1299, they summarily executed the captives together with the Chinese representatives, and then burned portions of Pagan.

The center of power in upper Burma thereafter shifted to the Kyauksè region, with successive capitals developing directly to the north. The inevitable Chinese invasion occurred in 1301. It encountered more spirited resistance from the mobilized Shan brothers' forces than had been anticipated, so that the project quickly ran aground. The Chinese attack was repelled; negotiations were initiated involving paying a substantial bribe to the discredited Chinese commander, and the invaders conducted a fighting withdrawal. China's remaining border Chieng-mien province was abolished in 1303, and Mongol rulers thereafter paid little attention to the region. Although the Shan brothers boasted perennially that they had defeated the Chinese invaders, they took care to send successive tribute missions to Peking to obtain authentication of their own authority. Burma was thus saved from Mongol-Chinese rule, but at heavy cost materially and politically. The revived Mon state of lower Burma resumed independence within restricted limits.

Two Centuries of Shan Rule in Central Burma

The ensuing two and one-quarter centuries of the history of central Burma were turbulent in the extreme. Although elite Shan influence remained pervasively dominant politically, it was highly fragmented, and the region continued to be strongly Burmese in language and culture. Two rival Shan-prince capitals were set up in 1312 and 1315 respectively at Pinnya and at Sagaing on opposite sides of the Irrawaddy River near the mouth of the Myitnge tributary at the mid-point of the westward bend. The first half of the century was one of chronic disorder. In 1364, the savage Maw Shan forces, invited from across the China border by one of the rival factions, sacked both capitals in turn, which led to the eventual establishment of a more defensible single upper-Burma capital at Ava. The use of the emerging written Shan language using the Burmese script spread in time throughout the adjacent plateau areas to the north and east of Ava.

The accession of the Ming dynasty in China in 1368 did little to

restore order along the Burma frontier. Mongol factions held out in
Yunnan until 1381. Meanwhile, the newly aggressive Mohnyin
Shans (centered at Katha downstream and to the west of Bhamo)
raided Shwebo in 1373 and attacked Ava itself in 1383. Fortunately
for increasingly Burmanized Ava, the several rival Shan tribes began
in 1385 to feud among themselves. An opportunity to reassert upper-Burma control over Mon-ruled sections of lower Burma developed after 1406, when Ava's forces administered a severe defeat on
enemy Shans to the north. The ensuing decade witnessed a massive
upper Burma invasion of the Irrawaddy delta, culminating in the
siege of Pegu in 1415. The attack failed partly because Pegu agents
persuaded the aggressive northeastern Shan chief of Hsenwei to
attack Ava. The Shan forces were checked near the present site of
Maymyo at the edge of the plateau, but Ava was forced to abandon
the siege of Pegu. For more than a full century thereafter, the
Peguan Mons were free to extend their seaborne commerce with
Indian merchants, and with the newly developing entrepôt center
of trade in the Malacca Straits. Early Portuguese reports from
Malacca in the 1500s indicated that the Peguans and their teak
ships, often for sale, were very highly regarded by all visitors.

Disorder in upper Burma became endemic after 1427. Ava was
chronically on the defensive, and on one occasion the vital Kyauksè
granary was threatened. Temporary relief came from policing actions initiated by Chinese border armies in 1438–1440, when the
Ming emperors shifted their attention from previous seaborne ex-
peditions to reopening the land route to the Bay of Bengal via
Yunnan and Burma. Chinese forces subdued both the border Maw
and Mohnyin Shans. When the Ava government became uncooperative in 1445–1446, they imposed tributary status on upper Burma
for approximately a quarter of a century. After 1469, the Mings
eventually lost interest in virtually all of southeast Asia, so that Ava
recovered complete independence and managed for a decade to
maintain order by its own efforts.

Disorder returned after 1481. Pressure from the Mohnyin Shans
became so severe by 1507 that Ava attempted to appease them by a
cession of territory. Chinese development around 1520 of a military
base at Tengueh near the Burma border helped but little in curb-
ing Shan belligerency. The Mohnyin tribesmen in 1527 finally succeeded in capturing Ava, sacking and destroying the city. They
continued in control of the site down to 1555. Following the debacle

at Ava, a host of Burmese refugees fled southward into the Sittang valley, where the minor principality of Toungoo had existed unobtrusively since the mid-fourteenth century. Toungoo produced two great leaders during the 1500s, who together achieved the second unification to Burma.

Emergence of Toungoo Dynasty Rule

A second exhibition of the explosive potential of Burmese energies occurred under the direction of successive leaders of Toungoo, Kings Tabinshweti (1531–1550) and Bayinnaung (1551–1581). The episode was associated with the activities of a number of Portuguese military adventurers in southeast Asia. The father of Tabinshweti, Min Kyinyo, initiated the expansionist program by seizing the politically and economically important Kyauksè granary area during or immediately following the Shan capture of adjacent Ava in 1527. Militarily trained Burman refugees from Ava joined the Toungoo forces, which quickly became the strongest army in all of Burma. So confused and fragmented was Shan-dominated upper Burma at the time, that Min Kyinyo elected to ignore any threat from the north and to direct Toungoo's expansionist efforts southward toward the prosperous but militarily debilitated kingdom of Pegu. He died in 1531 in the midst of such preparations, leaving the crown of Toungoo in the hands of his teen-age son, Tabinshweti.

During the century following Pagan's fall, the Mon state of Pegu had attained a high level of order and prosperity especially under the strong reigns of Binnya U (1353–1385) and Razadarit (1385–1423). Binnya U shifted the capital from Martaban to Pegu in 1369. For a time, he faced attacks from both Mon Chiengmai and Siamese Ayuthia, but these subsided when the rulers of Ayuthia became involved in the long-continuing efforts to establish effective control over Sukhotai and Chiengmai, and finally over Angkor by 1431. The principal threat to Razadarit's Pegu came from attacks from Ava in 1406 to 1415. For a century and more thereafter, the prosperous Pegu Mon domain extended inward from the mouth of the Salween and westward across the Irrawaddy delta to Bassein. It was administered under 32 provincial (myothugyi) units, and attained an enviable state of economic and cultural development. Indian cloth merchants came to Mon ports to obtain shellac, sampanwood, cotton, silk, and rubies. Mon trade with Malacca also prospered. A succession of devout Buddhist rulers revived religious contact with Ceylon. A newly arrived Malaccan Portuguese agent established a trading station at Martaban in 1519. It was thus a shocking experience for the Mon leadership of Pegu to discover in the 1530s that the previously feeble and presumably friendly Toungoo Burmans had developed into a formidable political rival.

Tabinshweti's Toungoo forces overran the western portion of the delta in 1535 and eventually captured Pegu itself in 1539. Dissident elements within the city may have contributed to its fall. The refugee Mon king made a desperate effort to solicit Shan aid against Toungoo, but the more responsible Mon leaders preferred association with civilized Burman leaders of Toungoo than with the half-savage Mohnyin Shans.

The final Burman attack on Pegu coincided with the arrival of an armed trading ship from Portuguese Goa, commanded by Fernando de Moraes. The Portuguese captain made the mistake of siding with the Peguan river defenders, only to suffer capture by the Toungoo army following the fall of Pegu itself. De Moraes was killed and his crew was promptly enlisted as an elite artillery corps in the victorious Burman army. The crew of another Portuguese trading vessel arriving at Bassein at the time barely escaped the same fate. Some Mon recruits joined the Burmans and Portuguese mercenaries in the capture of Martaban in 1541, after which all of the coastal cities from Moulmein southward to Tavoy offered their allegiance. After Tabinshweti had repulsed a belated Shan thrust down the Irrawaddy, he was formally crowned king of Burma at both Pagan and Pegu. The latter city became the new capital.

Instead of attempting immediately to carry his conquests northward against the Shans, Tabinshweti turned his attention in tentative fashion to Arakan in 1544 and 1546. Thereafter he undertook the far more ambitious task of capturing Siamese Ayuthia. The Burmese armies which invaded Siam via Tenasserim in 1548 were accompanied by a Portuguese artillery contingent of 180 men commanded by Diogo Soarez de Mello. The Siamese defenses proved stronger than anticipated, so that the attack ran aground. Part of the reason was that Ayuthia had also enlisted the assistance of some 50 Portuguese mercenaries, led by Diogo Pereira. The belligerent Europeans were developing an awesome reputation as a specialized military factor. The failure of the Ayuthia campaign undermined the self-confidence of the thirty-five-year-old king, who abandoned his governing duties in an orgy of self-indulgence. He was murdered by a Mon prince rival in 1550.

The confusion and turmoil which ensued following the death of Tabinshweti were brought to an end by his able military leader and brother-in-law Bayinnaung, who assumed the crown in 1551. He moved first to recover Toungoo, then Pagan and Prome, and finally ousted the Mon pretender from Pegu itself. The Portuguese forces of de Mello afforded him valued assistance. Bayinnaung's military efforts during the remainder of the fifties were directed against the northern Shan enemies whom his predecessor had ignored. He first captured Ava and the lower Chindwin valley, and then moved eastward into the Shan plateau area, where he enlisted considerable cooperation. Friendly Shan contingents were added to Burman armies moving eastward toward Chiengmai and eventually into the Laos country across the Mekong River. Bayinnaung's excessive involvement in the affairs of distant Luang Prabang and Vientiane Laos from 1560 to 1571 proved unrewarding, in spite of several victories in Laos.

More feasible and more profitable materially were Bayinnaung's successful efforts to capture Ayuthia. The first successful attack came in 1563–1564 via Chiengmai and Sukhotai. He had to repeat the effort four years later following a rebellion staged by the Siamese puppet ruler whom he had installed. Under a new Thai puppet, prince Tammaraja, and with the support of a Burmese garrison, Toungoo dynasty control persisted at Ayuthia from 1569 to 1583. During this period the Ayuthia government gained Burma's permission to improve its defenses in view of the aggressive moves of the Cambodians, who had reoccupied Angkor in the 1560s (previously lost to Siam in 1431), and were threatening Ayuthia. Tammaraja's youthful son, Pra Naret, was permitted to return from his six-year hostage residence in Burma to lead the defense against the Cambodians. Periodic rebellions in the Pegu capital which required Bayinnaung's attention, combined with his exhausting and profitless campaigns in distant Laos, depleted in time the resources of his Burman-Mon-Shan armies, although none dared challenge his authority during his lifetime.

Bayinnaung twice rebuilt the Pegu capital, which waxed immensely wealthy and impressive. European visitors during the 1570s were much impressed with the city. The Burman ruler also functioned as a vigorous patron of Buddhism. On one occasion he

reportedly offered to pay the Portuguese the sum of 300,000 ducats
to acquire the celebrated Buddha tooth which they had captured
at Jaffna in Ceylon. After the Europeans ground the tooth to dust,
the appreciative Ceylon government contributed the gift of another
tooth of allegedly superior authenticity, to gratify the needs of the
Burma ruler. Bayinnaung's Burma was the most powerful state of
southeast Asia in its day. At the time of his death in 1581, he was
preparing to invade Arakan, which was operating at the time in
league with Portuguese slave-trader adventurers. Even so, outside
the capital, the Mon country of lower Burma in the 1580s lay
ravaged and exhausted by the ruler's unrelenting demands.

The Decline of the Toungoo Dynasty

Following the death of the distinguished Bayinnaung, Burma was
convulsed by the inevitably gruesome ordeal of disputed succession.
The heir apparent at Pegu, Prince Nanda Bayin, was first challenged by rival relatives, an uncle viceroy at Ava, and then by two
brothers in charge of Prome and Toungoo. He liquidated a number
of court personalities at Pegu, who were accused of being a party to
the opposition. Nanda Bayin then managed to defeat the invading
forces of Ava's viceroy, after which the attacks of other rebels collapsed in 1584. Meanwhile, the supposedly pro-Burman authorities
at Ayuthia took advantage of the strife in Pegu to strike out for
freedom. They were led by the able Pra Naret. Nanda Bayin made
three abortive efforts to reconquer Siam, in 1584, 1586–1587, and
1592. In 1590, Prince Pra Naret became King Naresuen, inheriting
the throne of his father. He managed to recover Tenasserim up the
Martaban at the mouth of the Salween in 1593, and then inflicted a
paralyzing attack on Cambodia's Lovek capital in 1594. Thereafter
he staged periodic invasions of lower Burma as circumstances afforded him opportunity.

The collapse of Nanda Bayin's government came in 1599, when a
general rebellion developed led by the prince viceroys at Prome and
Toungoo. The latter prince attacked Pegu, enlisting the cooperation of the naval forces of the aggressive King of Arakan, who was
being assisted by a number of Portuguese adventurers. The rebel
Burmese forces captured and destroyed Pegu, carrying Nanda Bayin
away as captive to Toungoo, where he was summarily executed. At
the same time the Arakan naval forces seized Syriam, the port of

Pegu. When Naresuen's Siamese army arrived belatedly to share the spoils, it was defeated enroute to Toungoo, while the attending Siamese fleet was captured by the semi-piratical Arakanese forces.

Amid the ensuing confusion unified Burma fell apart, but the Mon inhabitants of the south were the principal victims. The Siamese took over the Tenasserim cities, and the once busy Irrawaddy delta ports silted up from lack of use. Visiting observers to Pegu in the 1590s reported that roads and waterways were clogged with material and human debris, while jungle-claimed rice fields were infested with wild cattle and tigers. The surviving leadership of the Toungoo dynasty eventually lost interest in the coastal region and shifted its center back upcountry.

A temporary legacy of the disruption of lower Burma's government was the assumption of control over the port of Syriam and environs by several Portuguese, who were associated with Arakanese occupation of the port. Philip de Brito and Ribeiro de Souza, who had been given charge of the customs house, decided in 1599 to identify with the local Mon population, harried as it was by the Siamese at Martaban, the Burmans from Prome and Toungoo, and the oppressive Arakanese governor. After ousting the titular Arakanese official, de Brito built his own fort and then departed for Goa to solicit official support, leaving de Souza in charge. During the ensuing three years, de Souza managed to defend Syriam from an angry Arakanese naval counter attack and from a land campaign launched by Prome. The enthusiastic Mons hailed de Souza as their deliverer.

The drama took a new turn when de Brito returned in 1602 with a Portuguese commission as captain-general with six ships bringing reinforcements and supplies. When it became apparent that Goa's objectives had little to do with protecting the rights of the Mon inhabitants, de Souza withdrew in disgust. De Brito continued as "king" of the Mons until 1613, extending his predatory control along the delta coast from Martaban to Bassein. His naval patrols forced all passing ships to pay tolls. He married his son to the daughter of the newly installed Mon chief of Martaban. The charade might have continued longer if the plundering de Brito had kept his hands off the gold, jewels, and temple bells (needed for cannon) of the Buddhist shrines and had refrained from efforts to impose Christianity, as prescribed by Goan authorities.

Toungoo forces levied an abortive attack on de Brito in 1610:

three years later a stronger Avan army led by a nephew successor of
Nanda Bayin, Anaukpetlun, captured Syriam with the assistance of
a Mon defector operating from the inside. De Brito was killed, and
his four hundred captured followers were transported as slaves to
the far northern Shwebo granary, to become an elite corps of
gunners and musketeers in the Burmese army. The captives married
Burman wives and eventually acquired the services of a Catholic
priest. The ousting of de Brito provided a basis for some semblance
of revived unified rule from the Ava government, which persisted
for more than a century thereafter. The explosive energies of the
Toungoo dynasty were nevertheless a spent force. Burma's attention
was later directed inward.

Institutional Development

The Toungoo dynasty managed to survive until 1752 partly because of the lack of any serious political rivals and partly because of
the maturity of its institutional development. Its partial recovery
from the fiasco of 1599 was the accomplishment of the nephew of
King Nanda Bayin, King Anaukpetlun, who assumed control at
Ava in 1605, reoccupied Toungoo in 1610, and overthrew de Brito's
adventurers at Syriam in 1613. He extended his control to
Moulmein in Tenasserim, leaving Siam in control of the remainder.
After returning to Ava, he directed his principal efforts eastward
across the Shan plateau extending by 1615 as far as Chiengmai,
where he installed his son as viceroy. The ancient Mon principality
apparently preferred mild indirect rule from Ava to more exacting
control by Ayuthia. It remained a part of the Ava domain until
1662. Anaukpetlun was also interested for a time in the economic
advantages to be derived from a revival of overseas trade not only
with the Portuguese, but also with the newly arrived Dutch and
English Company traders. In 1628, he actually shifted his capital
back to Pegu briefly. From there he began tentative preparations for
renewed military action against Ayuthia, in the time-honored
fashion.

This plan was abruptly terminated in 1629 by his murder at the
hands of a half-brother rival, Thalun, who was committed to a less
aggressive policy. An abortive Mon rebellion ensued, followed by a
mass exodus of rebel refugees across the Siam border. Thalun there-

upon abandoned efforts to collaborate with the Mons or to promote overseas trade. In 1635 he shifted the capital back to interior Ava. For more than a century thereafter the Burma state was inland centered, its policy becoming essentially isolationist, defensive, and xenophobic.

A major accomplishment of Thalun's reign was the perfecting of the governmental administrative system. It included the preparation of the first law code in the Burmese language, based in part on Wareru's earlier summary of the Hindu Code of Manu. Thalun then directed the famous revenue inquest of 1638, including a comprehensive inventory of land holdings and revenue sources. The seventeenth century apparently also witnessed the maturing of the elite ahmudan service status assigned to favored occupants of the royal granary centers, Shwebo, Kyauksè, and Magwe-Minbu. Multiple-family *asu* (royal service) units within the ahmudan system provided not only army officers and regular recruits, but also a self-supporting palace servant corps, including guard units, masons, carpenters, and menial caretaker personnel. Administrative developments also included substantial improvements in the governance of the dispersed athi subject population. It involved the appointment of *myowun* governors (town burden bearers) of provinces and palace-authenticated locally resident myothugyis (township headmen). Fiefdoms were assigned to royal relatives and to local princely retainers. Governmental administrative institutions thus became more firmly integrated.

The central agency of royal authority was the *Hlutdaw* (place of release), composed of four royally-appointed *wungyis* (great burden bearers; ministers) and their several *wundauk* assistants. The Hlutdaw exercised increasing authority under a succession of feeble kings. It functioned as the supreme executive organ, the final court of appeal, and the primary agency in the formulation of governmental policy. Individual wungyis took on special functional assignments at royal command. At the principal frontier entry points (in the delta and along the China border), provincial myowun governors acted as foreign relations buffers for the court. The interior palace counsellors (*atwinwuns*), also four in number, operated as an advisory privy council. The commanding general of the army (*Thenat Wun*) was a person of wungyi rank, and the colonels (*bohs*) associated with him were sometimes civilian political appointees, but all were bound by a special oath of allegiance to the king. The several regiments of the palace guard were commanded by military persons of high rank and prestige.

Serving under the provincial governors were the tax collectors and granary supervisors, the local police and military officers, the war boat commanders, the customs officials, and the port superintendent (*shahbandar* or ruler of the port), who was usually a multilingual foreigner. The governors presided over the provincial *myoyon* courts from which appeals could be carried to the Hlutdaw. Minor legal cases were decided, as a rule, by locally resident elders, functioning as arbitrator-consultants. The local myothugyi township headmen were assisted by census takers, household-tax collectors, and village constables. Burma's governmental system functioned effectively at the centers of authority and elsewhere when conditions were favorable. It was weak in its attempted avoidance of responsibility for external relations, in its lack of effective control over autonomous fiefdoms (*myosas*) and areas remote from the capital, and especially in the absence of any dependable arrangements for orderly succession to the kingship.

Also lacking at Ava was any systematic effort to assimilate the minority elements of the population. The Buddhist Mon and Arakanese peoples were hostile aliens, while the non-Buddhist Karen, Kachin, and Chin tribesmen and scores of other animist groups within the Shan plateau were for the most part regarded as beyond the pale of civilized Burman-Buddhist concern. Only the Shan wet-rice cultivators adopted Buddhism and the Burmese script. Superstitious animist and magical practices remained very much alive among all peoples of Burma. The essential cohesive factors within the state related to widespread male literacy as taught in the monastery schools, coupled with the general acceptance of the Buddhist faith and traditional loyalty to the divinely-sanctioned monarchial institutions.

Religious Organization

The order of monks, the Sangha, was revered by the people because it embodied the Buddhist ideal of unconcern with worldly desires. The monastic schools were attended by all village youth preliminary to their formal induction as ko-yin (novices) in the monastery proper at the age of 12 to 15. Public contributions to pagoda shrines and to needs of the monks ranked highly in the category of meritorious deeds. Devotion to the trilogy of Buddha, Dhamma (the Law), and the Sangha provided for the orthodox the sole means of escape from the endless burden of successive reincarnations, along with the sanctions for moral conduct of the eightfold path of righteous living. The abbots of the several monastery units exercised disciplinary control over the ko-yins and locally affiliated monks. Those refusing to accept such discipline could be disrobed, and in flagrant instances of defiance offenders could be forced to don the white robe of the pagoda slave.

Governmental control over the numerous and influential Sangha community was exercised through the office of the royally appointed *thathanabaing* (possessor of discipline and instruction). He presided as a kind of archbishop over a central religious council in which all important Buddhist sects were represented. Backed by royal authority, the thathanabaing and the district *gaingyok* section of the ecclesiastical hierarchy adjudicated disputes arising within the monastic community. They also supervised the annual examinations in the Pali scriptures required for entry into the various levels of the ordained clergy. Acting in cooperation with the Sangha council were two high governmental officials, the commissioner of ecclesiastical lands and the ecclesiastical censor. They kept records of monastery landholdings and the lists of all formally ordained monks, their ages, and dates of formal induction. The two commissions were properly staffed through district and local levels by royally appointed assistants and record clerks.

Traditional Burmese civilization reflected the psychological as well as the social influence of the long-extended and pervasive influence of Buddhist practices. The monastic system, which included for varying periods of time every Burman youth, functioned as a socially leveling system, an educational agency, and an instrument of moral discipline. The sons of princes and peasants experienced very much the same discipline as ko-yins in the monastery, involving full acceptance of reverence for monks and elders. The simple monk's robe combined with shaved heads and eyebrows reenforced the sense of personal anonymity.

In theory, the Burmese male enjoyed superior status over the female because he alone was capable of approaching the realization of the monastic ideal of the Buddhist faith. The wife customarily walked behind her husband and must never be elevated physically

above him. In actual life, females very much held their own.
Married women kept their maiden names, the title to their own
property, and an equal share of joint earnings. Burma's women
were earthy and mundane, pragmatic and thrifty, able to drive a
sharp bargain, to prepare food and clothing, and to care for
children. Uninhibited by the Buddhist exhortation to conquer desire, girls were free to make themselves attractive to men and to
adjust with self-confidence to their assigned life roles. Women were
inclined to be friendly toward male foreigners. A wife's tongue
could be very sharp, and divorce was fairly easy. Only the wealthy
could afford many wives, while ruling princes often became creatures rather than masters of their royal harems.

Burma's young men, by contrast, tended to oscillate between the
passive inactivity of the monastic ideal and the violent daring of
the bandit (*dacoit.*) One role was respected on religious grounds;
the other could be an admired expression of masculinity. Conduct in both instances reflected a considerable element of personal frustration, while the in-between roles of peasant, fisherman,
or cartman carried relatively little prestige. The average wife was
more steady of character and more responsible to her duties than
was her husband. The unrestrained violence of which Burmese men
were capable in their civil wars, in their destructive incursions into
neighboring countries, and their subsequent propensity for lawlessness under colonial rule—in flagrant violation of the Buddhist ethic
—were expressions of varying levels of psychological maladjustment.
Both sexes displayed the same refreshing sense of humor and paid
formal deference to status symbols and rank within their own
society. Burmans also exhibited a sense of proud disdain of their less
civilized tribe neighbors and were not unduly impressed by
foreigners generally.

The Last Century of Toungoo Rule

Few positive accomplishments can be ascribed to the successor-son
of Thalun, King Pindalé (1648–1661). He had the misfortune of
becoming involved in the feuding which developed in the late
1640s between the last surviving Ming Chinese refugee prince,
Yung-li, and the incoming Manchu dynasty. Yung-li held out in
Yunnan for more than a decade before being obliged to seek asylum

in Ava in 1658. His Ming supporters then raided Burma in a vain attempt to rescue their prince. Other complications developed in lower Burma when Mon army recruits mutinied, followed by an abortive Burman invasion of Siam. Meanwhile, direct Manchu intervention forced Ava to surrender Yung-li. The ineffective Pindalé was dethroned by his brother Pyé in 1661. When a major Chinese invasion of upper Burma threatened in 1662, Ava's fearful vassal ruler in Chiengmai sought protection from Ayuthia's kingdom of Siam.

The subsequent history of the Toungoo dynasty under a succession of feeble rulers was undistinguished. The Ava government administered little more in lower Burma than the Irrawaddy River corridor, the city of Pegu, and its port of Syriam. Following the turn of the century, the peace of upper Burma was disrupted by repeated raids on the part of looting Manipuri horsemen invading from India's border areas. The recurring raids were punctuated by periodic Shan rebellions, the risings sometimes extending down to the environs of Ava itself.

Burma's early commercial relations with European newcomers to southeast Asia after 1600, mainly Dutch and English, were far from promising. The Dutch Company operated a trading factory at Syriam from 1635 to 1679 in competition with Indian cloth merchants and locally resident Portuguese. An English factory, established at that port in 1647 was wrecked during the Cromwell-Dutch War of 1652 and was completely abandoned a decade later. The English Company tried again at Syriam in the 1680s, partly out of concern to develop a counterweight to contemporaneous French intrigues in Siam, which collapsed in 1688. In a formal agreement with the Burma authorities in 1709, British Madras gained access to the ship building and repair facilities at Syriam, but did not bother to set up a trading factory. After 1727, French ships from India also shared access to Syriam's repair facilities. Both European groups were obliged to leave lower Burma following the outbreak of civil strife during the 1750s.

The situation in Mon-inhabited lower Burma as described by European visitors in the early 1700s was very discouraging. The once-imposing city of Pegu was only a tiny fraction of its former size, while the surrounding countryside had reverted to jungle. Pagodas everywhere were in disrepair. The populous port of

Syriam was hardly Burmese at all, since the dominating merchant population was largely Muslim Indian, Armenian, and Portuguese. The section of the city protected by the stone fort constituted only one-fifth of the total inhabited area. The native population was thoroughly demoralized by the presence of so many foreign men, who experienced no difficulty in acquiring temporary wives for their indefinite stays. The descendants of the original Portuguese Christian community had become increasingly Burmese ethnically, and observers accorded little respect for the religious standards maintained by the resident Goa-recruited priests.

Ava in the north was forced increasingly on the defensive after 1714, when the governor of Pagan launched an abortive attack on the capital. Ava was powerless thereafter to curb the Manipuri raiders, who climaxed their efforts in 1738 with the capture and plundering of the city of Sagaing, directly across the river from Ava. Two years later, Shan tribesmen, assisted by locally colonized Mon slave troops, staged a rebellion directly to the north of Ava. Shortly thereafter, the Ava-appointed governor of Pegu rose in revolt. After the Mon forces repulsed an invading Burman army, the Peguans proceeded to nominate their own king, with one Binya Dala acting as chief minister. The Mon armies obtained artillery support by capturing the guns and the crews of six Ostend Company ships which happened at this inauspicious moment to venture into the port of Syriam. Meanwhile all European factories and churches at Syriam, together with ship-building facilities, were destroyed. In 1743, the Pegu forces moved north to capture both Toungoo and Prome, only to run aground thereafter.

The Mon rebellion revived in 1747, when Binya Dala pushed aside the incompetent king and himself assumed the Mon crown. From Prome and Toungoo, he inaugurated full scale attacks against the nearly defenceless Ava, which continued to be paralyzed by local disorders. The Burman capital finally fell in 1752, the event that marked the end of the Toungoo dynasty.

The relative ease with which the Mons captured Ava was highly deceptive. Binya Dala did not anticipate the spirited response which ensued. Burman leadership emerged more or less spontaneously in the person of the son of the myothugyi of Moksobomyo (later to be renamed Shwebo), the royal granary area located across the river to the north of Ava. After the initial Mon attack on Moksobomyo was repelled, the Burman countereffort attracted enthusiastic recruits in a determined move to retake Ava. Under the altered circumstances, the frightened Mon garrison elected to flee the city. Thus emerged the new Konbaung dynasty under King Alaungpaya of Shwebomyo (the city of the golden leader). His adopted royal title meant "Emerging Buddha."

IV A Century of Konbaung Dynasty Rule, 1752 to 1852

The vigorous Burman reaction to the presumptuous Mon capture of Ava in 1752 signaled another exhibition of the explosive energy latent in the mobilized nation. The Konbaung dynasty founder, King Alaungpaya and his brother and later successor, King Hsinbyushin, put down all internal resistance and carried their conquering armies into neighboring Siam. This time, Ayuthia was so utterly destroyed (in 1767) that the site had to be abandoned in favor of a new capital near present-day Bangkok a decade later. A tentative invasion threat from China diverted King Hsinbyushin's forces in 1767 from extending their Siam conquests beyond Ayuthia. Eventually, the perennial problems of royal succession undermined Burma's vaunted power, assisting the Siamese in recovering their independence. The new Chakri dynasty repelled repeated Burman invasions during the 1780s and 1790s. The prestige of the Konbaung dynasty faded almost as abruptly as it had risen.

As if seeking a consolation prize for their failure in Siam, the Burmans in 1784 shifted their attention westward to annex the previously independent state of Arakan, thus establishing a border contact with the newly occupied Chittagong section of British Bengal. Down to the end of the Napoleonic wars, border friction problems were contained by reciprocal concessions, but the two imperial powers eventually clashed in the 1820s. Burma's humiliating defeat by an invading British-Indian army in 1825–1826, supported and supplied by sea power and river steamers, was a shattering blow to the morale of the court. The British victors collected a large indemnity, annexed two coastal provinces, and were able to assume thereafter a kind of supervisory veto posture over the possible resumption of warfare between Burma and Siam. Successive coups at the Burma court in the 1830s and 1840s and their accompanying disorders aggravated the decline of political and military authority, rendering Burma powerless to resist the subsequent British occupation of all of lower Burma in 1852. Meanwhile

British colonial rule in the previously annexed coastal provinces had demonstrated what could be accomplished in terms of rice and timber exports under European direction and easy access to foreign commercial outlets.

The Reigns of Alaungpaya and Hsinbyushin

The enormously energetic Alaungpaya overcame formidable difficulties in his efforts to establish firm control over upper Burma in the face of renewed Mon attacks following their withdrawal from Ava in 1752. His two defensive campaigns against the Mons were diverted by efforts to curb the Manipuri raiders and tribal Shan revolts to the north and east. After the second decisive defeat of the Mon attackers, Alaungpaya was finally able in 1755–1756 to move southward down the Irrawaddy valley. His forces overran the lower valley and main delta region during the dry season of 1756 over to the Dagon shrine, which he renamed Rangoon, or "End of Strife." He was then obliged to turn back northward again for a last punitive action against the Manipuris, leaving the Mons still in control of their Pegu capital and the port of Syriam. His final campaign against the Mons in 1756–1757 was coupled with the defeat of French adventurer and supporter of Pegu, Sieur de Bruno, who enjoyed unofficial support from Pondicherry. De Bruno was apparently trying to duplicate the feat of de Brito at Syriam in the early 1600s. Belated assistance sent from Pondicherry arrived at Syriam only a few days following Alaungpaya's capture of the place. Two French vessels were decoyed into the harbor and run aground by Burmese pilots, to fall into the hands of the victors. For the final attack on Pegu, the Burman armies utilized to the full the 35 cannon, the 1,300 muskets, and the 250 enslaved fighting men taken from the French vessels. The capture of Pegu was a gruesomely bloody affair. Burman power had triumphed.

Two years later, Alaungpaya liquidated remnants of the British occupation of Negrais on the western end of the delta. Madras authorities had occupied Negrais in 1753 to offset the threat of de Bruno's French intrigue at Syriam. British agents meanwhile had tried to negotiate with the proud Alaungpaya but had failed to accede to his demand for a direct reply from George II and for firearms, largely because of the competing requirements of the crucial British war with the French in India. Following the elimination of the French threat at Syriam in 1756, the English Company authorized withdrawal from Negrais, but completion of the move was delayed out of concern to salvage some valued timber resources. The anti-British machinations of several renegade Armenian and French advisors to Alaungpaya precipitated the massacre of the survivors at Negrais in 1759. British India was in no position for rejoinder. The collapse of both the French and British interventions did much to bolster Burman pride and their disdain for the European foreigner.

Alaungpaya's untimely death occurred in the spring of 1760, following an abortive attack on Ayuthia. He was mortally wounded by the explosion of a carelessly handled siege gun, and died during his return trip to Burma. Three and a half years of political confusion ensued before King Hsinbyushin pushed aside a nephew rival and restored order in late 1763. The first move of the new ruler was to shift the capital from Shwebo to Ava; the second was to renew the war against Siam.

The Burman attack against Ayuthia in 1766 and 1767 was an overpowering effort. Utilizing the newly enlisted cooperation of the Manipuri cavalry and Shan levies, Hsinbyushin launched a major attack via Chiengmai and Vientiane from northern Siam, combined with a formidable advance via Tenasserim in the south. After enduring a year-long siege, Ayuthia fell in early 1767. The capture was accompanied by an orgy of looting and physical destruction, which left the place in complete ruins. Even though Burmese armies became heavily involved immediately thereafter in a distant war along the China border, it was more than a decade later, in 1778, before Siamese resistance forces managed to reoccupy the site of the previous capital. Siamese resistance found a leader in a part-Chinese army chief named P'ya Taksin, who set up a new temporary capital downstream at Thonburi, opposite what eventually became the royal capital at Bangkok.

The war with China from 1767 to 1770 developed primarily over aggressive Burman intervention in the Shan border areas and the consequent interruption of normal Chinese trading operations from Yunnan into the upper Irrawaddy corridor. The timing of the Chinese move during the course of the siege of Ayuthia was certainly more than coincidental. It may well have been made in response to a Siamese appeal for aid, but the supporting evidence is not available. Burman-Shan forces repelled repeated Chinese incursions from

Yunnan, although one of them penetrated to the vicinity of Ava. In the end, the Burmese commander obtained the withdrawal of the Chinese forces by entering into an agreement to reopen the trading route and to send decennial tributary missions to the Chinese capital. Hsinbyushin was highly displeased with the 1770 settlement, but could do no more about the matter in the face of the revival of Mon rebellion in lower Burma shortly thereafter. The defense of Burma proper of necessity took precedence over the deteriorating situation in Siam.

The Burman ruler's death in 1776 and the ensuing five-year interim period prior to Bodawpaya's accession in 1781, permitted P'ya Taksin to continue his successful guerrilla operations in Siam. He developed mental aberrations after 1780 and was pushed aside in 1782 by a coterie of nobles in favor of one of the princely military commanders, who took the title of Rama I as the first ruler of the Chakri dynasty. Although P'ya Taksin is still honored by the Thai as a national hero, his kingly status was less than authentic according to traditional standards. His harassing tactics in resisting successive Burmese invasions continued under the new Chakri leadership. The latter established a new capital at Bangkok, directly across the river from P'ya Taksin's Thonburi.

The Reign of Bodawpaya As Watershed

In a number of respects the reign of Bodawpaya marked a significant watershed in modern Burmese history. Bodawpaya's first important act as king was to conquer Arakan in 1784, which brought Burma into direct contact with British India. He then made a series of futile efforts to recover control in Siam. Four major invasion efforts (in 1785–1786, 1794, 1798, and 1802) produced negative results both politically and economically. Lower Burma in particular was impoverished by royal exactions levied in support of the successive campaigns. In the end, the Burmese retained control over the Shan plateau to the borders of Chiengmai and over the Tenasserim coastal district. A new center of border friction developed in Arakan and Chittagong, where opponents of Burmese rule found a base of operations in British India. Arakan grievances were many, including enslavement of several thousand captives and the theft of the prized Mahamuni Buddha figure. The failure of Bodawpaya's Siamese campaigns was partly responsible for the

ruler's costly decision to shift his capital from allegedly ill-omened
Ava to the new site of Amarapura, some ten miles to the north. At
the new capital, Bodawpaya constructed the pretentious Arakan
Pagoda to house the stolen image of the Buddha. With the Siamese
border more or less stabilized, the problem of relations with Arakan
and British Bengal became a matter of increasing concern.

For a number of reasons, the initial steps in Burmese-British relations proved manageable. When Michael Symes, as Company agent,
first visited Amarapura in 1795, his major concern was to forestall
possible use of Burma's ports by Britain's French enemy. Bodawpaya
at the time was still involved in his wars with Siam. Burma's
grievances relating to Arakanese rebel elements operating from
across the Chittagong border were considered sympathetically by
Symes partly because British authorities owed nothing to such semi-
bandit groups. The Calcutta authorities had already in 1794 turned
over three Arakanese rebel leaders to the Burmese. British assistance
along the Arakan border could obviously provide a basis for enlisting the cooperation of Amarapura in denying Burma's ports for use
by the French. The second Company mission to Amarapura by
Symes in 1802 and subsequent ones by John Canning (1803 and
1809) continued to be concerned primarily with preventing Burman cooperation with the French. Both negotiators gave satisfactory
assurances that rebel elements would not be permitted to use Chittagong as a base for attacks on Arakan. Relations were further eased
after 1803, when the principal Arakan rebel leader died. Burma's
near exhaustion following the repeatedly fruitless attacks on Siam
also contributed to the continuing détente.

Burma-Bengal relations began to take on a more abrasive character in 1811. The son of the deceased rebel leader, Chin Byan,
engineered a formidable invasion of Arakan provinces, including
the capture of the capital city of Mrohaung. The spirited Burmese
rejoinder of 1812 not only restored Amarapura's authority but
chased all rebel forces across the border into Chittagong. Relations
remained strained for several years thereafter. Amarapura accused
Calcutta of collusion with Chin Byan, who had actually offered to
make Arakan a vassal to India if the British would afford him protection. Canning's third mission in 1814 was obliged to admit evidence of some negligence on the part of British authorities, but he
argued that Chin Byan was being accorded asylum by Calcutta on
the grounds that his action was essentially political rather than

criminal. The crisis eased somewhat with the death of Chin Byan in 1815, but Burmese authorities developed thereafter an aggressive stance not only with respect to Chittagong, but also toward the India border states of Manipur, Cachar, and Assam, none of which were included at the time within the jurisdiction of the Company. Direct military confrontation eventually developed under youthful King Bagyidaw, who took over at Amarapura in 1819, following the death of his aged grandfather. The new king's first move was to shift the capital back to Ava.

The First Anglo-Burmese War, 1824–1826

Conflict with British Bengal first developed over control of buffer areas located inland from coastal Chittagong. The rulership of Assam had been contested since 1816 by various rebellious factions, not one of which proved capable of establishing itself. The original rajah of Assam, Chandrakanta, was ousted temporarily by a pretender, who tried in vain to solicit support from Calcutta and then appealed to Burma's Bodawpaya for aid. A Burmese invading force managed in early 1817 to install a new ruler at Jorhat, the Assam capital, only to see him expelled a year or so later. A second Burmese intervention was staged in 1819, this time restoring the original rajah to power before withdrawing. The political situation was highly confused.

The accession of King Bagyidaw to power in Burma shortly thereafter, in 1819, was preliminary to a more formidable Burmese military invasion of Assam in 1821, led by the able General Maha Bandula. Several refugee Assamese groups which had taken refuge across the Bengal boundary made a number of futile uncoordinated efforts to oust the unwelcome Burmese forces, that were living off the country in the same onerous fashion previously pursued in Siam. After two such incursions had been driven back into Bengal, Bandula registered a formal demand in 1822 that Calcutta surrender the rebel leaders to him, according to the previous pattern set in Chittagong. The borders of British Bengal were thus directly threatened by a fairly formidable and highly predatory Burmese army, although operating at a great distance from its Irrawaddy valley base. From this situation emerged Calcutta's conception of the counter-tactic of staging a direct invasion of lower Burma by sea.

A second area of tension developed meanwhile in Manipur and Cachar states, located between Burma's Chindwin valley and Bengal. Neither was claimed at the time as Company-protected territory. An excuse for the Burmese conquest of Manipur was provided by the refusal of the rajah of that state to attend the coronation of Bagyidaw in 1819. The invasion developed in 1821–1822. When the escaping Manipur forces fled westward into Cachar, plundering as they went, leaders of that state appealed to Calcutta for protection. Under these circumstances the new British governor-general, Lord Amherst (who took over in 1823), decided to extend Company protection to Cachar, to neighboring Janitia, and also to Assam. British-Bengali forces first clashed with the Burmese in Cachar, and managed with some difficulty to force the Burmese to return to Manipur. A third area of conflict developed in 1823–1824 over the island of Shahpuri at the mouth of the Naaf River on the Arakan-Chittagong border. Bandula himself was in command of the Chittagong campaign when the war began.

When Calcutta declared war on Burma on May 5, 1824, preparations for a direct invasion of the Irrawaddy delta by sea were already well under way. Some 11,000 British-Indian forces, previously assembled in the Andaman Islands, captured Rangoon on May 10, encountering little or no opposition. The onset of the rainy season immediately thereafter made impossible any further advance. Seaborne supplies were slow to arrive, and local anti-Burman partisans, Mons and Karens, remained aloof, refusing at first to provide expected assistance. The British thrust into lower Burma did have the anticipated effect of forcing the abandonment of Burmese operations along the entire Indian border area.

The crucial phase of the conflict developed at Rangoon following the end of the rains, from October to December, 1824. Preliminary Burmese attacks cautiously undertaken by wungyi (royal government) commanders against the city's depleted garrison forces might have succeeded if they had been more vigorously pressed. Fever and dysentery had taken a fearful toll, reducing the effective defense forces to a small fraction of their original strength. When the main Burmese army of 60,000 men arrived in early November, the available defenders numbered only around 4,000 men. The threat to the Rangoon garrison was grave.

Meanwhile Calcutta's problem of dispatching reinforcements had been seriously complicated in October by an embarrassing mutiny of the Bengal-stationed 47th Hindu infantry battalion ordered to relieve Rangoon. Part of the sepoy complaint was poor pay, but religious considerations were also important, since crossing the waters involved the threat of losing caste. In view of Rangoon's dire need of help, the British commander, Sir Edward Paget, dealt ruthlessly with the mutineers. When a battery of European-manned artillery opened fire on the protesters, the survivors panicked and fled. Eleven of the ringleaders were later executed, many native officers were dismissed, and hundreds of captive sepoys were sentenced indefinitely to hard labor. After some further delay, other forces were shipped to Rangoon, accompanied by gunboats. They arrived barely in time to assist the exhausted defenders in turning back the all-out assault of Bandula's forces starting on December 1.

The policies of Lord Amherst and Sir Edward Paget were subjected to sharp criticism by both the Company directors and the home government. The monetary costs of the Burma campaign were heavy as were the manpower losses sustained from both illness and combat. Critics argued that Amherst should not have provoked the Burmese in Cachar and should have avoided extending the protective obligations of the Company over other areas which he was unable to defend. Company officials went so far in 1825 as to veto a policy of additional territorial annexations. Lord Amherst himself was very discouraged, and the harrowing experience contributed to his early retirement as governor-general in 1828.

But the Burmese were also in serious trouble. Once forced to abandon their siege of Rangoon in December, they experienced difficulty in making an effective stand. The superior arms, discipline, and leadership of the pursuing Bengali forces, consisting of some 7,000 men plus the gunboats and river control, made the difference. General Bandula's death at Danubyu on April, 1825, threw Burmese forces into hopeless confusion and British forces managed to occupy Prome above the delta before the rainy season again halted ground operations in June. The determining factors were the seaborne supplies and reinforcements from India, plus control of river navigation, which permitted a sustained campaign extending through two successive rainy seasons. When the British-Bengali advance up the Irrawaddy Valley was resumed in late 1825, it was assisted by an armed river steamer provided by Calcutta. Meanwhile the Burmese hold over India border areas crumbled before local resistance, while invading British-Indian forces occupied important points not only in

Arakan but also along the Tenasserim shore of the Bay of Bengal.

The first efforts to negotiate a settlement failed, but they were resumed at Yandabo when it became apparent to the Burmese forces that they were powerless to halt the drive. The Treaty of Yandabo was signed on February 24, 1826. It imposed an indemnity of 10 million rupees (one million pounds sterling) plus the surrender of all Burmese claims to previously occupied Indian territories and to Burma's own provinces of Arakan and Tenasserim.

The principal casualty of the staggering and unprecedented Burmese defeat was the humiliation of the Konbaung dynasty. Ava resented particularly the imposed agreement to accept a British Resident at the capital. The Burmese Chronicles' account of the episode reflected such royal concern by praising King Bagyidaw's dedication to piety and to humanity in making his generous peace. He allegedly compensated the invading strangers for the vast sums which they had spent in the inconclusive enterprise, thus expediting their prompt withdrawal from the country. Unmentioned in the chronicles was the treaty's veto of future Burmese molestation of Indian as well as Siamese neighbors, and the surrender of coastal provinces.

Lord Amherst's decision to withdraw his forces quickly not only left the negotiation of a satisfactory commercial treaty virtually impossible, but also exposed to Burmese vengeance Karen and Mon allies in lower Burma who had actively assisted the British during the final year of the war. The invading forces withdrew southward to Rangoon upon Bagyidaw's payment of the first of several scheduled installments on the indemnity. Amherst was not prepared to risk additions to the heavy casualties already suffered, mainly from illness (some 15,000 dead of the 40,000 troops involved), by prolonging the occupation. The governor-general was congratulated by previously critical authorities on his successful conclusion of the operation, but he did not wish to incur any repetition of the kind of criticism which he had earlier sustained. Circumstances associated with the defense of Bengal rather than overt imperialistic intent had prompted British intervention, but the harsh terms imposed on the defeated state established the inevitable presumption of eventual British-Indian domination.

The interpreter and translator who assisted in the negotiation of the Yandabo Treaty was the American missionary, Adoniram Judson, who had been resident in Burma since 1813. When the war

began in May 1824, Judson happened to be present in Ava in connection with his third abortive attempt since 1820 to obtain from
the Burmese court legal authorization for his preaching activity at
Rangoon and to halt the officially-sanctioned persecution of the
handful of Christian adherents whom he had attracted. During the
first year of the war, Judson suffered rigorous imprisonment at Ava
along with other English-speaking foreigners and captive Indian
soldiers. He survived the ordeal only by reason of the assistance
afforded by Ann Judson, who was free to bring in food and other
necessities and to register appeals on his behalf with the authorities.
From May 1825, to his eventual release in November of the same
year, Judson was assigned to a more humane prison routine at
Amarapura, where he gradually regained his health. It was the Ava
government which requested his assistance as interpreter in the peace
negotiations.

The American medical missionary, Dr. Price, was also caught in
Ava during the war period and suffered imprisonment along with
Judson. Price later returned to Ava to serve as physician to the royal
court. The Judsons accompanied the retiring British-Indian army
back to Rangoon, and in 1826 transferred the direction of Baptist
missionary activities to British-annexed Tenasserim, with a later
projection into Arakan as well. Part of the irony of the American
missionary's plea for British colonial protection derives from the fact
that the Judsons in 1813 had twice been excluded from British
India, and went to Rangoon quite by accident on a Portuguese boat
sailing from Madras. The historical significance of the role of the
American Baptist mission in Burma will be considered in a later
connection.

From Bagyidaw to Pagan Min

The several years immediately following the withdrawal of British-
Indian forces from Rangoon in late 1826 witnessed the gruesome
suppression of Mon and Karen rebels who had dominated most of
the delta during the previous year. When Britain's John Crawfurd
returned southward from his commercial treaty negotiations at Ava,
he had to arrange for his passage to Rangoon by agreement with the
Karen rebels who then controlled the delta route. Subsequent Burman destruction of rebel villages throughout the countryside drove
some 10,000 Mon refugees across the Salween River into British-

occupied Amherst district (newly named). The harassed Karens took refuge in remote sections of the delta and in neighboring hill regions. Widespread starvation in lower Burma was prevented only by the government's importing grain from India. Use of the Mon language was thereafter banned throughout lower Burma. Alienation of Karens and Mons was intensified by the government's efforts to exact local contributions to help pay off treaty indemnity obligations. The authorities suppressed a final desperate Mon rebellion in 1836–1838.

King Bagyidaw's personal role in the Ava government disintegrated rapidly after the British refused to return Tenasserim in 1832, following the completion of the indemnity payments. Palace intrigue centered around the chief queen and her unscrupulous brother, as the king became progressively incapable of governing the country. Because the court clique were unreservedly hostile to the humiliating presence of any British Resident at the capital, Major Burney, the incumbent after 1830, tended to favor the usurpation of Prince Tharrawaddy, brother of Bagyidaw, as a desirable alternative. But when Tharrawaddy and his semi-bandit following eventually took over control in 1837, no improvement followed. Before and after the palace coup, the upper Burma countryside was engulfed in lawless violence, with virtually every village fending for itself, whether defensively or aggressively.

King Tharrawaddy's policies were persistently anti-British. He flatly disavowed the Yandabo Treaty, thus repudiating the legal basis for British-Indian control of Arakan and Tenasserim. He made the position of the British Resident so uncomfortable that Burney withdrew in 1837, to the dismay of Calcutta. His two successors followed suit by 1839. The Mon rebellion occupied Tharrawaddy's time from 1838 to 1840. He also moved to rebuild Amarapura as the new capital, the fifth such shift by the Konbaung dynasty since the establishment of Shwebo in 1752. When British-Indian forces became heavily involved in the war with China in 1840–1842 and with other troubles in Afghanistan, it appeared that the hostile Tharrawaddy might risk a direct attack on Moulmein and possibly on Siam as well. His complaint was that the British had failed to prevent Siamese incursions along the Shan states' borders. Diplomatic relations were severed for a time, with Bangkok offering to assist the British if hostilities developed. The Burmese move proved to be more bluster than substance, for Tharrawaddy became afflicted with the same kind of mental disorders which had incapacitated his brother Bagyidaw. Continuous intermarriages with close relatives at court was a probable factor in the mental illness of both princes.

In 1844 rival forces clashed with each other in a series of conflicts that elevated Tharrawaddy's son, Pagan Min, to the throne by 1845. During the ensuing seven years of Pagan's control, the government registered no substantial improvement in performance. He was displaced in 1852–1853 by a younger son of Tharrawaddy, Mindon Min, who had spent most of his adulthood as a Buddhist monk. The circumstances attending the change will be described in a later discussion of the origins of the Second Anglo-Burman War. Burmese military power by 1852 was a far cry from what it had been in the early 1820s, not to mention its prowess during the reigns of the previous century. Mindon's patient and considered efforts to revive the prestige and effectiveness of the monarchy were compromised by the advancing imperialist tide from India and eventually by Anglo-French rivalry which developed after 1870.

British Rule in Arakan and Tenasserim, 1826–1852

British-Indian rule in Arakan was in large measure a projection of the government of neighboring Bengal. The Burmese royal-sponsored administrative system of myowun and myothugyi was abruptly pushed aside in favor of the semi-feudal Bengal *zemandari* landlord rule. Local officials collected land taxes and supervised the rapid expansion of rice cultivation and export, while Company representatives cared for police and courts. Indian labor and capital were brought in to develop cultivable lands and water controls. Akyab developed during the ensuing twenty-five years into the largest rice-exporting center in the world. The English Company itself realized after 1836 some 600,000 rupees profit annually. The indigenous population protested the exploitive alien domination, resorting finally in 1838 to a desperate but futile rebellion. Political unrest died down thereafter in view of the total 450 percent increment in rice acreage, which eventually attracted Burmese immigrants.

Tenasserim's history under early British rule was quite different. The population welcomed relief from its traditional status as a bone of contention between Burma and Siam, but it developed economically much more slowly than Arakan. During the initial decade, the courts, police, and revenue services were based on adaptations of indigenous custom utilizing resident Burmese officials. Contract labor from India was used to develop rice acreage and to construct roads, but the immigrants degenerated in time into a hopelessly disorderly rabble recruited largely from the jails of the port cities of south India. The government of the province ran a chronic operations deficit, a fact which encouraged hope on the part of Burma's government that the British Company might surrender control when the indemnity was fully paid off. A tentative British suggestion that Tenasserim might be exchanged with Siam for the Malay state of Kedah angered the Burmans very much. Supplementing the steady expansion of rice production, the profitable exploitation of teakwood forests started in 1829. Particularly useful economically in Tenasserim were the arriving immigrant Chinese, who moved northward from Penang Island.

The first British administrator, N. D. Maingy, originally from Penang, was obliged to retire in 1835 as a result of complaints registered by the British-Indian business community. It demanded a more authoritative and clearly defined legal and administrative structure, with less resort to improvisation. A decade later, the colonial system had become so unpopular that many of the Mon refugees who had left Burma after 1826 crossed the Salween River back into Burma despite the hazards involved. Exasperated Karen villagers, forced to work for timber operations, retaliated by setting fire to much of the remaining teakwood forest, to the dismay of the profiting timber merchants. Maingy's successor, Blundell, had a difficult time. He was caught between the demands of the cost-conscious government of Bengal, resident British businessmen, and decaying indigenous social institutions.

In spite of the difficulties, the economic gains for Tenasserim were such that the population more than doubled between 1835 and 1852. By then the colonial authorities were generally aware that the really profitable development of the economy in rice, timber, and trade, called for the control of the hitherto neglected lower Burma delta and the adjacent hill regions. The vast Irrawaddy delta dwarfed the agricultural opportunities available in Arakan, and the watersheds adjacent to the lower Salween valley were full of valuable timber, easily accessible. Distraught Burma by 1852 was in no position to mount serious opposition to further colonial advance, while it could be assumed that dissident Mon and Karen residents would probably welcome British deliverance.

Under the protective encouragement of British colonial rule in Tenasserim, the American Baptist Mission began to make substantial progress. Animist Karen residents of the area proved to be far more responsive to the Christian message than Rangoon's Buddhist Burmans had been. Karens generally cherished no loyalty to the Burmese kings or to Buddhism, and most of Tenasserim's peoples welcomed deliverance from the interminable feuding between Burman and Siamese rivals for control of the region. Among the Karens, the missionaries fitted well into an ancient tradition that a younger brother would some time bring back to them their long-lost sacred book. When entire Sgaw Karen villages began to respond affirmatively to the missionary call, it became urgently necessary to teach the potential converts what the Christian faith was about. American missionaries, utilizing the Burmese script, reduced both the Sgaw and Pwo languages to writing and began the translation of the Bible into both tongues. The next step was to set up schools as a means of promoting literacy.

Missionary work among the Sgaw Karens tended in time to dominate the American Baptist program. Whereas Judson's lifetime of scholarly achievement had focused on the mastery of Burmese, Sanskrit, and Pali languages, including the preparation of his monumental English-Burmese dictionary and Bible translation, he received little positive response from Buddhist Burmans. His own repeated return visits to Rangoon were unproductive, and the Arakan mission, which he also supported vigorously, was similarly unsuccessful. What was happening among the Karens was the emergence of a kind of rudimentary nationalism, led by educated Christian Sgaw sponsors. But the sentiment was more anti-Burman in tone than positively cohesive. It did not bridge the gap between the Karen groups themselves. Despite the heavy attrition suffered by American missionary personnel from disease in the hostile climate, new recruits maintained the staff at a score or more throughout the 1840s. Judson himself lost three wives during the course of a quarter century. Missionary work among lower Burma Karens was to expand after 1852.

V The Reigns of Mindon and Thibaw, 1852–1885

Burma's history from 1852 to 1885 witnessed the country's progressive decline from national independence to a semi-vassalage relationship with the expanding British colonial dominion, and finally to its eventual incorporation as an integral part of the British-Indian empire. British control over lower valley exits to the sea after 1853 denied to the interior kingdom any fruitful economic or diplomatic contacts with the outside world. The new British policy of encouraging exportation of rice surpulses from lower Burma aggravated the chronic food deficit of upper Burma and also produced in time a debilitating exodus of Burmese cultivators southward to newly developing lands of the delta. The opening of the Suez Canal in 1869 made possible the marketing of Burma's milled rice in Europe, while the increasing utilization of Indian coolie labor after 1880 on the docks, railways, and interior water transportation, and at harvest time increased the disparity between the two regions.

The conciliatory policies pursued by the tactful King Mindon (1853–1878) prevented during his lifetime any overt confrontation, and the immediate international circumstances which attended the disorderly accession of King Thibaw postponed the clash for several years thereafter. The final British move to conquer the Burma kingdom in 1885 was precipitated in part by Anglo-French colonial rivalry over access to the presumedly profitable trade with southwestern China. The French annexation of Tonkin province in 1883–1884 gave them commercial access via the Red River corridor to China's Yunnan province, which also lay adjacent to Burma. Even more provocative were the concurrent attempts of Paris representatives to establish commercial and diplomatic contacts with the Mandalay government. Locally developing quarrels between Rangoon and Mandalay over allegedly illegal timber exports afforded a plausible justification for the final British-Indian move against King Thibaw's government in late 1885, followed by outright annexation

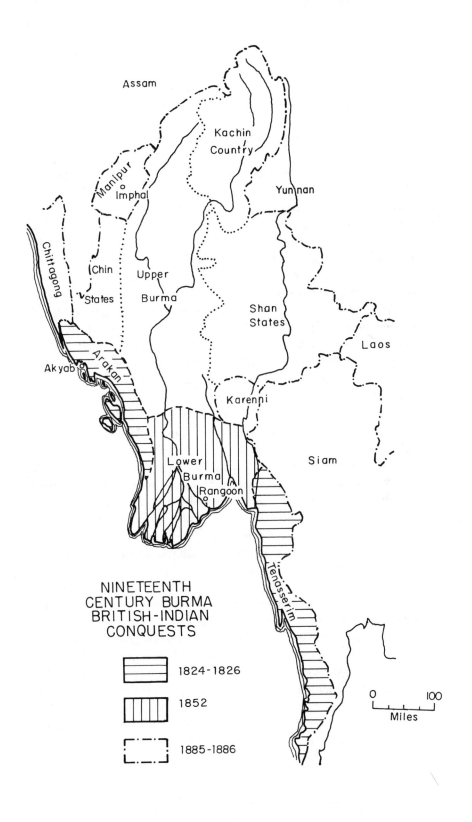

Assam

Kachin
Country

Manipur
o
Imphal

Yunnan

Chittagong

Chin

States

Upper

Burma

Shan
States

Laos

Arakan

Akyab

Karenni

Siam

Lower
Burma
Rangoon
o

Tenasserim

NINETEENTH
CENTURY BURMA
BRITISH-INDIAN
CONQUESTS

1824-1826

1852

1885-1886

0   100

Miles

of Burma to India in early 1886. Historical developments during these crucial years need to be examined in some detail.

The Second Anglo-Burman War

The second war developed out of local friction at the port of Rangoon. Both port officials and foreign traders were to blame. The turbulent spirit characteristic of visiting merchant crewmen, violently jealous of each other and disrespectful of port rules governing debt payments and smuggling, was paralleled by the irregular actions of poorly paid officials, who levied arbitrary exactions in fines and bribes on foreigners accused of port violations or criminal misconduct. Ship captains complained of official harassment in the opening of mail, the search of shipping offices, and accusations levied against anyone adjudged vulnerable. Under such conditions, the volume of trade at Rangoon declined sharply after 1848. Friction at Moulmein centered on British complaints that teak log rafts originating far upstream were being diverted to the Burmese port of Martaban on the western shore of the Salween river mouth.

The situation at Rangoon came to a head in 1851, when two British ship captains were accused of criminal drowning of a pilot at the river entrance and the death of a crew member in port. The captains were assessed fines totaling around 1,000 rupees as a condition of proceeding with their trading operations. Upon the receipt of these and other complaints and without making any serious investigation of circumstances, the Calcutta government decided to regard the actions of the Rangoon authorities as an insufferable and deliberate derogation of British prestige. Although ostensibly not intending to precipitate a war, Governor-General Dalhousie took the dubious step of despatching two naval vessels to Rangoon under the volatile Commodore Lambert to demand the replacement of the offending governor. After the Burmese accepted his initial demand, Lambert raised further objection because the dismissed myowun was not publicly disgraced and because his replacement refused to adopt a properly subservient attitude. Without awaiting orders from Dalhousie, the truculent commodore declared the port of Rangoon under blockade, destroyed by gunfire the port defenses, and seized a Burmese war vessel to be towed downstream. Both the Calcutta and London authorities reprimanded Lambert for his unauthorized actions, but they kept their disapproval secret while exploiting the situation which he had created to enhance trading access to lower Burma and to vindicate imperialist considerations of face.

Preparations for a limited war were pushed vigorously in India. Aware of the hardships of climate and illness previously encountered in 1824–1825, Dalhousie gave serious attention to medical, food, and housing needs, while counseling avoidance of a protracted and costly land campaign. The British ultimatum, delivered in February 1852, demanded payment of an indemnity of one million rupees, which was a thousand times the size of the original fine against the two ship captains. When the time limit expired, British naval forces in April and May occupied the widely separated ports of Martaban, Rangoon, and Bassein. After recommending to London the indefinite continuation of such occupation, Governor-General Dalhousie travelled to Rangoon for a personal inspection of the situation. His report, submitted in August, urged that the entire province of Pegu be annexed unilaterally. Following the cessation of the rains, the city of Prome was accordingly occupied, and Pegu was captured in mid-December.

For a time, the military situation became highly embarrassing for the British, mainly because the required resources for full conquest were not available. Calcutta was also averse to becoming involved in the developing strife between Karens and Burmans in the delta area, since Company officials wanted to avoid incurring the costs of an extended campaign. That contingency was surmounted when dissident political and military elements at the capital, including members of the Hlutdaw council, moved to oust the disreputable King Pagan early in 1853 in favor of Mindon. Organized resistance to the British collapsed in the south. Dalhousie then decreed India's unilateral annexation of lower Burma northward to an interior line running east and west some fifty miles above Prome and Toungoo. He left the adjacent Karenni state, located between the Sittang and Salween valleys, as an autonomous vassal state. More than four years were needed to subdue political dissent in lower Burma and considerably longer to suppress lawlessness, but the way was open to a substantial experiment in economic development.

The Reign of Mindon

The new king, Mindon Min, was a younger son of Tharrawaddy by a lesser queen. Having spent most of his adult years in a mon-

astery retreat, he had never anticipated the possibility of an eventual
accession to power. Faced with the immediate task of ending
anarchy in upper Burma, Mindon and his advisors called off the
British war. As a man of personal integrity and as a devout Buddhist,
Mindon moved to restore order, to improve governmental administration and to stimulate upper Burma's economy, but the difficulties
were many. Mindon respected the imposed southern boundary, but
he refused as a matter of personal prestige to legalize the de facto
British occupation of lower Burma by signing a formal treaty. He
annoyed Dalhousie further by affirming his expectation that British
India would some day return the seized territory to its rightful
owner, hopefully without strife or bloodshed. At first, Dalhousie
claimed that the treaty was both unnecessary and useless, but he
nevertheless tried repeatedly to get one, even to the point of offering
to provide Mindon's army with muskets and ammunition. It was
to no avail. In contrast to his relationship with Dalhousie, the "de-
ceitful" Mindon cultivated relations of personal friendship and
mutual respect with the new British commissioner of Pegu, the Burmese-speaking Major Arthur Phayre. On the occasion of the major's
visit to the Burma capital in 1855, in a futile effort to obtain a treaty
of cession, the two lingered long to discuss the merits of the Buddhist
faith. Mindon resisted persistently the counsels of belligerent court
factions who proposed to take advantage of successive British embar-
rassments in Crimea in 1854–1856, during the India Mutiny of 1857,
and the second China War of 1858–1860.

As a man and as a ruler, King Mindon was far more reputable
than his immediate predecessors. Born to a lesser queen, he was lucky
to escape the blight of mental instability and inbreeding which had
impaired the competence of both Bagyidaw and Tharrawaddy. In
areas of personal integrity and trustworthiness, he exemplified the
values of the Buddhist faith, to which he continued to be a devout
adherent and practitioner. He was a man of peace, coveting neither
wealth nor power, and despite his devotion to traditional values, was
a proponent of governmental and econmic reform. The tragedy of
his reign from the Burman point of view related to his inability to
prevent the dominance of the British-Indian presence in lower
Burma and to the jealousies which persisted within his court.
Burma's attempted constructive adjustments to outside world demands, in terms of governmental change, economic development,

expanding trade, and broadened diplomatic relations were rendered more difficult by the interior location of the new capital (Mandalay), with British India controlling the only feasible outlets to the sea.

King Mindon's first major move, dictated by traditional considerations, was the building and adorning of Mandalay, several miles north of Amarapura. The burdensome task was not completed until 1858. Meanwhile he sent a high-level mission to Europe to bring back recommendations relating to needed improvements and innovations, both governmental and economic. In 1856 a French mission returned the visit bearing presents to the Burma court, to the great annoyance of British authorities. A tangible result of early French contacts was the eventual delivery to Mandalay in 1859 of a French river steamer purchased by Burma. It was delivered by a French army general, who brought along artisans to service the craft. A few months later, the British themselves offered to provide Burma with the first of several additional steamers.

In 1861, King Mindon introduced the use of coined money and undertook to substitute fixed salary stipends for both fief-holding princes and high public officials, who had previously been accustomed to living off the resources of their assigned jurisdictions. In order to generate public revenues to cover these and other additional costs, Mindon initiated in 1862 a household tax (*thathemeda*), which varied from area to area in accordance with estimated indexes of production and prosperity determined at harvest time. Ahmudan service personnel who moved away from the royal granary areas were required to pay the household tax in the districts of their new residences.

Such well-conceived reform efforts were only partly successful. Local myothugyis and other tax collectors continued to be compensated with 20 percent of their receipts. They also cheated by falsifying the number of households within their respective jurisdictions. The total funds required for the reforms were simply not available to meet salary needs and other costs, including capital construction and economic development expenditures. The benefits of office-holding continued to be available at higher levels of control, even though Mindon assigned to high-ranking traveling officials the duty of reporting directly to him on the conduct of provincial governors and criminal court judges. Efforts to augment revenue income by additional earnings from royal monopolies over timber, petroleum, and precious stones, plus the assessment of moderate dues on external trade were largely ineffective.

Although British authorities objected initially to Mandalay's imposition of duties on trade with lower Burma, a series of commercial agreements alleviated the difficulties. The treaty of 1862 admitted an official British Resident to Mandalay, accorded free passage of British steamers up the river, and permitted the departure of Burmese immigrants who wished to enter lower Burma. Subsequently, Burmese authorities tried to slow down the southward movement by restricting the emigration of wives and children, but to little avail. The British offered such immigrants access to undeveloped land and exemption from land and head taxes covering substantial periods of time. A later agreement of 1867 permitted British steamers to proceed upstream as far as Bhamo, near the Yunnan China border. Mindon refused the British request to permit shipment of Indian opium to the China market via Burma. The treaty also permitted the residence of an official British agent at Mandalay, with limited legal jurisdiction over British subjects living in the capital. To balance the British presence, Mindon permitted the residence at Mandalay of a French vicar apostolic, Monseigneur Bigandet, along with an Italian priest named Abbone and other Catholic missionaries at Bhamo. An Anglican clergyman, Dr. Marks, also resided at the capital.

Mindon's conciliatory policies and reforming efforts were opposed by hostile elements at his court, who staged a serious rebellion within the palace in 1866. The rebels invaded the Hlutdaw council chamber and murdered the presiding heir apparent (*Einshemin*), a brother of the king, and several of his supporters. They failed to capture Mindon as planned, and fled southward on a commandeered royal steamer, while the army remained loyal to the king. The two sons of Mindon who were involved in the rising were interned in India; one of them later defected to the French at Pondicherry. Meanwhile, the Burma army suffered progressive decline in both discipline and morale, due in part to attrition within the ranks of the traditional ahmudan service residents on the royal granaries. Many royal service families intermingled with the general athi population and migrated southward into British Burma, where cultivable land was more readily available.

In the years following the rebellion, the new Chief-Commissioner Fytche and the Mandalay Resident Colonel Sladen pressed vigorously for a reduction of royal monopolies and for lowering of frontier trade duties. The resulting expansion of the volume of trade encouraged the entry of large British firms interested particularly in river traffic, the timber trade, and possible commerce with China. Increased British interest reflected official concern over the news of French explorations up the Mekong River valley. The aggressive British agent at Mandalay, Colonel Sladen, staged his own exploration into Yunnan in 1868–1869 and otherwise offended Mindon by his increasingly arrogant behavior.

Mindon's most significant action as royal patron of Buddhism was his convening, in 1871, of the Fifth Great Buddhist Council at Mandalay. He financed the reproduction of the entire Tripitaka scriptures on 729 marble slabs, protected by a veritable forest of pagoda sheds grouped together at the base of Mandalay Hill. He also contributed a bejewelled *hti* umbrella to top the Shwe Dagon pagoda at Rangoon. He then tried to patronize the revival of Burmese vernacular literature. Throughout the quarter-century of his rule, Mindon preserved both the dignity and independence of his country, even though time was running out on his courageous performance. He provided a pattern for Premier Nu to try to emulate in the 1950s.

British Rule in Lower Burma, 1852–1878

Although organized resistance to British control in lower Burma ceased in early 1853, the establishment of an effective substitute for the traditional Burmese administrative system was a difficult task. Below the top levels of the ranking British commissioner and the district deputy commissioners, local administrative posts had to be filled with Burmese personnel. The language barrier was a major problem. Experienced persons were not available because all men of myowun rank and their official assistants, plus many of the myothugyis, withdrew to upper Burma at the end of the war. Indigenous officials who remained behind were generally a disorderly lot, many of them using their armed retainers to prey on the local population and to undermine British authority. It was five years before political disaffection was brought under control, and much longer before

order was completely restored. In 1858, a troublesome Karen rebellion developed along traditional lines in an abortive attempt to
set up a Karen dynasty at Pegu.

The colonial administration which eventually emerged utilized
the services of Burmese at various levels. Township officials
(*myooks*) were enlisted from former myothugyi ranks and from
younger trainees. Competitive examinations accorded preference to
candidates competent in arithmetic, in techniques of land surveying,
and in grasp of basic English. Those selected were placed on salary
and usually held office indefinitely if their performance records
justified it. Myooks supervised tax collections and handled petty
civil and criminal cases in court. Serving under them were the circle
headmen (*taikthugyis*), whose principal duties were to keep the
records of ownership of the expanding rice acreage and to collect
taxes thereon. Taikthugyis were held strictly to account for their
performance on pain of fine or dismissal from office. At the village
level, police duties were entrusted to meagerly compensated *gaungs*,
who reported to the central police authorities. Finally, the largest
taxpayer of the village (*kyedangyi*) received authorized remunera-
tion for assisting in local tax collections and for entertaining
district officers on tour. Most of the Burmese officials under the
system lacked prestige, and social cohesion generally tended to dis-
integrate under artificially imposed authority. This problem worsened after 1871, when the pace of economic development accelerated. The effectiveness of colonial administration thus owed much
to the generally high competence of British deputy commissioners,
who exercised virtually plenary authority at the district level.

The substantial if gradual economic gains realized in British-
administered lower Burma were concentrated mainly in the areas of
agriculture, timber extraction, and transportation. The population
actually doubled during the first decade of British control, due in
part to immigration from the north and from the entry of Indian
laborers. From 1852 to 1872 rice acreage increased threefold. It
continued to expand afterwards as the Suez Canal made European
markets more accessible. The export of rice from Rangoon, which
had been prohibited under Burman rule to ensure ample food for
the interior, attained impressive proportions. All teak trees were
declared the property of the government, but timber operations
were encouraged under leasehold permits granted for the most part
to large British firms. The Scottish-owned Irrawaddy Flotilla Com-

pany took over the major share of the river traffic extending northward into upper Burma, thus eliminating the jobs of thousands of
river boatmen. Railways were constructed northward to Prome and
Toungoo, financed by interest-bearing bonds. Rangoon port and
the city itself were rebuilt along European lines. The material
advantages of expanding production and trade were unevenly distributed, but the impact was felt throughout the countryside and in
upper Burma as well.

The negative side of development was social disintegration, which
was the result of population growth and the progressive debilitation
of religious sanctions and monastic discipline. Outwardly little
seemed changed. The monks made their daily rounds and were
accorded support by the people. They also continued to function
as the primary agents of popular education. Shrines were visited on
holy days, and annual religious festivals were regularly celebrated.
Religious standards in lower Burma nevertheless suffered substantially from the absence of the disciplinary functions traditionally performed by royal commissions assigned to supervise
monastic property holdings and the registration of properly
ordained monks. Orthodox standards of monastic conduct gave way
under pressure of social change and also by reason of the decline of
discipline within the Sangha itself. Persistent British efforts made
during the 1860s failed to influence the pongyi kyaung schools to
expand the content of their curriculum to include geography, arithmetic, and elementary science. Families that wanted their sons to
qualify for government jobs sent them to more efficient lay or missionary schools. Religious traditionalism still showed remarkable
vitality despite the steady erosion of standards.

Anglo-French Imperialist Rivalry

The vulnerability of the kingdom of Burma to pressure from
British-Indian authorities was enhanced by the development of
Anglo-French rivalry in southeast Asia. Beginning in the late 1860s
the two competed for access to trade with the border provinces of
southwest China, especially Kweichow and Yunnan. The revival of
Chinese trade with Burma was long hindered by the continuing
activities in central Yunnan since 1855 of the Muslim-Panthay
rebels, a carryover from the Taiping Rebellion era. Following the
conclusion of the aforementioned British-Burma treaty in 1867, the

British Resident at Mandalay, Colonel Sladen, was sent on an exploratory mission to make contact with the Panthays. His entry into Yunnan in early 1868 was accompanied by the dispatch from Shanghai of a British consular representative named Cooper. Sladen succeeded in reaching the Panthays and solicited their willing assistance in reopening the Burma trade, but he encountered serious hostility from official Chinese and Shan partisans on his return trip to Bhamo. Cooper's party failed to reach Burma at all, and finally exited to India via Nepal in July 1868.

The French counterpart of the Sladen-Cooper venture was the more ambitious exploratory mission of naval officers Lagrée and Garnier in 1867–1868 from Cochin-China up the Mekong valley into south China. The move was sponsored by the Paris Geographical Society, which was always headed by a retired naval officer. Lagrée died enroute, and Garnier eventually made his way to Shanghai. The French explorers discovered that the Mekong River was not navigable, and that commercial access to southwestern China from the South China Sea was through the Red River valley and Tonkin. The French expedition produced no immediate results because Paris had advanced no previous claim to Tonkin, and Louis Napoleon's government was then seriously concerned with events in Mexico and in Europe. Garnier took leave from the navy, and acting under the auspices of the Paris Geographical Society spent several years writing and publishing his magnificent two-volume report on the expedition. He returned to the Far East in a private capacity in 1873. French competition was held in abeyance for some time thereafter by the overthrow of Louis Napoleon's government during the Prussian War of 1870–1871, and by the subsequent occupation of France for several years by Bismarck's troops.

Meanwhile, Colonel Sladen's overoptimistic report covering trade prospects with China aroused mixed reactions. British commercial interests at Rangoon advocated immediate assumption of control over Burma's relations with the outside world, in a move calculated to ensure their own unimpeded access to Yunnan's trade. But authorities in India faced more pressing problems elsewhere, and Britain's Shanghai traders took a dim view of the future of trade with Yunnan. The region at the time was convulsed by civil strife, and the prospect of serious rivalry with the French over the area's trade seemed remote. European interest in southwestern China revived in 1874, when a French trader-adventurer named Dupuis, acting under sponsorship of the Chinese military governor of Kweichow, opened trade down the Red River to Hanoi. Dupuis was arrested on his second attempt by the Vietnamese authorities, and a crisis ensued. When the French governor at Saigon enlisted the aid of Garnier and several score volunteers to rescue Dupuis, the audacious Garnier was killed outside the Hanoi citadel. In the final settlement of the affair, the harried Hué government granted the French theoretical rights of commercial access up the river and conceded to France legal control of Cochin-China.

When the Panthay rebellion collapsed in Yunnan in 1873, the British in their turn assumed that the time was appropriate to renew efforts to open trade contacts with China through upper Burma. The project enlisted strong commercial backing in England as well as in Rangoon. Burma's King Mindon also agreed to assist the endeavor by providing steamer passage up the Irrawaddy to Bhamo for Colonel Horace Browne's Sikh military escort. He also provided a cooperating contingent of 250 Burmese troops, financed by a special household levy imposed at Bhamo. The British plan was similar to that of Sladen in 1868. Consul A. R. Margary, a Chinese language officer, was directed to proceed up the Yangtse Valley from Shanghai and across the several mountain divides to Bhamo, whence he would accompany Colonel Browne's group on the return journey as guide and interpreter. Margary reached Burma on schedule, but only because successive Chinese officials preferred to let him pass rather than to follow Peking's order to stop him. The attempted return journey proved disastrous for Margary. Shortly after leaving Bhamo and prior to his entry into Yunnan, he and several advance companions were massacred in a Chinese ambuscade. Colonel Browne's Sikh-Burmese escort managed to escape by bribing local Kachin tribesmen, who set fire to the jungle where the Chinese forces were concealed. Now both the British and the French had martyrs to the expansionist cause: Garnier and Margary. Prestige considerations tended to take precedence at Rangoon over any realistic estimate of the dubious profits to be made from the exchange of Burma's salt and cotton for China's silk and tea.

Although the British had no possible grounds for complaint with regard to Burma's cooperation in the Margary-Browne expedition of 1873–1874, friction developed over other matters. In 1872, Mindon had dispatched a high-level diplomatic mission to Europe, headed by his confidant, the Kinwun Mingyi, in an effort to break through the diplomatic boycott imposed by the Indian authorities. It managed to conclude an innocuous treaty with Prussian-occupied France and another with newly unified Italy, but the mission was denied contact with the British Foreign Office. The Burmans were entertained instead by several chambers of commerce in Britain. With some European help, the mission formulated plans to send Burmans abroad for study of economic and governmental problems and also fashioned a fairly comprehensive program of administrative reform. British Rangoon became annoyed late in 1873 when a French emissary passed through lower Burma en route to Mandalay to exchange treaty ratifications and to listen to Mindon's appeals for diplomatic and military assistance. The French gesture lacked substance because France itself at the time was still occupied by German troops, and President de Broglie was strongly opposed to imperialistic ventures.

British-Indian relations with Burma took a gratuitous turn for the worse in 1875, when Calcutta authorities ordered the British Resident at Mandalay to refuse to comply with the traditional requirement to remove shoes when entering the throne room. The move had the effect of canceling future royal audiences for the Resident, thus in effect severing direct diplomatic communications. Growing tensions tended to aggravate Rangoon's concern over allegations of French intrigue and hostile Catholic missionary activity in Burma. The Kinwun's reform party within the Mandalay court was thrown sharply on the defensive, so that intrigue between rival palace factions became rife. When King Mindon's health began to fail, with no prince clearly designated to succeed him, the confusion was compounded. Mindon's death in September 1878, and the accession of the youthful Prince Thibaw marked the beginning of the end for the Burma kingdom.

The Reign of Thibaw, 1878–1885

The surprising elevation of the inexperienced Thibaw, fresh from a long monastery assignment, was in part the result of the initiative of his new mother-in-law, the chief queen Sinpyumashin. She had no son of her own and was allied with a henchman and fellow conspirator named Taingda. Opposition reform elements at court, led by the Kinwun Mingyi, accepted Thibaw's elevation to the kingship to avoid civil strife and in the hope that they might be able to influence the impressionable youth in the determination of policy. Thibaw himself proved to be a cipher in the situation, for he was no match for the domineering chief queen and his own wife, Supayalat. Thibaw's mother had been a faceless Shan princess whom Mindon had divorced for alleged moral irregularities. The more eligible Nyaungyan prince refused the summons to appear at the palace, thereby avoiding probable death at Taingda's hands. He escaped to British Burma and later to Calcutta. Eight other captured princes were put to death in gruesome fashion in February 1879, among a total of thirty-four elite victims. A number of personal friends of the king, who had warned him of the dangers of petticoat rule, were also executed. The despondent ruler allegedly took refuge in alcohol.

The shocked reaction of the British authorities to events in Mandalay in March and April 1879, produced an abortive effort to enlist support from moderate elements in Mandalay for the substitution of Prince Nyaungyan for Thibaw. Proposals of intervention ran aground for various reasons. The Indian government at the time was involved in a war in Afghanistan, and London was also diverted by the Boer rebellion in South Africa. Furthermore, the aftermath of the critical European Balkan crisis and the Congress of Berlin of 1878, was no time to take on a difficult and possibly costly intervention in Burma. A diplomatic break nevertheless occurred in October, when the British Resident, Colonel Browne, withdrew from Mandalay in anticipation of intervention. London's negative reaction was subsequently strengthened by the accession of the anti-imperialist Gladstone as Britain's prime minister in 1880. The faltering efforts of the still struggling Kinwun Mingyi to carry through his administrative reforms with Thibaw's help ran firmly aground. His objective was to recast the central administration along functional cabinet minister lines under a responsible premier. He managed to maintain a measure of personal influence, but only by refusing to force the issue.

Meanwhile the countryside was engulfed in an epidemic of violence and banditry, aggravated by irresponsibility at top official levels. Virtually all administrative posts were up for sale by agents of the powerful ally of Queen Supayalat, Taingda, so that the purchasers had to recoup their costs through their own irregular conduct of affairs. The situation was particularly bad in the upper Sittang valley adjacent to the British-ruled Toungoo district, which was the center of the teakwood industry. The irregular export of logs down the river afforded abundant opportunities for profit on both sides. It was out of this situation that the crisis of 1885 later emerged. The Rangoon business community wanted full access to the wealth of upper Burma and to the possibilities of trade with Yunnan China. British opinion also became increasingly concerned over the sharp acceleration of French imperialist activity and intrigue, starting in Tonkin around 1881 and extending by 1885 into independent Burma as well.

An important factor in promoting French imperialist aggression in Tonkin came from Germany's Prince Bismarck in 1879. He asked the French ambassador at Berlin to find out whether or not Paris was interested in Tonkin, with the clear implication that if France was not concerned then Germany would become involved. The probable German motive was to divert the French from concern over their European losses, including Alsace-Lorraine, and possibly also to stimulate Anglo-French friction over neighboring Siam and Burma. Paris responded in 1879 by shifting the responsibility for colonial administration of Cochin-China from naval officers connected with the ministry of marine to civilian officials responsible to the ministry of colonies. The Paris authorities after 1880 promoted a relentlessly aggressive stance against Tonkin, which eventually developed wide imperialistic implications. The policy led to an undeclared French war with China in 1883, and to repercussions extending westward into Laos, Burma's Shan states, and to Mandalay itself. British concern over possible French designs in Burma was no doubt exaggerated, but colonial interests at Rangoon welcomed an opportunity to challenge assumed French machinations when a quarrel with the Burma government developed in the summer of 1885.

Liquidation of the Kingdom of Burma

British colonial frustration over seeming inability to keep even with French commercial and political penetration of the south China border area mounted during the first half of the 1880s. One proposal coming from Hong Kong was to exact from China, as part of the long-delayed Chefoo Convention in settlement of the Margary affair dispute, permission for uninhibited British trade from the Burma side. This would match what the French had obtained via Tonkin in 1884. But the theoretical Burma kingdom lay athwart the only feasible trade route to China, and the French were themselves becoming increasingly involved in negotiations with Mandalay.

Starting in 1882–1883, Burma itself took the initiative in attempts to establish its independent identity. The first move was an unsuccessful effort at New Delhi in 1882 to negotiate a settlement with British authorities which would guarantee Burma's continuing political existence. The next step was to send a major diplomatic mission to France, which reached Paris in August 1883. The mission encountered numerous difficulties and delays, which postponed the actual signing of the new commercial treaty until January 1885. In the meantime, a French Foreign Office official named Deloncle visited Mandalay in July 1884, transmitting the allegedly unofficial suggestion that France might enter into some kind of alliance guarantee in return for Burma's recognition of French control over the Kengtung region of the Shan plaetau contiguous to the Mekong River. In response to London's repeated inquiries concerning the protracted activities of the Burma mission, the French Foreign Minister, Jules Ferry, maintained that the new treaty agreement was purely commercial and involved no political or military arrangements. London's suspicions were subsequently marginally confirmed when it was learned in July from secret Mandalay sources that Ferry had also agreed in a separate letter, technically not part of the treaty, to send requested arms to Burma via Tonkin and the Shan states as soon as quiet was restored in northern Vietnam. The legal validity of the letter was subject to question because Ferry meanwhile had fallen from power in March 1885.

Anglo-French rivalry in Burma was further exacerbated following the arrival in Mandalay in June 1885 of an aggressive new French consul named Haas, who had been sent by the new French Premier Freycinet. During his initial month's stay, Haas negotiated two supplementary loan agreements, calling for the construction of a railway from Mandalay down to the Toungoo border and for the establishment of a Burma state bank. The loans would be serviced by customs duties levied on river trade and by taxes on oil extraction and the output of Burma's ruby mines. At the end of July, a Burmese official departed for Paris to exchange ratifications. From the British point of view, the negotiations of Haas discounted more recent assurances given by the Freycinet government, as well as the latter's eventual repudiation of the actions of Haas and his recall from Burma in October. The action came too late to dissipate the mounting pressure for a British move into upper Burma.

Manadalay itself provided a timely excuse for British action by the decision of the Hlutdaw in August to levy a heavy fine of 2.3 million rupees against the Bombay-Burmah Trading Corporation for illegal traffic in teak logs above the Toungoo border. The alleged violations involved several special agreements reached in 1882 and 1883 for lump-sum payments covering undersized logs and others not technically dutiable at the official rate. If dishonesty had indeed occurred, it was shared by conniving Burmese officials, who were profiting personally from the arrangement. But the size of the assessed fine was flagrantly exhorbitant, and the blame was placed exclusively on the British firm. The move was made more sharply punitive when log-raft shipments on the Sittang River ready to move downstream were held up until an initial installment was paid on the assessed fine. The issue should have been capable of settlement by negotiation, for the facts were subject to verification. Moderate elements at Burma court, including the Kinwun Mingyi, eventually indicated a willingness to settle for less than 10 percent of the original demand, but many British welcomed an excuse to attack Thibaw's government.

Earlier British suggestions that French influence at Mandalay be undercut by the elevation of the Nyaungyan prince ran aground in early 1885 when the prince died in Calcutta. His half-brother, the Nyaung Ok prince and virtually the only alternative, had previously shifted his residence to French Pondicherry. Since no British-influenced prince was available, India's government authorities favored the outright annexation of upper Burma, although they were duly warned by informed associates in Burma concerning the difficulties which such a policy would entail. An essential British concern was to eliminate for all time the political and commercial threat of French intrigue at Mandalay. A twenty-day ultimatum was delivered on October 22 demanding the installation of a British Resident at Mandalay and the submission of all future questions of Burma's foreign relations to the government of India.

On November 12 British forces embarked upstream and encountered little resistance. Mandalay fell in late November. King Thibaw and his principal wives and advisers were captured and taken to Madras. The elimination of the Konbaung dynasty was an accomplished fact by the time Gladstone's victorious Liberal Party returned to power in London in January 1886. The only decision which the British parliament took with reference to the third Burma war was to rule that the costs of the operation were chargeable to the revenues of the government of India because the action had allegedly been taken to ensure India's security.

VI The Impact of Colonial Rule to World War I

Economic Development in Lower Burma to 1885

The progressive expansion of rice cultivation which occurred in lower Burma once British pacification was achieved, far exceeded the fairly impressive performance of Arakan and Tenasserim prior to 1852. The gains realized in lower Burma were particulaly dramatic because of the economic decline which the region had suffered during the previous quarter century as a result of cultivator displacement and heavy government exactions. British policy ended the widespread practice of family-staffed subsistence production of rice by encouraging the production and export of grain. Colonial authorities offered higher prices for exportable surpluses, opened new lands for cultivator development, and made available in return attractive consumer imports.

Substantial inducements were offered to attract cultivators from upper Burma. Immigrants were largely exempted from the payment of land taxes for twelve years, the period traditionally required for acquiring occupancy ownership, and also from direct capitation or household taxes for five years. Upper Burma boatmen, who became jobless because of the increasing use of river steamers, found new employment in the delta, transporting paddy and consumer goods to and from the principal ports of Rangoon and Bassein. Many boatmen doubled as small-scale rice brokers, using capital funds made available by millers and trading firms. After 1862, the Mandalay government cooperated by legalizing immigration of laborers southward, even though families were forbidden to follow. In actuality, wives and children managed with little difficulty to evade the prohibition. Eventually British steamers operating as far north as Bhamo provided virtually gratis transportation downstream for cultivator and trader immigrants, with Rangoon authorities paying the costs. During the 1860s, nearly all of the expanding rice acreage in lower Burma was developed by indigenous labor. Railway lines were extended up the Irrawaddy valley, reaching Prome by 1877, and up the Sittang to Toungoo by 1884, facilitating both trade and immigration. Lower Burma's 1881 census reported some 12 percent of the population as upper-Burma born, with the same group constituting around 60 percent of all new residents.

During the early seventies, the number of immigrants from the north could no longer meet the heavy seasonal demands for labor at planting and harvest times, nor could they man the expanding transportation services, docks, rice and timber mills. To meet such needs, a substantial stream of Indian laborers began to be attracted to Burma, coming mainly by steamer from Calcutta and Madras. British authorities at Rangoon made several halfhearted efforts in the mid-seventies to regulate labor recruitment in India, but it proved more convenient to leave the matter to private contractors. The latter advanced funds to cover migrants' debts and interim living expenses, later recouping such costs by withholdings from wage payments. During the late seventies, such arrivals from India averaged around 15,000 persons annually, a figure which was far exceeded in the early 1880s.

In 1880, transportation costs from Indian ports to Burma were reduced by half as the result of the inauguration of competitive steamship services. Shortly thereafter, the Rangoon government offered for a time to defray a fraction of the cost of passage. The number of migrant laborers accordingly jumped from 20,000 in 1879–1880 to more than four times that number by 1883–1884. Males outnumbered females by 20 to 1. Most of the newcomers stayed for two or three years before returning home with their accumulated savings. Except for their widespread employment in harvesting operations of November-December, they found jobs mainly in the cities. Many worked in rice and timber mills, on the docks and railways, on public works development projects, and as house servants. They contributed little directly to the development of new land for cultivation, but filled important economic roles in which the Burmese were not interested.

The increment in cultivated rice land in lower Burma averaged around 150,000 acres per year from 1874 to 1884, and the total acreage expanded by some 75 percent during the same period. The rate of increase slowed down during the disorders after 1885, only to augment substantially after 1890.

The Pacification Period, 1886–1889

The British decision to annex the Burma kingdom was carried through in spite of warnings advanced by officials who knew the country best. Commissioner Bernard and other informed persons were convinced that the governance of upper Burma would entail far more difficulty and expense than had been encountered in lower Burma, and with minimal revenue gains to balance the costs. But no satisfactory substitute prince for King Thibaw was available, and Rangoon business interests were in no mood to risk dealing with another uncooperative ruler. In support of the annexation policy were considerations based on the remarkable economic progress realized in British lower Burma since 1862, which had attracted so many migrants from upper Burma. From the British point of view there were many reasons to assume that intelligent Burmese would tolerate, if not welcome, escape from Mandalay's unprogressive rule.

The disorders which engulfed Burma during the early months of 1886 were in part a projection of the growing lawlessness of previous years, greatly aggravated by the collapse of police control. Following the fall of Mandalay in late November 1885, most village communities in the north began to fend for themselves. Village gangs staged foraging parties against their neighbors. The epidemic of violence in upper Burma became directed in time against the British-Indian conquerors, partly because they employed such harsh tactics to curb local disorders. The army simply shot on sight villagers who were found possessing arms. Minor offenders were flogged, and villages suspected of harboring rebels were burned. From the Burmese point of view, the spread of anarchy could be properly ended only by installing a new king in the palace, one who could appropriately embody the symbols of kingly authority. If the corrupt palace clique which had surrounded the king could have been eliminated, Thibaw himself would probably have been acceptable to most Burmans.

In the absence of any princely authority at Mandalay, the harsh measures employed by the occupying army stimulated the hostility of Burmans generally toward the common alien enemy. It was one thing for Burmans to distrust the government of Queen Supayalat and her Taingda henchman and to migrate southward for economic and security reasons. It was another to contemplate the destruction of their identity as a Buddhist nation under British-Indian control and to envisage the dire consequences which would result from the abandonment of royal support of the Buddhist establishment. Burman social and political values differed sharply from those which appeared to be reasonable to British residents at Rangoon, despite some measure of agreement on economic development.

The optimistic affirmation by India' viceroy, Lord Dufferin, in late February 1886, that he saw no evidence of partisan opposition to the proposed British annexation of the Burma kingdom was based on wishful thinking and a complete misunderstanding of the mood of the people. By June of 1886, upper Burma was in utter confusion, and police authority in lower Burma was also becoming seriously impaired. Those Burmese who were inclined to assist the alien government, officially or otherwise, became objects of popular intimidation and violence. The ultimate cost to the government of India of four years of pacification activity amounted to some ten times the initial estimates. Burma's revenues after 1890 assumed the continuing policing costs. Occupation forces, which numbered at peak strength more than 40,000 troops, were deployed at hundreds of posts distributed along the main lines of communication.

Because the rebel bands lacked coordination as to both objectives and leadership, resistance began to decline in the spring of 1887. The arms and discipline of the British-Indian troops were superior, and the disorder produced dire economic stress. The government's initiation and completion of the railway line from Toungoo northward to Mandalay afforded employment for many otherwise destitute villagers. In lower Burma, widespread use was made of Karen volunteer police drawn from communities which had suffered violence at Burman hands. Hostile Burman gangs were often led by Buddhist monks or renegades posing as monks. Karens volunteering to oppose them were frequently recruited and led by Christian pastors and occasionally by American missionary personnel. In 1887, the colonial government ceased recruiting Burmans into the army in favor of Karen volunteers and, somewhat later, turned to Kachin and Chin tribesmen as well. One small Karen unit was used by the British army in upper Burma in 1887. Pacification policies thus stimulated the emergence of Karen nationalist sentiment which tended to bridge linguistic factions and Christian and non-Christian groups.

Pacification of the Shan states was effectively accomplished in 1887 and 1888 by British mediatory efforts applied within the local politi-

cal context. The Shan States Act of 1889 provided for the appointment of a British superintendent and subordinate officials. They
would determine the size of annual tribute payments levied on the
several states covering five-year spans, coupled with some essential
modifications of the customary law. Direct control continued to be
exercised by Shan *Sawbwa* chieftains, whose jurisdictions were
clearly delimited territorially. The trans-Salween state of Kengtung
was brought under British control in 1890; the Siam boundary was
fixed in 1892; the Mekong River was designated as the boundary of
French-claimed Laos in 1894 and 1897. In the far north of Burma,
military pressure was exerted in 1892 against Kachin tribal groups to
force their acceptance of British authority to mediate their long-
term differences with neighboring Shan peoples. The Chins were
also brought under indirect control.

Lawlessness continued longest in lower Burma, especially in the
Irrawaddy valley area below Prome, where land titles were insecure
and Karen-Burman hostility was rife. Burma proper could never be
the same following the alien conquest. Traditional symbols of authority were destroyed and nationhood was undermined, along with
the sanctity of customary social and legal institutions.

The Pattern of Colonial Administration

The essential task of devising a system of colonial control for
upper Burma and peripheral regions afforded the occasion to revamp
the largely demoralized lower Burma administration as well. The
reorganization task was assigned to Bernard's replacement as commissioner, Sir Charles Crosthwaite, who took over in 1887. Relying
on his previous experience in India, Crosthwaite decided that governmental authority needed to be strengthened at the grass roots
level by expanding the authority and responsibility of appointed village headmen (*thugyis*). They were asked to function as tax collectors, police officers (rather than mere informers), and as petty
magistrates. They were held responsible for their official conduct
to colonial officials of the central government. Under the new Burma
Village Act of 1889, the village headmen in effect were asked to
function as lesser myothugyis or taikthugyis. They were permitted
to carry around the coveted silver-mounted *dah* (large knife) and
the red umbrella with gilt flaps, which were calculated to enhance
their personal prestige. At the same time, they were forbidden as

government officials to exercise any political role. In upper Burma, cooperative myothugyis from the older order were permitted to stay on indefinitely, depending on their proper performance of duties, but their authority henceforth was confined to territorial boundaries rather than being based on personal prestige as headmen.

In compensation for his many duties, the new lower Burma headman received a 10 percent commission on tax collections plus exemption from payment of personal taxes. The pre-1885 five-year exemption from capitation taxes for newly arrived settlers from upper Burma was abolished. Thugyis were also empowered to require from resident villagers unpaid assistance in community defense against predators, for upkeep of footpaths and ox-cart roads, ferry operations, and the care of public wells and burial grounds. They must also collect vital statistics and enforce minimal sanitary and health regulations. Crosthwaite's new system was conveniently simple and uniform, but many of the 17,000 village tracts failed to provide effective incumbents who could perform their assigned tasks and enlist villager support. The gap between village officials and the alien central authorities became too wide for intermediate district officials to bridge. Officials who were designated annually as derelict for non-performance of duties, and village tract communities that were made liable to official discipline, usually numbered well over a hundred. In 1907, the Village Act was made equally applicable to upper Burma in the interest of administrative uniformity. An effective central administration served the needs of the expanding economy, but government continued to function ineffectively at the village level.

Colonial government became increasingly impersonal and alien to traditional standards. The originally plenary authority of the district deputy commissioners was diminished in time by the development of functional agencies of administration. The expanding volume of governmental business made the trend unavoidable. The important responsibility of maintaining land surveys and tax assessments, for example, was assigned in 1894–1895 to the land records department. Special duties were later entrusted to revenue-collecting agencies, to public health and veterinary officers, to departments of public works, agriculture, and education, and to specialized civil and criminal courts functioning at various levels. All such services were eventually associated with the expanding central secretariat at Rangoon, which far outstripped in its complexity and size anything that court reformers of Mindon or Thibaw had ever had in mind. However appropriate the new colonial system may have seemed for the needs of an increasingly complex society, its effect contributed confusion and bewilderment to the indigenous population. The average Burman had understood the plenary authority of the deputy commissioner, who corresponded to the traditional Myowun, but officials of the manifold functional agencies proved incapable of enlisting local cooperation.

Particularly bewildering was the new westernized law and court system. It was geared to handle the enormous volume of civil and criminal cases generated by the rapidly changing economic and social order. Earlier colonial law codes of the 1860s and 1870s had respected customary rules relating to inheritance, marriage, and religious matters. Down to 1891, colonial courts acknowledged as legal the arbitral decisions of village elders and the rulings of surviving myothugyis. By the turn of the century, however, court proceedings were divorced from the exercise of executive authority. After 1905, all fulltime judges at the district level were included within the special judicial branch of the civil service.

The application of an impersonal and alien law by professional judges and lawyers became in time for the Burmese a technical game, which had little relevance to traditional ideas of justice. The oaths which witnesses were obliged to take before testifying in court carried no effective moral sanction, so that perjury became the rule. At lower levels, judges and witnesses were amenable to bribery, and lawyers profited from fees collectible from the crowded dockets of the courts. Increased civil litigation and criminal trials were associated with the cumulative alienation of land holdings within lower Burma and with the violence which accompanied an increasingly disorganized social order. Judicial integrity was generally maintained at upper levels of the courts, but appeal judges often had little understanding of the confusing and contradictory evidence available to them. Basic concepts of British common law, such as the guarantee of freedom within the law, judicial independence from political interference, and respect for valid evidence were all properly appreciated by legally-trained Burmans, but not by the mass of the litigants.

Indigenous representation at the government level came about slowly. Following India's granting of legislative autonomy to Burma in 1897, the Burma governor appointed a legislative council of nine members. Included were four non-official members, one of them a Burman and another a Shan. When the council's membership was increased to 17 in 1909, two elective members were included, one selected by the Burma Chamber of Commerce and the other by the Rangoon Trades Association, both British. Thirteen additional members were authorized in 1915, more widely representative but all appointed by the governor. Interests were better represented than people, and the council's actual authority in any case was minimal. The governor could ignore the advise of the council, while his own decisions were subject to veto by the government of India and by the secretary of state for India in London.

Colonial administration felt obliged to pay special deference to the British business community at Rangoon, as when the latter pressed in the 1890s to construct a gratuitous northern railway to the Salween River east of Lashio or advocated the dubious advantages of eliminating the Burma kingdom after 1885. Particularly influential were the Bombay Burmah Trading Corporation, the Irrawaddy Flotilla Company, Steele Brothers, and later the Burmah Oil Company. The situation afforded virtually no opportunity to take into account the wishes of Burmese leadership, largely unorganized. Municipal corporations, which were authorized to function as early as 1874, were run for the most part by and for the alien residents, subject to central supervision. Administrative and governmental innovations were generally too massive and too arbitrarily introduced to be effectively assimilated by the nation as a whole.

Economic Accomplishments

Economic expansion in such areas as rice production, milling, and export trade were resumed following pacification in 1889, and similar expansion occurred in other areas during subsequent decades. The process owed much to the accelerated enlistment of Indian labor under indigenous contractor direction, to the availability of credit from Chettyar moneylender services, to British industrial promotion, and to improved marketing and transportation services. The smaller rice mills located on river banks or at railway stations outside the port areas (Henzada and Toungoo were examples) were usually manned by Burmese labor. The use of Indian labor was concentrated in the larger urban centers of lower Burma. Upper Burma shared belatedly in the agricultural expansion at the fairly constant rate of one-fifth of the total gains realized, with principal emphasis placed on cotton production, groundnuts, and oil seeds.

The average annual acreage increment devoted to rice during the period from 1894 to 1904 was some 188,000 acres. The gains declined thereafter to 140,000 acres per year from 1905 to 1914, and to half that amount during the war years, 1915 to 1919. Meanwhile other exports (timber, minerals, oil, and rubber) contributed substantially to the expansion of foreign earnings. Exports had been valued at only 93 million rupees in 1896, compared with 275 millions in 1906 and 381 millions in 1916. During the post-war period, rice shipments accounted for 50 percent of total exports by 1926 and for only 37 percent a decade later, when total exports reached the value of 567 million rupees. Asian markets for Burma's expanding rice exports increased from 50 percent of the total in 1900, to 60 percent in 1914, and 70 percent in the 1930s. Despite all the hardships and political unrest which were associated with depression conditions after 1930, Burma's economy continued to demonstrate surprising vigor. Local purchase of imported consumer goods invariably lagged far behind the value of export totals, but the demand for foreign goods nevertheless acted as an incentive for additional effort.

The annual migration of laborers from India increased roughly in proportion to expanding production generally. The peak of the early subsidized immigration from India in 1883–1884, amounting to 83,000, was dwarfed in subsequent decades. The average number of arrivals annually from 1891 to 1895 was 130,000 and for 1901–1905 some 180,000. The figure rose to 336,000 from 1911 to 1915, and to more than 400,000 annual arrivals during the twenties. Most immigrants still came as contract laborers recruited and controlled by Indian managers. During the thirties, the number of annual departures roughly balanced the number of arrivals, but the total number of Indians resident in Burma at the outbreak of the war in 1941 was well over one million. Labor immigrants usually arrived following the end of the rainy season in October and November, in time to participate in seasonal rice harvesting and milling operations. Emigration began in April and May, when such job opportunities tapered off.

Burmese labor mixed little with the Indians except marginally during harvesting operations. Burmans disliked living apart from their families, especially if it meant working with Indian coolie labor. Burmese peasants were perennially in debt to employer-land-

lords and to Chinese storekeepers, who provided them with food supplies to tide their families over to harvest time. When the laborers
were paid following the harvest, accumulated debts were subtracted
from the amounts due as wages. When the available land for new
development became less attractive to prospective owners, cultivators
tended to assume the status of mere tenants, exposed to rack-renting
and to consequent chronic indebtedness. Younger men, who were
usually unemployed following the harvest period, spent their free
time during the hot season attending pye dramatic performances and
gambling, or else turned to more exciting violence and thievery.

Despite the declared British objective to promote cultivator
ownership, land titles tended increasingly to gravitate into the hands
of speculators and lending agencies. Few Burman occupants of new
land remained for the twelve-year period needed to qualify for full
ownership rights. Lands acquired by moneylenders through mortgage foreclosures were usually taken over by large-scale speculators
for possible sale to new occupants or for annual rental to tenants.
Even in good times, the gradual increment in the wholesale price
of paddy payable to the cultivator ran far behind rising rental costs.
From 1890 to 1904, for example, rental levels in lower Burma increased some 60 percent and by another 50 percent by 1909, while
the sale price for paddy rose only 14 percent during the same extended period.

Higher prices which were paid for non-rice products in upper
Burma during World War I assisted the liquidation of indebtedness
on many family-owned plots, while the wartime rice surpluses of
lower Burma were unsaleable. After the war, agriculture expansion
in lower Burma resumed boom proportions, but it was accompanied
by the same abuses of tenancy and mortgage foreclosures. The rising
level of land values, as measured in terms of rental income, sustained
the development boom to the end of the twenties. Individual cultivator occupants were often intimidated by large gangs in the employ
of speculators, who also profited from connections with corrupt officials. Some Karen villages in the fertile delta area managed to
develop and defend their valuable holdings by cooperative effort
on a community basis, but this was not the rule.

Successive annual settlement department reports prepared after
1900 revealed the dimensions of the land alienation and tenancy
problems. In one representative district, three-fourths of the resident
cultivators had enjoyed occupancy rights of one year only, while

only 6 percent had worked their holdings for as many as five years. Indian Chettyar moneylenders held most of the outstanding mortgages, but they were described as less grasping than their Chinese and Burman counterparts. The Chettyars preferred not to foreclose mortgages if land occupants could continue to make reasonable payments on their indebtedness. During the depression years of 1905–1907, many land speculators were caught in the squeeze between declining paddy prices and poor share-cropper performance. The problem was aggravated by the government's demand for continued full tax payments without regard to declining cultivator income as a result of low prices, crop failures, or exhorbitant interest rates.

Prevailing business practices contributed significantly to the victimization of debt-ridden tenant cultivators, who had to sell their harvested paddy for immediate cash. British ricemilling and exporting firms resorted from time to time to collusive buying to keep the price of paddy low, a practice contrary to the interests of both the Chettyars and the farmers. Generally speaking, the British business community at Rangoon, which outnumbered the civil service personnel, managed to exert effective opposition to appropriate reform proposals. Business favored strong police controls, easy money, systematic land tax collections, and low-priced Indian labor. Meanwhile they developed minimal contacts with the local population, even during extended periods of residence in Burma.

Agricultural Reform Efforts, 1890 to 1915

The related problems of agricultural expansion were examined repeatedly by the colonial government after 1890. They included the failure of peasant occupants to acquire firm title to their lands, the steady drift from cultivator to non-cultivator ownership, and deficient credit resources. Officials of the revenue service, the land settlement agencies, and even the regional commissioners and governors themselves took the leadership in the search for remedial measures. Most of their efforts ran firmly aground on administrative difficulties, official need for more revenues, and concern over possible slow-down of the rate of agricultural expansion. Throughout the quarter-century prior to 1915, the views of opposition elements (landlords and moneylenders) were more strongly represented in the appointive legislative council than were the disorganized and

inarticulate interests of the people who might have benefited if
successive remedial proposals has been approved.

The first important reform effort was the Burma Agricultural
Bill of 1891, proposed by the financial commissioner D. M. Smeaton.
It would restrict the sale of land by a cultivator to a non-agricul-
turalist unless express approval was obtained from a revenue officer,
and the tract would also be subject to the preemptive right of
repurchase by lineal descendants of the original owner. Lender
income would also be limited to usufruct mortgages based on annual
output, with all solvent mortgagees guaranteed occupancy for some
15 years. The bill would have made borrowing more difficult for
the cultivator, particularly to finance such extravagant outlays as
weddings, initiatory *shin pyu* ceremonies, and holiday observances.
Smeaton's proposal remained under consideration by the government of India for five or six years, only to be abandoned in 1897,
when Burma was accorded legislative autonomy.

Meanwhile, a similar proposal was half-heartedly initiated by
chief commissioner Sir Frederick Fryer in 1896. All cultivator-occu-
pants of twelve-years standing would have their rentals set by settlement department officers of the district, following prescribed rules
relating to productivity. Such holdings would be declared heritable
but not otherwise transferable except by court decree for non-pay-
ment of rent. When this measure was adjudged by subordinate
British officials as being radical and premature, Fryer advised the
India authorities to ignore it. His later proposal of 1900 provided
only for security of tenure conditioned on payment of "fair rent"
as determined by government officials. This one also encountered
strong official resistance and was rejected by the Burma council. The
pattern of Irish land reform efforts approved by London's Parliament is clearly discernible here.

The same fate overtook the Burma Tenancy Bill of 1906–1908,
even though it enjoyed the active support of the governor, Sir
Herbert Thirkell White. It proposed to protect occupants of particular plots from rental increments over a five-year period, except
as revenue officers might rule otherwise under special circumstances.
In the absence of organized indigenous backing and in the face of
strong opposition within the business-biased legislative council,
White's proposal ran aground.

Governor White in 1906 also championed a Land Alienation Bill,
persisting in this effort up to 1910. He proposed to accord to agri-

culturalists who sold their land the right to repurchase their holdings on approximately equal terms during the course of a designated period. Usufruct mortgages should extend for one year only, and co-heirs of the original vendor would share the repurchase privilege. Here was a deliberate attempt to restore a significant principle of Burmese customary law. The proposal died in 1911, although not until it was reviewed at length by both the government of India and the secretary of state for India in London. A tax relief measure was also brought forward by land settlement officer John S. Furnivall in 1911. It would apply in times of crop failure and was coupled with cultivator access to cooperative credit and to cotton ginning facilities. This proposal was flatly rejected by the Burma government's reviewing committee. The interests of the Burmese cultivator here as always took second place to the need for accelerated agricultural development and government revenues.

Two experimental efforts were tried out on a restricted scale in efforts to encourage cultivators to acquire firm title to their lands. One was the so-called "patta system," which accorded relief from payment of taxes during the early period of land development, in return for denial of the occupant's right to borrow money on land security. As might have been anticipated, the system benefited only the minority of fairly well-to-do farmers, and it was eventually abandoned in 1907. An alternative government-estate program was conceived in 1910 and finally implemented in 1915. The estates were established in marginally located but contiguous areas which had earlier been set aside as fuel reserves. Estate occupants were tenants of the state, which undertook to provide essential credit needs on reasonable terms using the improved lands as security. A states colonies department was charged with keeping such land rents in line with cumulative improvements realized on the land itself. Rental income revenue was used for the development of state-financed facilities for water control, transportation, and other community needs. The plan was well conceived in theory, but the several estates were widely scattered, limited in size, and difficult to administer. The total area of estates land was never more than a tiny fraction (some 2 percent) of the millions of acres under cultivation.

The most extensive agricultural reform effort for Burma was borrowed directly from the India Cooperative Societies Act of 1904, an outgrowth of the India Famine Commission Report of 1901. As a result of persistent encouragement from the Burma department of agriculture, the cooperative movement finally got under way. In 1910 the government established the Upper Burma Central Union Cooperative Bank. This institution and its successors were intended to supply the credit needs of hundreds of local cooperatives otherwise unable to generate sufficient share capital. The number of such societies reached 1,250 by 1915, some 3,300 by 1920, and more than 4,000 in 1925, when the structure began to fall apart. Credit resources were overextended during the World War I period, and administration suffered from operational confusion and ignorance prevailing within the several societies. The bookkeeping was carelessly done, and loan renewals were extended overgenerously. The audit of the Cooperative Bank assets in 1928–1929 found that the participating institutions were bankrupt. The recession of the early thirties completed the debacle. Approximately one-third of the societies were later salvaged, but the government sustained heavy losses. Even at the peak of the cooperative movement in the early twenties, its resources provided only a small fraction of the credit needs for Burma's agriculture. In addition to the perennial shortage of funds, what was lacking in the Irrawaddy delta was the necessary feeling of mutual trust and cohesion among prospective members.

Generally speaking, the ruling hierarchy within colonial Burma was interested only peripherally in the promotion of cultivator welfare. Enhancement of total output, expansion of trade volume, and the collection of maximum tax revenues were clearly the overriding concerns. Economic reform proposals, usually formulated by perceptive British officials who were aware of the need to establish more equitable regulations to safeguard cultivators, usually ran aground in the face of opposition from legislative councils representing hostile business interests. Even in situations where the Burma governor exercised his prerogative to ignore council opposition and to forward the reform proposal to superior authorities in India and London, the same British interests could exert pressure to prevent approval. Comparable organized Burmese support for such reforms was lacking.

Aspects of Cultural and Religious Decay

Cultural decline became increasingly evident after 1885. It was due in part to the disappearance of the royal court, which had long sponsored artistic craftsmanship, music and dance, and superior literary talent. Under colonial rule, proficiency in the traditional arts and in Burmese literary communication ceased to be an important avenue toward social and vocational advancement. Destruction of the court also meant the disappearance of the governmental commissions designed to regulate monastic properties and the authenticity of Sangha ordination records. During the troubles of 1886–1887, Commissioner Bernard successfully enlisted the assistance of the thathanabaing in upper Burma to restrain monk-led violence, but the same religious leader, when brought south, was not able exert a substantial influence on the belligerent pongyis of lower Burma. Commissioner Crosthwaite, after 1887, refused to accord any official support to the disciplinary authority of the Buddhist hierarchy and subjected the monks themselves to the direct surveillance of the police and secular courts. The post of thathana-baing fell permanently vacant following the death of the last incumbent in 1895. Monks as a group continued to enjoy the respect of the Burman Buddhist community and to exert a humane and charitable influence, but the relentless trend was toward laxity and loss of discipline.

In the educational field, the traditional monastic pongyi kyaung schools for Burma's youth became increasingly irrelevant to growing literacy demands and to considerations of social or vocational advancement. Among the elite, knowledge of English took precedence over proficiency in Burmese or familiarity with the Buddhist scriptures. To complicate matters further, schooling in an alien English language medium in Anglo-vernacular and American missionary schools subjected students to personal frustrations and to separation from their more traditionally-educated parents. By 1910, government and missionary-operated schools had taken over virtually all secondary education, which became largely divorced from traditional moral and religious norms.

In business operations, few Burmans could compete with foreign elements of the population (Indian, Chinese, or British). For a Burman Buddhist, the search for wealth alone violated traditional social values. Moreover, it was usually accompanied by deliberate exploitation of fellow Burmans, and often by thievery and violence, making it revolting to most, although an increasing number engaged in its pursuit. The self-respecting Burman continued to cherish traditional social customs and held on to his animistic beliefs long after their rationale had been discredited.

The magnitude of the task of social reintegration and national revival under alien rule was staggering. Beginnings of the process were feeble and halting. In 1897, a small group of Western-oriented Burmans at Moulmein formed a society to promote a modernized educational program to be conducted under lay Buddhist sponsorship, hoping to match the standards of the best of the missionary-operated schools. They urged Burmans to curb excessive expenditures on prestigious weddings, funerals, and initiatory rites for youth in order to provide the funds needed for better schools. The response was limited; only four or five urban groups responded meaningfully. An alternative approach was projected in 1904 in the organization at Rangoon college, a teaching branch of the university of Calcutta, of a Student Buddhist Association. It sponsored meetings and lectures on religious and cultural themes, but again the results were minimal. Meanwhile, monastic schools refused to modernize their curricula to include arithmetic and geography and flatly refused to submit to government inspection in order to qualify for public funds.

More significant politically than educationally was the organization in 1906 by European-educated Burmans of the Young Men's Buddhist Association. The lay membership of the YMBA assembled locally from time to time to discuss religious, artistic, and literary topics. The fifty branches, located in as many urban centers, sent delegates to annual sessions of the General Council of Buddhist Associations. So suspicious became the British authorities, that they forbade Burman employees of the government from participating in the activities of the YMBA chapters. The GCBA became within a decade one of the few *bona fide* spokesmen for emerging nationalist sentiment.

From similar roots but operating within a broader context emerged in 1909 the Burma Research Society. Sympathetic British officials such as H. Clayton and John S. Furnivall helped sponsor the project. The research society was forbidden to consider potentially divisive economic or political questions; even archeology was frowned upon for a time. Thus limited, the society managed to enlist the continuing support of Burman members of the civil service as well as Burmophile British representatives. Governor White himself served for a time as a patron of the society and acted on occasion as presiding officer at its sessions. Part of the support and interest generated by the group was due to growing popular concern to develop a distinctive Burmese ethnic and cultural identity separate from that of India. These tentative beginnings of national revival were overtaken by the events of World War I.

Developments During World War I

The most significant initial impact of the World War I on Burma was in the economic field. Lower Burma's rice surpluses became unsaleable abroad, partly from collapse of world markets and partly due to the lack of shipping facilities later in the war. For rice-growing lower Burma, this meant cumulative debt, increasing mortgage foreclosures, and default on tax payments. By comparison, upper Burma was relatively prosperous, the economy being buoyed by increasing British investments in minerals and oil. The market for upper Burma's agricultural production in cotton, sessamum, sugar, onions, pepper, and tobacco held up well, so that prices kept pace with rising living costs. The influx of newcomers to urban centers of upper Burma, reversing the previous southward population movement, produced a boom in real estate prices. This was coupled with increased speculation generally, an orgy of gambling, and accompanying lawlessness. Thus the epidemic of crime which had previously characterized lower Burma began to spread to upper Burma as well.

Despite these disturbing economic developments, the war was half over before any significant political impact was discernible. Most of the basic social tensions had little direct connection with the British presence, apart from the required payment of taxes, which was eased somewhat in 1916. Anti-alien sentiment was directed mainly against resident Indian laborers and Chinese shopkeepers. Immediate enemies of the cultivators included Burmese landlords and the Chettyar moneylenders. Relations between the older and younger generations were strained, and students generally were frustrated by the experience of forced instruction in an alien English language, and by the lack of jobs at the end of the study program. The goal of student endeavor was usually to qualify for the colonial civil service, and the successful encumbents were the object of envy and emulation. Public issues were neither defined clearly nor openly discussed. Indigenous political parties were lacking, along with popular concepts relative to the nature and value of representative government.

Nationalist sentiment started crystalizing in 1916, when a younger faction within the GCBA raised the issue of prohibiting the wearing of shoes within pagoda premises. The issue intrinsically was unimportant except for considerations of face. The British were being forbidden to do something that related to Buddhist sensitivities and national pride, so that shoe wearing became a symbol comprehensible to all. The clamor continued long after the government, in 1918, conceded that local monastic authorities were free to prohibit shoes on pagoda premises if they wished to do so.

During the final two years of the war, literate Burmans also became cognizant of declared allied war aims, especially President Wilson's advocacy of self-determination. They read for the first time accounts of the Japanese victory over Russia in 1905 and saw German prisoners of war arriving to work on the new Shan states railway. More important after 1918 was the growing Burman awareness nearer home of the Congress Party's demand in India for constitutional reform. Potential political leaders, like U Ottama, studied in India during the period.

The war period also saw the arrival of Governor Sir Spencer Harcourt Butler, who had previously been posted in India but knew very little about Burma. His vigorous advocacy of Burma's social and economic progress within the imperial connection reflected his concern to divert public attention from political matters. He adjudged Burma to be far behind India in experience with self-government and therefore saw no immediate need for governmental reform. He nevertheless endeavored to promote cooperative effort to improve industry, education, and public welfare generally as a means of attaining Burma's "shining destiny." In 1916 he purchased a 400-acre site on the outskirts of Rangoon for the establishment of a national university. In his view nationalist freedom to create a better life was associated with opportunities afforded within the British imperial system and loyalty to the beneficent king-emperor. He proposed to inculcate social responsibility, moral concern, and public spirit by the preparation of a manual of civic duties derived from Burma's own historic experience, including an anthology prepared from the country's choice literary treasures. Some fifty lectures were planned for public use covering empire history and stressing governmental, economic, and strategic goals. As interpreted by Governor Butler, World War I was a struggle between British freedom and Prussian autocracy. He argued that the cooperative role

played by both India and Burma in that struggle should earn for
them a respected role within the empire. He acknowledged that
alien-sponsored missionaries had contributed useful educational services, but insisted that empire citizens should henceforth take over
as heads of all such schools. Butler's efforts were effusive and labored.
A mild rejoinder to the governor's spate of imperial propaganda
was entered by several understanding Indian civil servants of long
experience, such as H. Clayton and John S. Furnivall. They pointed
out that patriotism must rest primarily on love of one's own country
and its valued traditions. This would then have to be combined
with loyalty for civilized society throughout the world, for which the
British Commonwealth ostensibly was endeavoring to serve as
trustee. Only if Burma's own patriotism could be reconciled to
Commonwealth loyalty, they argued, would flags and ceremonies
serve useful ends. There existed a vast gap between the idealized
exhortations of Governor Butler and the concurrent insistence of
GCBA spokesmen that visiting Britishers must not wear shoes on
pagoda premises. Attempts to arrive at a meeting of minds during
the intervening decades proved to be extremely difficult.

VII Constitutional Change Between World Wars

The period between the wars can be divided into three major segments. The years 1919 to 1930 saw the formulation and application of Burma's version of India's dyarchy reform program. The ensuing six years (1930–1936) witnessed the Simon Commission's review of dyarchy in operation and London's consideration of recommended changes, culminating in Burma's separation from India under the new constitution of 1935. This middle period was also attended by varied expression of economic and political unrest. The final six years prior to the outbreak of the East Asian war in late 1941 saw the attempted implementation of responsible constitutional government coupled with increasing domestic political tension and subsequent efforts to exploit Britain's involvement in the European war after 1939.

At the outset, in 1919–1920, articulate Burmese public opinion demanded and was promised, in London, constitutional concessions comparable to those which the British Parliament had accorded to India in 1919. The new dyarchy reform pattern kept the most important ministerial posts (police, courts, finances) in the several provincial governments under the governor's control. But by the time the Burmese negotiating delegation returned from London in early 1921, the Gandhi-led Indian boycott of the entire reform program had changed the picture. The shooting down of hundreds of protesting Punjabis at Amritsar in April 1919, had produced such a profound revulsion of Indian opinion that it carried over to Burma as well. A majority faction of Burmese villagers, led by India-influenced monk agitators and others who were hostile to the colonial government and distrustful of London's political intentions, opposed any participation in the dyarchy reform program and any talk of Burma's separation from India. Better informed Burmese political leaders favored separation from India partly for economic and social reasons, and a number of them opted to participate in the new legislative council, some for objectives of personal or group advancement and others to strive for expanding self-government within the existing governmental framework. From 1923 to 1930, Burma's semi-representative dyarchy government managed to function by following a noncontroversial legislative agenda. Meanwhile the frustrated majority of boycotting Burmans split into quarreling factions.

The visit of the Simon Commission in 1930 and subsequent discussions in London did little to clarify the political atmosphere in Burma. A series of anti-Indian riots erupted in Rangoon, precipitated in part by economic depression conditions of 1930 and 1931, to be followed by a religiously inspired rebellion. The price of rice exports plummeted, and the rate of land alienation to moneylenders reached an all-time high. In 1932, the distraught villagers abandoned their futile political boycott and elected their own anti-separationist majority to the legislative council, committed to full independence as soon as the way seemed clear. Since Burma's continuing status as part of India was clearly out of the question, the London authorities approved Burma's own separated constitution of 1935, granting elected assembly control over the entire cabinet. The governor retained broad emergency powers.

The year 1936 featured the first elections under the new constitution and the significant Rangoon university student strike. The latter marked the political emergence of the Thakin Dobama Asiayone (We Burmans Party) that was to dominate the postwar political scene. Following the elections of 1936, Premier Ba Maw, a European-trained former anti-separationist, of socialist inclinations, managed to organize a coalition cabinet, capitalizing on the inability of political rivals to cooperate among themselves. Forced out of office in early 1939, Dr. Ba Maw later joined hands with the Thakins in the fall of the same year to agitate for Burma's postwar independence.

The Question of Governmental Reform

Interest in democratic constitutional reform was very limited among Burmans at the end of World War I. British Secretary Montagu's initial proposal for Indian reform, made in 1917, called for wider participation by Indian personnel in all branches of government, looking toward the eventual goal of responsible self-rule within the empire. The only positive response in Burma at the time was made by the moderate YMBA delegation which proceeded to

Calcutta in December 1917 to talk with Lord Montagu. The group asked that Burma be separated from India to become a distinct nation within the empire. In view of this limited initial response, the report of the London Parliamentary Joint Committee Report on Indian Constitutional Reform, published in 1918, concluded that Burma's political evolution "should be postponed for separate and future consideration." Shortly thereafter the new governor, Sir Reginald Craddock, was asked by Lord Montagu to formulate a separate reform scheme deemed to be suitable for Burma.

It was not so much the details of the Craddock reform proposals that aroused Burmese anger, as his patronizing approach and insulting innuendos. Craddock was an India-born Englishman who had spent a total of thirty-three years in that country; yet he was completely lacking in sympathy for Indian nationalist aspirations. As governor, he expressed concern that Burma be spared what he termed the poisonous turmoil of political agitation that was emerging at the time in the subcontinent. He argued that, under the guidance of trusted British officials, Burma could in time become accustomed to elective institutions and live down its dismal reputation for criminal violence, gambling, and thriftlessness. He noted also that the country lacked India's experience since 1882 in the operation of local boards and councils and that not enough Burmans (some 400 only) had received higher educational training, which would be needed to man a representative type of government. He favored the "highest degree of self-government which they [the Burmese] were competent to exercise," but British authorities would make the final decisions. The Burmese were furious over the governor's suggestion that they were less competent than Indians to govern themselves and must therefore become reconciled to an indefinite period of British tutelage.

Craddock advocated that Burma's self-government program be limited largely to local circle and district boards, which would function in an advisory capacity to regional bureaucratic governmental agencies. His proposed central assembly would include representatives from the thirty-one districts, from a score of urban constituencies, a half dozen special interest groups, plus twenty-two official appointees of the governor, but with no legislative power and authorization to give advice only when requested to do so. The widespread distrust and anger generated by Craddock's approach went far to destroy whatever *rapport* had developed previously between articulate Burman leadership and the governor's office under Butler and Whyte.

The immediate rejoinder to the Craddock proposal was Burman insistence that they be included in the complete India reform program, even if it meant some delay in making the necessary adjustments. This alternative was argued at length and with conviction in 1919. Burma's deep-seated concern not to become a permanent part of India was nevertheless qualified here and later by the fear that political aspirations entertained by an isolated Burma could too easily be ignored.

While the Burma delegation at London was arguing the case for inclusion, events in India contributed a new trend to public opinion. The turning point was the Amritsar massacre of April 17, 1919, when British-Indian troops fired some 1,600 rounds of ammunition point blank into an unarmed protesting assembly. This drove Gandhi into the political arena and led to the general rejection throughout India of London's newly approved dyarchy reform constitution. Ensuing Indian elections were widely boycotted. When the Burman delegation returned triumphantly from London in early 1920 with the promise that Burma also would be offered a measure of self-government comparable with India's, they found the popular mood ominously altered. A radical grass-roots nationalist movement led by monks and other traditionalists and reacting directly to political developments in India had decided to reject the reforms and to join the Gandhi boycott. The English-educated and reformist middle class of professional men, editors, and government employees was at first too small and too far out of touch to enlist any popular following. This group's influence was nevertheless due to expand.

Various local considerations also contributed to the changed point of view. During 1920, elite discontent came to focus on several decisions reached by colonial authorities with respect to the new university of Rangoon. It was to be a strictly residential institution, operating under more exacting matriculation standards and examination expectations than Calcutta had required. Burmese critics countered with the charge that the same authorities who had alleged that Burma had too few degree holders to merit a constitution equal to India's were apparently seeking to perpetuate such disabilities by abruptly raising standards. YMBA leaders staged a public protest meeting on August 1, 1920, which denounced the proposed University Act. In an ostensible effort to shield the infant institution from political influences, the act would limit indigenous representation on the university council to 5 of 46 members and to a mere 2 of 24 seats in the senate. Opponents then recalled that Governor Butler in 1916 had advocated establishing a new university as a means of promoting the imperial idea. When the act was formally approved on August 28, 1920, without taking such protests into account, the university itself became a political issue.

On December 4, just three days before the scheduled formal opening of the institution by Governor Craddock himself acting as Chancellor, the university students went out on strike. The strike was apparently instigated primarily by off-campus political agitators, but under the pressure of patriotic appeals all students fell in line. The movement quickly spread to public and mission high schools in nearby Rangoon. In a short time, virtually the entire male student population found living accommodations in monks' quarters at the Shwe Dagon pagoda. Food was provided by a supporting popular effort. The political excitement thus generated afforded ample opportunity for India-oriented advocates of home rule to propagate their cause. Because Christian and non-Buddhist Indian students became involved in the movement, the GCBA decided to substitute the word "Burmese" for "Buddhist" in its traditional designation.

The resulting movement to establish a system of non-government national schools enlisted for a time substantial lay donations and pongyi educator participation. Only a few such institutions managed to survive, for the sponsors early discovered that national spirit was no substitute for classrooms, teachers, textbooks, and operating funds. The university and school strikes were short-lived, but the movement was an important step in the birth of a new type of revolutionary nationalism, youth-led and heedless of both parental and governmental control. December 4 was later designated as national day.

At the opposite end of the social spectrum, Burma's rice cultivators were becoming involved in a grassroots pattern of political protest. When the world market for rice became available at the end of the war, the government's control board assumed monopoly control over all grain exports. The objective was two-fold: to prevent private speculators from realizing enormous profits from rice exports, and to hold down food prices domestically for the benefit of urban labor in particular. The difference between the price paid to cultivators and that gained from sales made overseas provided a windfall profit to the government's control board of some 92 million rupees within two years. The millers, shippers, and the government all profited at the expense of the cultivator, who received little more than the cost of production.

Such circumstances afforded opportunity for leaders of the GCBA to sponsor the organization at the village level of a large number of *Wunthanu athins* (national-interest defender organizations) to challenge alleged governmental exploitation. For most cultivators, it mattered little that the accrued profits from rice exports were to be spent on railway and road construction and other public works, including a grant of ten million rupees to the rural cooperative societies. When the full-blown program to boycott the dyarchy-reform elections got under way in 1922, the Wunthanu athins were prepared to play a significant role. In many situations they fell under the control of political pongyi agitators, who added the charge that Buddhism was in danger as a result of alien rule and resulting national impoverishment.

When the investigating British Burma Reforms Committee arrived in Burma in late 1921, it encountered an unanticipated situation of political turmoil. The GCBA leadership flatly refused to cooperate, and few Burman leaders outside of the association were willing to testify. London's reluctantly granted dyarchy reform proposals were found to be highly unpopular; events had outrun parliament's leisurely timetable. Those Burmans who did testify before the committee stressed the importance of including the ministries of forests and education within the several governmental functions to be transferred to indigenous control.

Some of the most penetrating comments came from sympathetic and informed Britishers, like John S. Furnivall. He advocated the need to transfer at the earliest opportunity all routine functions of government except the police and courts to the control of ministers responsible to the proposed elected assembly. He would also limit suffrage rights to the informed and more responsible elements of the population, who would be free later to decide how and when popular participation should be further extended. He contended that Burma's peasant population was more concerned that the price of rice be regulated by an understanding administration than in casting votes for ambitious political aspirants to any legislative council. If popular elections were staged prematurely, the frustrated and confused electorate would be more likely to respond to demagogic and obscurantist political direction than to intelligent national leadership. He also cautioned that local district boards should not be saddled with responsibilities which lay outside their immediate interests and competence. Unfortunately, such informed counsel was disregarded. The pattern had already been set, involving the use of convenient taxpayer suffrage rolls, postponement of separation from India, communal representation plus governor appointees in the legislative council, and the retention of the governor's control over military and police authority, the courts of law, public works, taxation and finances.

Proliferation of Political Factionalism

Political alignments in Burma coalesced into a number of general categories during the course of the formulation of the new constitution and following its inauguration in January 1923. The most radical and irresponsible group was led by political pongyis recruited mainly from younger elements of the Sangha monkhood and led by the revolutionary U Ottama. Prior to his return to Burma in 1921, Ottama had lived for a number of years in Japan and Calcutta. In India, he had been in close touch with the Hindu Mahasabha organization and became its elected president for Burma. He was thoroughly familiar with Congress Party's objectives and tactics. By alleging that Burma's Buddhism was endangered by alien rule, he attracted an undisciplined following among the restive younger monks. His partisans denounced the dyarchy reforms, demanded home rule, agitated for nonpayment of taxes, and condoned intimidation and violence to achieve their ends.

Ottama's monastic following, in 1921, dominated many of the GCBA-sponsored Wunthanu athins and in 1922 asserted control over the general council of *Sangha Sametggi* (associations). To the great distress of the responsible senior Sayadaw heads of monasteries, the GCSS sponsored an obscurantist monks' rebellion. The government's attempt to curb the agitation by arresting the rebel leaders (U Ottama in particular in 1921, 1924–1927, and 1928–1939) only advertised the movement and made martyrs of U Ottama and U Wisara, who both eventually died in jail. Pongyi radicals exploited popular faith in both astrology and magic; they constituted a kind of traditionalist threat to the smaller group of westernized Burman elite. Although less radical leaders of the GCBA did not

approve the political methods of U Ottama's following, they felt
obliged to pay deference to his influence in order to avoid alienating
the villagers. Overt denunciation of pongyi radicals had to be
avoided by all aspiring politicians. The more dedicated proponents
of home rule like U Chit Hlaing, a well-to-do educated Mon, allied
himself with the GCSS efforts within the Wunthanu athins to boycott elections, but he did not sanction the tactics which Ottama's
followers frequently employed.

Governmental repression was severe. Persons suspected of revolutionary intent, under terms of India's Rowlatt Act and later
amendments, could be arbitrarily imprisoned for fifteen days and be
subjected thereafter to parole restrictions and indefinite detention
even though they had committed no overt criminal offense. Burma's
Anti-Boycott Act of 1927 eventually authorized severe penalties if
boycotts were perpetrated for "purely political" purposes. A frequent pongyi tactic was to challenge the authority of local village
headmen, who were vulnerable as government officials. The usual
approach of Chit Hlaing's followers was to advocate boycott and
home rule but also to denounce official fraud and corruption along
with all popular expressions of crime. Some members of the GCBA
corresponded directly with sympathetic members of the British
Parliament as a means of bringing their views to public attention in
England.

During the course of the 1920s, the GCBA itself split into four
principal fragments. An important minority group of twenty-one
recognized leaders defected in 1922 to form the so-called "21 Party"
nationalists in the first legislative council, dedicated to work for
home rule within the constitutional system. The majority GCBA
constituency continued to work within the Wunthanu athins in
partial alliance with the monk-influenced agitators. A major split
within the GCBA ranks developed in early 1924, when U Ottama's
radical wing stirred up a riot in Mandalay, the incident which led
to Ottama's second incarceration. In February 1925, a moderate
faction broke away from U Chit Hlaing's majority following to set
up the Home Rule Party led by Tharrawaddy U Pu. A month later,
an ultra-radical faction led by U So Thein defected from the
dwindling majority. Thus did confusion proliferate.

The new Home Rule Party abandoned the boycott tactics in 1924
and stood for election the following year. Meanwhile, a somewhat
less radical defector group founded the Swaraj Party, following an

Indian pattern. It attracted the support of a number of able Europeanized Burmans, including Dr. Ba Maw and U Paw Tun, who later became the party leader. The Swaraj group managed in 1925 to elect nine members to the new legislative council, but they did not seek office and were too closely tied to Indian connections to attract any wide popular following in Burma. Clearcut issues tended to be lost in the growing political confusion, as factions coalesced around rival leaders and emotion-laden symbols. When denied government posts in the second assembly in 1927, the moderate Burman group united to form the People's Party.

At the extreme left of the political spectrum, a fanatical secretive faction called the *Bu athins* appeared as early as 1924. It was a conspiratorial movement, addicted to violence, intimidation, and defiance of governmental authority. The members denounced taxation requirements, Chettyar moneylending operations, and the governmental requirement of licenses to fish. Police repression forced the Bu athins underground, where political protest tended in time to mingle with criminal activities generally.

The Provisions of the Dyarchy Reform Constitution

Under the Burma constitution of 1922, the legislative council included a majority of members elected from general constituencies (58 of 103). Fifteen additional members were elected communally, seven others by business groups and the university constituency, and twenty-three officials were nominated by the governor. The general suffrage was based on available tax rolls, with urban constituencies somewhat overrepresented. The rolls for upper Burma included a large number of women householder taxpayers. The constitution provided that two of the four main cabinet ministers would administer the so-called transferred subjects, which included excise tax collection, agriculture, forests, education, health, and non-irrigation public works. These two ministers would function under responsibility to a majority vote of the council. The other principal ministers for home affairs (police), finance, labor, and irrigation controls would continue to be under the governor's control. Hence the term dyarchy. The governor retained his authority over peripheral tribal areas of Burma, and was empowered to veto all items of legislation. He could also certify on his own authority essential items of expenditure omitted from any council-authorized budget.

Other matters such as foreign relations, coinage and currency, law, income tax, communication and transport, and civil service selection continued under control of the central Indian government.

The efforts of the election boycotters were generally effective. Less than 7 percent of the eligible voters went to the polls in 1922, 16 percent in 1925, and 18 percent in 1928, when the elected membership was raised to 80. Voter intimidation was hardly necessary because few Burmans wanted to vote in any case. The fact that suffrage rights were based on the payment of unpopular direct capitation and household taxes tended to discredit the voter privilege itself. Villagers associated with the Wunthanu athins preferred to challenge the taxes directly rather than to elect candidates to a legislative council which exercised no real power. More than half (30) of the initially elected general constituency candidates were persons who were locally influential but who lacked party affiliation. They included two Christian Karens. The "21 Party" elected the other 28 members, but it could exert no effective control over the thirty independents.

The cooperative spirit engendered initially within the first council owed much to the efforts of returning governor Sir Spencer Harcourt Butler, who succeeded the unpopular Craddock in January 1923. He appointed one member of the nationalist "21 party," U Maung Gyee, to be minister of education. He also managed to do much to relieve tensions by broadening university controls and even enlisted financial support for a number of qualified national schools which had managed to survive. Butler appointed other respected Burman leaders, including U May Oung, founder of the YMBA, to ministerships responsible to the governor. One of his appointees died in 1924, and May Oung himself died in 1926 at the age of 46. Comparable replacements were difficult to find. The honeymoon with Governor Butler proved short-lived.

Functioning of the Dyarchy Reforms

Aside from the adjustments made in the area of education, the nationalist minority of the first legislative council pursued opportunist tactics. The main political objectives were to embarrass the government and to establish some *rapport* with the boycotting Burman constituency. Principal targets of criticism were the colonial police, the high salaries paid to European supervisors, alleged governmental overattention to political suppression, and the continued arbitrary detention of suspected offenders. Budgetary needs for the police services were denied and had to be certified by the governor as a consequence. In an effort to enlist villager support, the nationalists also demanded repeal of the capitation tax, discontinuance of the outlawry of the Bu athins, and return to the local selection of village headmen. These tactics were too superficial to attract favorable attention within the radical Wunthanu athins, but they generated sharp opposition from representatives of business interests, minority groups, and officials within the council.

In the 1925 election of the second council, the three nationalist parties gained 45 of the 58 general constituency seats (25 of the "21 Party," 11 Home Rulers, and 9 Swarajists), reducing the number of alleged independents from 30 to 13. But ten defections occurred when an effort was made to force all members of the projected United People's Party to decline acceptance of office. A well-to-do moderate Burman faction, called the Golden Valley Party, eventually absorbed most of the available appointments to ministerial posts, high court judgeships, and other attractive offices of government. The GVP also helped provide a continuing council majority for the governor's supporters. The heterogenous character of the coalition majority forced the avoidance of legislative reform proposals such as the land mortgage bank, and the Agrarian Bill of 1927 designed to assist cooperatives. Abandoning their socially-oriented proposals, the Burman legislators finally began to demand priority access for indigenous applicants for civil service jobs over incumbent British and Indian officials. The People's Party went financially bankrupt during the course of the 1928 elections and was thereafter split by personal rivalries.

The years 1927–1928, following U Ottama's second release from prison, witnessed a resurgence of crime and intimidation throughout the lower Burma countryside. Pongyi politicians attacked the authority of headmen and urged nonpayment of taxes, while the courts fined entire village units for suppressing evidence of anti-tax agitation. Such tactics led to the third incarceration of U Ottama in 1928, and to the death in prison in 1929 of U Wisara, who refused as a prisoner to doff his monk's robe and staged a fatal hunger strike. Even more ominous were the continuing erosion of headman authority and the rumored emergence at Shwebo of a princely pretender to the throne of a revived Burma kingdom. The rumors were associated with magical tattooing rites calculated to produce invulnerability to firearms.

One of the most unfortunate results of the experiment of the 1920s in governmental reforms had to do with the faltering operation of the Burma Rural Self-Government Act of 1921. It had grown out of Governor Craddock's earlier proposals for circle and district boards, designed to serve as training grounds for self-government. The scheduled popular elections of 1922 for circle board members attracted so little interest that more than half the places had to be filled by official appointment. Many village headmen were elected and later confirmed to office, contrary to the rules. Circle boards did virtually nothing except to designate respectively two members of each circle to sit on district boards. The functions assigned to the district boards were varied and numerous. Their responsibilities included health and sanitation measures, veterinary services, vernacular education, upkeep of secondary roads and waterways, collection of ferry and bazaar rentals, and the administration of cattle pounds. Government officials were ordered not to interfere with local boards unless aid was requested, which was seldom done.

The second round of circle elections encountered no dearth of candidates. Self-seeking individuals had become aware of the possibilities of favoritism and graft in connection with the expenditure of funds provided for district projects. The boards were responsible to no articulate local opinion and also encountered little restraint from official sources. Except for some of the unpaid school teachers who sought membership in the boards for promotion of their personal interests, few reputable persons participated. Little or no legitimate compensation was available to board members, and yet all were subjected to intimidating abuse at the hands of spokesmen for the Wunthanu athins. The rule disqualifying village headman participation contributed to the fiasco, even though many were illegally elected.

The introduction of elected town committees in 1922 contributed similarly to the deterioration of municipal administration. After 1923, when the participation of European residents was virtually eliminated, inefficiency and corruption proliferated everywhere. The official ratings for municipal corporation performance declined from a 65 percent having a satisfactory record in 1922–1923 to less than 50 percent receiving such rating after 1927. Neither local government officials nor any responsible citizenry were able to control the rampant dishonesty which developed. An estimated nine-tenths of class I judges accepted gratuities from litigants. Water services, lighting, and trash collection suffered as did street and school maintenance. John Furnivall's criticisms of the Craddock proposals, made in 1921, were amply corroborated. He had meanwhile resigned from the land settlement service in discouraged protest.

Burma's governmental and political problems at the end of the twenties were seriously aggravated by worsening economic conditions. The price of paddy at Rangoon declined by one-third between 1926 and 1930, due in part to collusive buying practices by the four principal European rice-exporting firms. All agricultural elements felt the pinch; the cultivators, landlords, and moneylenders. The firms were acting legally, and worldwide price trends were measurably to blame, but their complicity generated psychological tinder for political explosion. The same period of 1928–1929 witnessed the collapse of the network of agricultural credit cooperatives as a consequence of cumulatively careless lending practices and irregular accounting. The world depression, which broke for Burma in 1930, completed the economic collapse.

The Simon Commission Investigation of 1929

The India Statutory Commission, headed by Sir John Simon, was dispatched by London in 1928 in accordance with specifications within the India Act that a review of the dyarchy reforms should be made after ten years. The commission's arrival in Burma in February 1929 was well advertised because the group had spent much of the previous year in India. Despite considerable effort of compromise, Burman nationalists failed to reach any general agreement over what position they should assume with respect to constitutional revision. The basic disagreement lay between the better informed spokesmen, who favored separation from India under varying degrees of self-rule, and the distrustful pongyi-led anti-separationists. The latter group, reflecting influences from India, discounted British intentions to make any substantial concessions to Burma apart from London's decisions regarding India. One fragment of the

GCBA coalition, led by U Soe Thein, rejected ineffective boycotting tactics, although still continuing to oppose separation and to encourage peasant protest.

The three Burmans selected by the legislative council to be part of the Simon Commission were all drawn from the pro-government group. The four ethnic minority representatives included a Karen, an Indian Hindu, a Muslim, and a Eurasian. The 82 percent of eligible voters who had boycotted the 1928 elections and many of the 18 percent who had voted were not represented at all on the commission. It is therefore understandable why Burmans nationalists regarded the cards as stacked against them.

The views of local British residents were thoroughly explored by the commission. They were far from unanimous. The most extensive and best informed statement was prepared by selected senior officers from various branches of the India civil service. They declared flatly that it was a matter of political necessity that Burma be accorded constitutional advances comparable to any that would be given to India, the ultimate goal to be a fully responsible government within the empire. They denounced as mischievous nonsense the suggestion that Burmans were on trial to prove their fitness for self-government, but they also declined to propose any time schedule. Until Burmans acquired the essential political and administrative experience, the governor would have to maintain control over police and finances and continue to protect the various racial, religious, and economic interests of minority groups. The position was informed and moderately stated, in an obvious effort to find some basis for accord with Burman opinion.

Spokesmen for the elite British chamber of commerce also affirmed their sympathy for Burma's political aspirations, but not very convincingly. They put major emphasis on attaining separation from India, but for fiscal and commercial reasons which had little in common with considerations which motivated the Burman separationists. The chamber nevertheless rejected any effort to curtail the immigration of Indian labor or Chettyar moneylender operations.

Far more stridently hostile was the memorandum submitted by the Association of Professional and Business Men in Burma, which reflected the embittered views of former Governor Craddock. It declared that the dyarchy reforms had been a sad mistake, and that no further extension of self-government should be contemplated by

London, despite all the political clamor. They pointed out quite correctly that experiments with the rural and municipal councils had failed dismally, and argued that the performance of the Burman members of the legislative council had been grossly incompetent. Local political bosses of the Wunthanu athins were declared totally unable to comprehend the basic issues involved. Their picture of public irresponsibility, spreading lawlessness, and demoralized courts, included no effort to assess the causes or to suggest remedial measures. They implied the need to revert to autocratic rule in an effort to hold the lid down. The gap between the conciliatory civil servant point of view and that of the resident British business community of Rangoon was obviously very wide.

The moderate Burmans who associated with the Simon Commission were understandably incensed by the deprecatory British allegations regarding Burma's incapacity for self-rule. They argued that Burmans would respond affirmatively to reform proposals which were relevant to their basic needs. They attributed the admitted failure of local government to popular opposition to dyarchy reforms in general, to the mistaken assignment of unsolicited and onerous responsibilities to inexperienced district councils, and to the lack of official supervision over the handling of available funds.

The most comprehensive statement of the nationalist Burman point of view was made by a coalition group calling itself the Separation League. The league included spokesmen of the Provisional Congress Committee, the People's Party of the legislative council, the British Burma Association, the Karen National Association, and the radical but participating U Soe Thein branch of the GCBA. The moderately-worded initial statement presented by the Congress Committee declared that Burma's desired separation from India would call in time for surrender of the governor's responsibility for foreign relations and his power to veto legislation. All six ministers of the cabinet should, in the immediate future, be made responsible to the legislative council majority. The council itself should also exercise the initiative in proposing future constitutional changes, subject to ultimate approval or rejection by London. The proposal called for a five-year limit to the governor's existing authority to nominate the official bloc membership of the council but conceded that some form of minority representation would have to continue. The league denounced bitterly the continuing efforts of Indian politicians to perpetuate Burma's distrust of British intentions and urged London to counter such effort by issuing a statement pledging sympathetic consideration of a separated Burma's new constitution. Prolonged delay in London, such as had occurred from 1918 to 1922, would only serve to confirm popular suspicions and distrust.

The detailed constitutional proposals of the league were based on the new governmental system of Ireland and included several conciliatory items. All members of the new bicameral Burma parliament should swear allegiance to the British monarch and Commonwealth, but they would enjoy complete freedom of speech within the walls of the two chambers. Burma's parliament would be empowered to initiate future constitutional changes, subject to eventual British approval, and would exercise full control of developmental access to the country's lands, forests, minerals, waters, and power resources. The entire cabinet under the proposed constitution would be responsible to a majority of the popularly elected lower house, whereas the governor and the high court would be responsible only to the crown. The league also proposed, for bargaining purposes, that Burma's international boundaries should revert to pre-1825 status and include India's Naga Hills area, Manipur, and Cachar. The document was skilfully drawn.

More openly anti-Indian and less concerned with reconciling Burman and British opinion was the statement submitted by the "Burma for the Burmans" league. The group consisted mainly of Rangoon intellectuals who lacked formal organizational backing. They included government officials, newspaper editors, employees of British firms, and opposition members of the legislative council. The statement scorned the role of the obscurantist pongyi agitators and other politicians like the Swarajists, who allegedly took direction from Indian sources. They demanded immediate separation from India and an abrupt ending of Indian immigration, but advocated no specific governmental reforms.

The proposals by ethnic minority factions, including Hindu and Muslim Indians, Shan chiefs, Anglo-Indians and Anglo-Burmans, and two Karen factions, presented a highly varied picture. The Karen spokesmen in particular were scornful of the allegedly dishonest and hypocritical Burman participation in the dyarchy reform government and reaffirmed unqualified loyalty to British rule. The anti-separationist majority Burman group, which chose to boycott the commission, received no hearing whatever during the course of the investigation.

The conclusions regarding Burma's reforms as set forth in the final report of the commission, published in 1930, reflected local British opinion far more accurately than they expressed Burman views. Affirming that all articulate Burmans favored separation from India, the report strongly recommended that course, accompanied by assurances regarding the progressive character of the new constitution. It nevertheless discounted the allegation that Burmans were opposed to continued Indian labor immigration, and argued on the contrary that Indian participation had really been the measure of the country's economic development. Because the governor's responsibilities could not be abruptly terminated, the report cautioned against making any premature announcements about the precise nature of the contemplated reforms.

The three Burma volumes of the commission's report (seventeen volumes all told) failed completely to gauge the undercurrent of angry unrest beneath the surface. Burma government's own annual administrative report for 1929–1930 also reflected little sense of apprehension. It stated that the Simon Commission Report had been well received in Burma and commented reassuringly that factional differences and personal rivalries had kept opposition political groups divided and ineffective. British readers of the report could not possibly have anticipated the storm which broke out in 1930–1932. In terms of revealing political realities in Burma, the proverbial mountain had labored and delivered a mouse.

Internal Upheavals, 1930–1932

One of the principal developments during 1930, following the Simon Commission investigation, concerned the changing role of the General Council of Burmese Associations. The boycotting tactics of the organization had by then reached a dead end of futility and frustration. At the village level, the pongyi agitators of the U Ottama school, highly aggressive and culturally reactionary, advocated direct action and overt rebellion, exploiting all forms of tradionalist symbols and superstitions. U Chit Hlaing and others of his type could not function in such a political climate. In its relations with the government the moderate GCBA also faced a discouraging situation. Having denied themselves participation in the legislative council and the Simon Commission, they were now excluded from the newly selected delegation to attend the London roundtable conference scheduled to convene in November 1930. They had got no-where with their anti-tax campaign and had generated little political awareness of any alternative methods or possibilities. If the influence of the mass of Burma's population was to become effective, positive objectives and more fruitful tactics would have to be devised.

For other reasons than pragmatic failure, the continuing pressure of Indian politicians against Burma separation was becoming increasingly unpopular. Distrust of British intentions tended to conflict with Burman dislike of Indians generally. At a time of increasing unemployment, Burmese tenant farmers faced growing competition from discharged Indian industrial workers for access to paddy and sugar lands, where rentals were already too high. Indian money-lenders in 1929 foreclosed mortgages on some 230,000 acres of rice land, and the rate increased alarmingly in 1931, when paddy prices collapsed from 130 rupees per 100 baskets to a mere 77 rupees. Destitute tenant farmers who were obliged to seek rice loans to tide families over to the next harvest had to repay accommodating shop-keepers two baskets for one. For these and other reasons, the two principal factions of the GCBA decided in 1930 to abandon boycott-ing tactics and to try to come to an understanding with the Burman leadership within the legislative council. The Soe Thein faction alone continued its cooperation with pongyi agitators.

Burman leadership associated with the separationist faction had a better understanding of the total political problem. They were determined that India's future constitution must not be permitted to set the boundaries for Burma's political aspirations. The Simon Commission hearings had convinced them that the British economic community centering at Rangoon was the major barrier to Burma's eventual achievement of self-government. Local British advocacy of separation for Burma, it was noted, involved no curtailment of Indian laborer immigration or economic participation and called for no substantive constitutional concessions. The understanding of the country's basic problems demonstrated by long-experienced British civil servants in their search for rapport with responsible Burman leadership obviously carried little weight with the new governor, Sir Charles Innes. He was far more closely associated with the membership of Rangoon's exclusive European clubs. John Furnivall had suffered virtual ostracism by the British community since the 1920s, and Judge Maurice Collis (author of *Trials in*

Burma) experienced the same treatment in the early thirties. British face had to be maintained.

Burmese economic differences with the British business community were easy to identify. For one thing, Indian labor competition kept wages very low. The collusive buying practices of British rice exporting firms contributed to reducing paddy prices paid to the cultivators even before the depression. Meanwhile the British corporations which dominated the chamber of commerce continued to pay handsome dividends to stockholders, even through the depression. Under such circumstances, nationalist leaders became increasingly resentful over British moralizing about rampant crime in the countryside and petty corruption within the district councils. They charged that the system itself contributed to the impoverishment of the indigenous population and to social disintegration. Leaders of the Separation League were not revolutionaries, but they were committed to exploit all legal channels, including communication with Labour Party friends in London, to achieve their constitutional and economic reform objectives. Unfortunately, the events of 1930–1931 were outside their control.

A shift to other than political methods to vent cumulative Burman frustrations began with the dock riots of May 1930. Striking Indian dock workers, who had been replaced temporarily by Burmese labor, precipitated a violent response when they returned to taunt the discharged strikebreakers. Once started, the rioting became highly contagious. Fighting raged unchecked in Rangoon for two days as frenzied Burman mobs hunted down panic-stricken Indians. Several hundred were killed, and thousands of Indians had to find asylum with the British authorities until popular anger subsided. Only two Burmans, who got into a fight with the police, were subsequently prosecuted. A month later, Burmese prisoners in the Rangoon central jail mutinied against their newly appointed Indian superintendent.

Racial strife became endemic in 1931. Rioting against Chinese shopkeepers developed in Rangoon and neighboring towns in January, driving many of them to seek refuge within the capital. In March and April 1931, Burman cultivators in the sugar cane areas along the Pegu-Toungoo district borders attacked Indian farmers, who had moved there recently in large numbers. Such incidents were racially and economically motivated rather than politically.

They contributed to reducing the size of the annual immigration flow from India to around 250,000 in 1930–1931, down from the previous annual level of 400,000. Departures of Indians for several years thereafter tended to equal arrivals.

Meanwhile, an overt rebellion, long contemplated by the political pongyis, broke out in December 1930. It was led by Saya San, who posed as Burma's new king. He was a native of Shwebo (original home of the Kongbaung dynasty), a well-known practitioner of Burmese medicine, a former pongyi and anti-tax agitator of the U Soe Thein GCBA. At a newly constructed foothill jungle palace in lower Burma's Tharrawaddy district, he assembled all the traditional trappings of royalty: multiple wives, the white umbrella, the symbolic crown and sword, and the galon (garuda) bird symbol of a Vishnu avatar, plus tattoo artists and astrologers. He despatched pongyi agents to dozens of Wunthanu athin centers, extending into upper Burma, in a concerted effort to spread the rebellion once it started in Tharrawaddy. Very secretively, he announced his kingly accession at exactly 11:33 P.M. on October 28, the astrologically propitious time. The rebellion itself broke on December 22, while Governor Innes was in London attending the first roundtable conference.

The rebellion followed traditional patterns; it had no direct relevance to political reform agitation or to anti-Indian rioting. Participants were fortified by magical amulets and charms and had their bodies tattooed to make them invulnerable. Their dependable firearms numbered thirty guns at the outset, plus accretions gained by planned raids on the premises of permit holders, including village headmen. They enlisted the aid of the spirit of the European forestry officer whom they killed along with his five assistants.

One mass peasant rising, numbering 700 men, took place in Pyapon district south of Rangoon, where Chettyars had recently foreclosed mortgages on wide stretches of rice lands. Within the ensuing months, a dozen other outbreaks occurred at centers previously visited by Saya San's agents. All such situations were fairly quickly brought under control by well-armed government troops assigned to the task. The latter numbered some 8,100 by June 1931, to which were added seven battalions of reinforcements sent over from India. Saya San was captured in upper Burma in August 1931, and his revolt faded out by April 1932. Karen volunteers assisted the regular troops in the defense of isolated villages and in anti-rebel operations generally. The result was a limited revival of the Karen-Christian hostility to pongyi-led rebellion, which had previously surfaced in the 1880s.

The impact which the abortive Saya San rebellion had on the country as a whole was more psychological than political. A Burman had dared proclaim himself king, challenging directly the might of the greatest of Europe's colonial powers. The event contributed an emotional link, hitherto lacking, between traditionalist villagers and Rangoon's westernized elite. This happened in spite of the obvious military madness of the endeavor.

Two very different and at the time unimportant politicians volunteered to act as legal counsels for Saya San. One was Dr. Ba Maw, European-educated and Christian-trained, and the other was a third-rate court pleader named U Saw. Both were to emerge as influential political leaders later in the decade. Ba Maw had been temporarily associated with the Swaraj Party and then with the U Soe Thein GCBA, prior to its outlawry during the rebellion. He exploited his day in court in the tradition of the Dreyfus trial in France, with which he was familiar. Saya San's conviction for treason was pronounced by a Burmese judge, and appeals were carried to the high court in Burma and even to London's privy council. At the time of San's eventual execution in 1937, Dr. Ba Maw was serving as prime minister of the first cabinet under the revised constitution.

The government's efforts to counteract the psychological impact of the rebellion were not fully successful. Governor Innes returned from London in January 1931, and moved immediately to relieve popular economic distress by reducing fractionally the tax obligations of fifteen depression-ridden districts of lower Burma. He also provided additional funds for agricultural loans. But he refused to endorse a more comprehensive staff proposal to legislate permanent safeguards to prevent further land alienation. He was also unable to give Burmans any assurances regarding London's plans for a separate constitution. His most repressive move was to enact the Criminal Law Amendment Act of 1931, which empowered special judicial commissioners to arrest and try persons suspected of intending to violate the criminal law. This action provoked angry protests within the legislative council.

The two principal factions within the GCBA, including U Chit Hlaing's large following, not only denounced the rebellion but also discontinued anti-tax activities. Abandoning election boycott tactics,

Chit Hlaing formed a loose federation with the Swarajist Party, led
by U Paw Tun. In September 1931, five representative anti-separationists, including Dr. Ba Maw and U Chit Hlaing, were selected
to attend the special Burma roundtable conference which was to
convene at London later in the year.

Roundtable Conferences and Constitutional Plans

The first India roundtable which was staged in London from
November 1930 to January 1931, paid scant attention to Burma's
constitutional problems. The conclusion was reached at the outset
that the country would have to be separated from India, but under
conditions which would be determined later. The three Burman
representatives from the legislative council, all of them Separationists, commented that if Burman opinion was to be mobilized to
support such a change, some official assurances were urgently
needed that the country would not be accorded treatment inferior
to that given to India. A cable denouncing the separation proposal,
sent to London by its Burmese opponents was not deemed worthy
of serious consideration. Selected powers which would be reserved to
the governor covering finances, trade, defense, and minority protection were to be held over for later definition. U Ba Pe tried in
vain to persuade the British chairman to expand his initial affirmation that "Burma's constitutional advance would not be prejudiced
by separation" to read "Burma's claim or right to self-government
would not be jeopardized." The second wording carried unacceptable implications for London with regard to the future status of
India as well.

The most adamant opponent of U Ba Pe's proposal was Governor
Innes himself. He argued that the determination of the character
of Burma's future constitution could not even be discussed by the
roundtable conference until his own views and that of India's authorities were presented in private to His Majesty's government in
London. The Labourite secretary of state for India, Wedgewood
Benn, who was destined to be replaced during the course of the year,
was somewhat more accommodating. He proposed the phrase that
"the objective after separation will remain the progressive realization of responsible government in Burma." He also suggested, to
Governor Innes' annoyance, that public opinion in Burma would be
consulted at some future time. The negative mood of Governor

Innes was not improved by the outbreak of the Saya San rebellion, which he was obliged to face on his return to Rangoon in January 1931.

The convening of a special Burma Roundtable conference was announced by Secretary Benn in August 1931. The conference assembled in November following the accession of Ramsay Mac-Donald's new National Government. Five of the twelve Burmans selected to attend it were anti-separationists. Governor Innes was also present, along with a dozen representatives from various minority groups in Burma. The Burman delegation agreed before-hand that they would reject any constitutional offer which stopped short of full responsible government. The separationists prepared a specific draft constitution for consideration. British spokesmen took the counter position that the conference agenda called only for canvassing the opinions of those present, without prejudicing in any way the ultimate authority of the sovereign Parliament in London. They also refused to be bound by any previous statements or promises. They ignored the provocative Burman demand that Governor Innes be replaced and that a joint commission be convened to examine the causes of the Saya San rebellion and to recommend measures to promote pacification.

The five anti-separationist representatives contributed little to the discussion of the constitutional issue. They denounced the existing government as repressive and indifferent to the interests and wishes of the Burmese people. They refused in advance to accept any constitution which failed to grant full dominion status self-government. British spokesmen challenged their assumed exercise of a veto and their implied suggestion that the Burman delegation alone could presume to speak for the country.

Prime Minister MacDonald's announcement on December 1, 1931, at the conclusion of the concurrent India conference, that India's future constitution would involve safeguards with regard to external affairs, finances, and defense, changed somewhat the context of the Burma discussions. It undercut any Burman expectation that retention of the India connection would promote Burma's goal of complete self-government. But British spokesmen also refused at this juncture to affirm that a separated Burma's constitution would not be inferior to that given to India. In the end all but one of the Burman delegation (U Chit Hlaing) conceded that the governor must continue to exercise some reserved powers. The concluding

sessions were occupied by Burman complaints concerning the dominant economic role played by foreigners and denunciations of
minority claims for communal representation. The final pattern
which emerged contemplated establishing a partly-nominated senate
to balance the fully elected assembly, with continuance of the
governor's powers to cover the protection of minority rights, including foreign commercial interests.

Prime Minister MacDonald's concluding statement to the conference was conciliatory in tone. He declared that the London
government would take steps to provide Burma with a government
responsible to a representative legislature, and that the potentialities
for its future alteration would belong to the Burman people. He also
suggested that the next general election could determine whether
the people really wanted separation from India. MacDonald's full
statement was translated into Burmese and distributed widely.
Back in Rangoon in January 1932, the Burman delegation agreed
(with the single dissent of U Chit Hlaing) to go along with the
MacDonald offer. The legislative council itself later concluded
that it provided an acceptable basis for future negotiations.

The Anti-Separation League and the Elections of 1932

Indian politicians refused to give up Burma following the roundtable conference. It appears doubtful that the opposition to separation from India could have been revived without such instigation
by outside agitators. The Congress Party sessions held at Karachi
in April 1932, approved a resolution supporting Ba Maw's contention that rejection of separation at the time need not require, as
London was arguing, that Burma be permanently and irrevocably
associated with India. A group of well-financed Indian promoters
founded an Anti-Separation League in July 1932, headed by Haji
of the India-to-Burma Scindia Navigation Company, who had
attended the roundtable conference, along with Pillay, who was
Indian representative in the legislative council, and Tyabji, the
Congress Party leader in Burma. For some 1,000 rupees per month
Haji hired U Su's services and also enlisted the assistance of both
U Chit Hlaing and Dr. Ba Maw.

The Burmese response was not unanimously enthusiastic. Dr. Ba
Maw was capitalizing at the time on his notoriety as the legal counsel for Saya San and was inclined to assume a more aggressive role.

He flatly rejected London's quite generous offer of a constitution for separated Burma; he would also reserve Burma's freedom of action to withdraw from India at some future time. U Chit Hlaing reaffirmed his group's rejection of the British constitutional offer and aligned with the league, albeit with no great amount of enthusiasm. U Su was particularly effective in upper Burma, while Ba Maw concentrated his efforts on corralling a GCBA and pongyi following. Together, the league campaign achieved a 40 percent participation of eligible voters in the forthcoming 1932 elections.

Completely contradictory to the expectations of London and of many Burman observers, the anti-separationists achieved a majority of 49 elected seats in the new legislative council, compared to 29 for the separationists and 9 neutrals. The conservative Golden Valley Party returned no candidates at all. Effective use of Indian Congress Party funds in upper Burma, where distrust of Britain was strongest and anti-Indian feeling less intense, was largely responsible for the outcome. Within the majority group, Ba Maw's faction was somewhat stronger than that of U Chit Hlaing. Under the circumstances, the pro-government faction had to solicit cooperation from nationalist elements within the council, but it managed to do so with some success. U Kyaw Din, a prominent member of Ba Maw's following, accepted the post of education minister in December, 1932.

Shortly after the newly elected council assembled in December, it rejected by majority vote both of London's alternate proposals for early separation from India or for unconditional federation under India's new constitution. Ba Maw then obtained unanimous approval of his own resolution of December 22, declaring that, in the absence of a satisfactory constitution, Burma would prefer federation with India, but on condition that the country be permitted to secede at a later date by vote of its own legislature. In an effort to strengthen their case, Ba Maw and U Chit Hlaing traveled to India in early 1933 and talked informally with some two score Indian assemblymen. The latter registered no objection to Burma's later secession from India if done on terms acceptable to the India federation, a reply which fell substantially short of the visitors' expectations.

The matter came up again in March. The secretary of state for India, Sir Samuel Hoare, asked the Burma council to indicate its preference between the two alternatives previously offered, warning that London's action on the new constitution would be deferred in the absence of a reply. He added the previously denied assurance that Burma's separate constitution as planned would be almost identical with that of India. The council's majority leadership thereupon asked the governor to call a special council session for April 25, and prepared a resolution for consideration at that time. The proposal asked that a conference be convened to "formulate a constitution affording a basis for the systematic growth of Burma towards full responsible government as a separate identity within a reasonable period." The equivocal wording of the resolution aroused a storm of angry anti-separationist sentiment, both within and outside the council, some of it artificially inspired. Dr. Ba Maw himself had helped draft the resolution, only to find that he had thereby alienated his supporters in doing so. Radical pongyi and GCBA remnants cried foul and emphatically reaffirmed the earlier December 22 statement. The entire Indian delegation within the council reacted negatively, presumably on orders from the Congress Party directorate.

When the special session of the council finally convened on April 25, neither Ba Maw nor Chit Hlaing was willing to discuss the compromise resolution at all. As a result, the opposing separationist faction embarked on a filibuster to prevent the issue from coming to a vote. U Ba Pe led the effort, assisted by the British president of the council and by the Swarajist faction, who shifted their support to the separationists. The speakers severely criticized Ba Maw for repudiating his previous insistence on federated Burma's right to secede from India. The debate also fully exposed Haji's role in the development of the upper Burma faction of the anti-separationists. Critics charged that the effort was part of Indian intentions to entrench themselves indefinitely in the economic life of lower Burma. GCBA partisans attacked the authors of the new resolution from the opposite side of the political spectrum. They castigated anti-separationist turncoats in such derisive terms that the venerable Chit Hlaing stalked out of the chamber. The slanging session was finally ended by action of the new governor, Sir Hugh L. Stephenson. The anti-separationist majority was in complete disarray, unable to reach agreement among themselves, much less to plot a future course for the country.

Secretary Hoare subsequently submitted the question of Burma's future constitution for consideration by a parliamentary joint committee in July 1933. The group promptly reaffirmed Parliament's exclusive competence to decide the issue, but nevertheless requested representative Burman spokesmen to come to London the following December for a further exchange of views. When the group convened, U Chit Hlaing and Dr. Ba Maw argued that the anti-separationist victory in the 1932 election must be respected, and that Burma's clear right to secede from India in the future must also be acknowledged as a feasible alternative. U Kyaw Din, the third anti-separationist spokesman, and a close associate of Ba Maw with whose consent he had accepted the post of minister of education the year before, admitted that his previously entertained doubts regarding British intentions had largely been dispelled and that he now favored separation. After two days of such testimony, the joint committee moved on to consider, in secret, particular aspects of the proposed constitution. After nine days of serious discussions, the conferees finally approved the idea of separation, and Burman members urged that the new constitution be implemented as early as possible.

Persistent proponents of anti-separation, especially in the Wunthanu athins, could find many reasons to distrust their supposed representatives in the council. That body seemed to have few answers to peasant needs. Burman landlords within the council regularly sided with alien interests to block successive tenancy-relief proposals that were designed to protect both land and produce from forced sale, to facilitate repurchase of lands through a government-sponsored land mortgage corporation, and to scale down debt obligations generally. Meanwhile, paddy prices in 1933 reached an all-time low of 60 rupees per hundred baskets (22.5 cents per basket), leaving most peasant-tenants with no alternative but to dispose of their jewelry savings, to limit family consumption of fish and cloth, and to withhold as much as possible from the portion of the rice crop claimed by the landlords.

One tangible agricultural gain was realized not through the council, but through the initiative of the Burman registrar of lands, U Tin Gyi. He managed to revive some 1,500 of the bankrupt cooperative societies by drastically scaling down their outstanding debts (mainly owed the government) and by amortizing payments of the residue over a fifteen year period. But such aid was minuscule in terms of the total problem. By 1936 the Chettyar moneylenders had acquired title to some 25 percent of the paddy land of lower

Burma, and they could legally have taken over much more than that. As late as 1936, the price which the peasant received for paddy was still only 90 rupees per one hundred baskets.

Popular disillusionment with the role of the council was aggravated by the unseemly scramble for high office on the part of erstwhile champions of the popular cause. The top prizes were three in number: the two ministries of forestry and education, with 5,000 rupee monthly salaries attached, and the presidency of the council itself. Each carried perquisites for distribution to friends. The immediate target of the critics was U Kyaw Din, the education minister, who had repudiated his allegiance to Dr. Ba Maw and turned separationist in London. The other incumbent under attack, minister of forestry Joseph Augustus Maung Gyi, a former member of the Golden Valley Party, provided an even more vulnerable target. U Ba Pe and Dr. Ba Maw cooperated in the attack, arguing that neither of the Burmans in charge of the two transferred-subject cabinet posts enjoyed popular backing or majority council support. The objections of the critics were essentially personal and not associated with any particular legislative proposals. U Kyaw Din pointed out that he had not changed policy any more than Dr. Ba Maw had done, while J. A. Maung Gyi simply announced that he left the outcome of the controversy to Karma. Following the approval of the no-confidence motion in April 1934, Be Pe became minister of forests and Dr. Ba Maw minister of education. The new incumbents managed to survive until after new elections were held in 1936, but they had to weather successive attacks by political enemies within the council.

The ousting of council president Oscar de Glanville proved to be a more difficult matter, for no good excuse was available to nullify his earlier election to the post. The attack was led by U Saw, a follower of U Ba Pe and one of the most sinister creatures in Burma's political jungle. His method was to ignore de Glanville's authority as presiding officer by provoking disorder and sabotaging the conduct of official business. The president survived the initial attack with Governor Stephenson's assistance, but succumbed to a subsequent attack in February 1935. U Chit Hlaing thereupon became the new president, a post which he had held briefly in 1932. Directly prior to the elections of 1936, Ba Maw and U Chit Hlaing joined hands with some European council members in an abortive effort to oust Ba Pe from the forestry post. Alone among the nationalist leaders, U Chit Hlaing continued to enjoy wide popular respect for his long dedication to the nationalist cause.

The 1935 Constitution and Its Implementation

A period of seventeen months elapsed between the joint committee conference of December 1933 and the final approval of the new constitution in May 1935. During this time, the London Parliament was itself subjected to political pressures from business and commercial interests of Rangoon, which had no difficulty finding spokesmen within the ranks of Parliament. Former Governor Craddock was one of the participants. They insisted that strong deterrent authority be placed in the hands of the governor, including power to postpone for several years any Burman legislative action which might affect trade with India or the entry of Indian laborers. They reasoned that agreements on such matters as trade and immigration should be worked out by negotiation between the two new governments. During the concluding phases of the debate, parliamentry opponents persistently attacked the new Burma constitution on the grounds that it failed to grant adequate protection to British interests within the country. The final version reflected such influences.

The innovations contained in the constitution of 1935 can be briefly summarized. An expanded nine-member cabinet would be selected by the governor in consultation with the majority party leader of the fully elected house of representatives. Except in categories which were explicitly reserved for the governor's decision, he would accept the advice of his cabinet, which in turn would continue in power so long as it could command majority support within the house. Membership within the house was expanded to include 33 new general constituencies, mainly rural, and 12 single-member districts reserved for Karens. Karens resident outside their own districts would vote in the general constituencies. Other designated minority and business representatives were to be elected on a national basis. Half of the new senators would be elected by the house and half appointed by the governor from a selected list of wealthy persons, including all ethnic groups. The senate was designed to check political vagaries on the part of the house, and was clearly fashioned to safeguard property interests.

The powers which were reserved to the governor were extensive.

He was charged with the duty to preserve financial stability, to maintain law and order, to protect minority rights and the integrity of the public service, to exercise exclusive control over the Scheduled (tribal) Areas, and to preserve fair trade practices. He could exercise plenary authority in emergency situations. He could also veto any legislative enactments, as could the London authorities.

Although the constitution opened the door for wider Burman political participation in governmental affairs, it was in no sense a radical document. Cabinet members could intiate reform legislation within the bounds of their responsibilities and were expected to supervise the administration of their respective governmental jurisdictions. In actuality, most of their time would have to be spent keeping their individual political fences in repair so that they could maintain themselves in office. The new constitution left routine administrative procedures in the hands of the traditional civil service, whose appointment and discipline were still under the governor's control. The most vulnerable aspect of the administration lay in the lower level of the courts, which were graft-ridden, and in the seriously impaired authority of the village headmen. The high court was made completely free from political control, and the upper levels of the civil service theoretically so.

Accompanying provisions set forth by the London Parliament included allocating 7.5 percent of the external debt of India as Burma's responsibility. The sum included the cost of servicing bonds covering railway construction costs and also the expenses sustained by India in the conquest of Burma. Finally, the Burma legislature was forbidden for three years to make any alteration of trade relations with India or of rules governing Indian immigration. The Burma constitution, like that of India, was a tribute to British skill and patience in reaching compromise adjustments. Both also reflected the limitations involved in the exercise of sovereign control at so great a distance, both geographically and culturally, by a Parliament at London burdened with many other important responsibilities.

Following the promulgation of Burma's new constitution in 1935, important changes took place within the country's political spectrum. Such issues as election boycotts, pongyi-proclaimed threats to Buddhism, anti-tax agitation, overt rebellion, and the quarrel over separation from India, were no longer relevant. A variety of new political alignments emerged, while sensitivities within older organizations were sharpened.

Karen Nationalism

One hitherto unmentioned aspect of the changing political climate was the increasingly aggressive role assumed by the National Karen Association. It favored separation from India, but wanted to keep the British around indefinitely out of fear of what could happen to the Karens under Burman rule. The Association had been organized in 1881, in an attempt to bridge the gaps between Christian and non-Christian Karens and among the three principal Karen language groups. Animist Pwo and Bwe Karens were jealous of the leadership assumed by the better-educated Christianized Sgaws. Development of an integrated Karen identity was the principal goal. The influential Christian minority of the Karens owed most of their progress as a people to the work of American Baptist missionaries among them, going back to the 1830s. The American mission had provided both religious and educational training. The Karen national movement owed much to increased security and economic opportunity afforded them by British rule, including access to service in the exclusively Karen regiments of the colonial army. Although leading American missionary observers doubted the wisdom of encouraging Karen nationalism (see Harry I. Marshall, *The Karens of Burma,* 1922), the general British practice was to take advantage of Karen religious distrust of the Buddhist Burman majority in enlisting their loyalty. Karen-Burman antagonism had been exacerbated during the 1920s by partisan pressures exerted by political pongyis within the Wunthanu athins. A principal issue was the general neglect of Karen language schools by the dyarchy district councils. Karen military contingents has participated actively in crushing the Saya San rebellion. From the viewpoint of Burmese nationalism, Karen communalism had reached the point of diminishing returns by the 1930s.

Efforts to reverse the communal trend in favor of a broader Burmese national identity were generally ineffective in terms of the total problem. Officials and faculty of Judson College on the university campus made deliberate efforts to discourage communal segregation in athletics, departmental clubs, rural reconstruction efforts, and student activities generally. Participants came to know each other as individuals. Burman Buddhists constituted the largest single fraction of the Judson College enrollment, followed by the largely Christian Karens, then by Indians, Chinese, and tribal groups. The process of amalgamation was nevertheless slow, and the downward social penetration of such an elite effort was limited. Karen students tended to be timid and somewhat clannish, attributes which were employed as a kind of defense mechanism. Deeply-rooted social and cultural factors were involved.

Official Karen spokesmen both at Rangoon and at the London conferences made no secret of their distrust of Burman rule and insisted on provisions for special communal representation. Many of the older generation agreed with Dr. San C. Po (*Burma and the Karens,* 1928) that the growing sense of Karen identity should be explicitly recognized by the establishment of an autonomous state comprising the entire Tenasserim Division. They later obtained twelve separate Karen constituencies in the 1935 constitution.

British enlistment of educated Karen participation at the upper levels of government dated from the second decade of the century. Representatives were appointed to the advisory councils of successive governors, and several Karens were elected from the general constituencies of the dyarchy legislative councils. After the 1932 election, Saw Pe Tha was selected as deputy president of the council, and he was later included in the first cabinet under the new constitution. But the long-term prospects that may have seemed possible in the 1930s of achieving a substantial measure of political and social integration between the majority of Buddhists and the 1.5 million Karens of lower Burma were shattered by tragic events occurring during the Japanese conquest. The rift would survive as one of the difficult problems facing independent Burma.

Student Unrest and the University Strike of 1936

Students did not constitute an important element of Burma's political unrest down to 1936. The reasons were mainly social and economic. Matriculants at Rangoon university, as a rule, came from middle and upper class homes of varied ethnic groupings. Parents were concerned that their young people take advantage of the opportunities for upward social and vocational mobility afforded by high school and university training. University students were a select group drawn from the better schools, many of them missionary-sponsored. A premium was placed on competence in English and on ability to cope with the prevailing examination routines.

A rigorous process of elimination prevailed within the university, for standards were relatively high. Fewer than 50 percent of the second-year candidates passed the intermediate tests, and only 60 percent of those who persisted through the four-year regimen attained the coveted A.B. degree. Only the very best male students continued into the five-year Honours program, which could qualify them for participation in the Burma civil service examinations. Students who were thus vocationally motivated were usually not inclined to become involved in political activities which could jeopardize their studies and their subsequent job opportunities whether in industry or government service. The founders of the university in 1920, it may be recalled, had been much concerned to insulate the institution from political influences—the administration as well as the student body.

The rising tide of student unrest originated, for the most part, from within the educational system itself. The peer group exercised the decisive influence, subordinating both parental controls and outside political stimulation. The frustrations encountered were numerous and cumulative. Students had to study and communicate in an alien English tongue, and they faced the ever present threat of examination failure. The inevitable emphasis on rote memorization of accumulated notes covering anticipated questions, all of which held little intrinsic meaning or value, bred growing discontent within the system itself. The examinations were a dreaded ordeal, for particular tests usually lasted for three or four hours. Frustrations grew during the depression of the early thirties, because job opportunities dwindled at a time when the number of applicants expanded. Holders of high school diplomas, intermediate certificates, and bachelor degrees were themselves not assured of suitable jobs, quite apart from the large number who were repeating the exams for the second and third times.

After 1930, unrest began to take on political overtones, both in high schools and at the university. Students would downgrade high academic performers who tended to be wary of becoming involved in political activity. By 1935, student leaders had also developed disrespect for nationalist leaders, especially within the legislative council, who exploited their presumed roles as political leaders to gain high government office. Student opinion found opportunity for free expression in the new structure of the Rangoon University Student Union, which was funded by private donors in 1928.

The Dobama Asiayone (We Burmans Society) had been started in the early thirties, but it took final form in 1935. It amalgamated with several other protest groups, including the All Burma Student Movement. The members adopted the practice of calling each other by the title "Thakin" (master, sahib), which was widely prescribed when speaking to British personnel in upper Burma. The term became a symbol of youthful defiance of the educational regimen and of colonial rule generally. As ardent nationalists, the Thakins pledged to accept the full risks of political activity and to seek no personal advantage at the expense of their nationalist ends. Their appeal at the outset was limited to fellow Burman students, for few minority elements were involved. Efforts to establish contact with peasant groups ran aground because of villagers' distrust, and student agitators also had only limited success in trying to foment labor strikes.

On the university campus, the Dobama Asiayone took over the leadership of the student union organization in the fall of 1935. Thakin Nu, a graduate law student who had taught for a time in one of the national high schools where U Thant was principal, became president of the union. The younger Thakin Aung San, an intensely partisan individual, was secretary of the union and editor of its *Oway* journal publication. He was assisted by Ba Swe, who was also the leading Thakin labor organizer. Thakin Kyaw Nyein, an honors student in English, aided Thakin Nu. Thakin Than Tun, destined to become leader of the Communist Party of Burma, headed the Dobama group on the nearby Teachers' College campus.

During the course of the ensuing school year, the union building became a forum for discussion of a large variety of political and international topics. Democracy against fascism was a favorite theme, along with problems of Chinese-Japanese relations, Mussolini's venture into Ethiopia, and Stalin-Hitler relations. The Oxford Union tradition of freedom of comment was honored. Marxist literature also became available to the Thakins, centering in the Leftist Reading Club located off campus. Several Burman participants in the two London roundtable conferences brought back communist literature from England, along with the socialist writings of China's Sun Yat-sen, India's Palm Dutt, and Britain's Lytton

Strachey. Sinn Fein literature had been examined earlier; the Dobama Asiayone designation itself had been borrowed from Irish writings. Additional communist literature was purchased by funds realized from the sale of the remaining stock of the executed Saya San's medical books.

The Leftist book club included some 200 members by 1937. Only a small fraction of the Thakins could be characterized as Marxists, for the situation in Burma had little relevance to the concept of class struggle in an industrial society. Nevertheless, the term "socialism" came to denote in a general way the idealized opposite of exploitive imperialist capitalism, which Thakins characterized as Burma's principal enemy. The student indictment of colonial rule thus developed an added ideological dimension.

Toward the end of the school term, in late February 1936, a controversy developed between the leaders of the student union and Principal Sloss of University College. It was precipitated by Thakin Nu's extravagant denunciation of an unpopular professor, a Burman, and a demand that he be dismissed on moral grounds. Principal Sloss reacted belligerently, declaring that he would not be intimidated by political pressure. When face thus became involved, Nu aggravated the tension by charging inaccurately that Principal Sloss was challenging student political activity itself. Nu was then expelled from the university as was also Thakin Aung San, whose student union paper, *Oway*, published an anonymous and even more scurrilous attack against the same faculty person.

The controversy quickly took on wider dimensions. Student protagonists called a mass meeting at the union on February 25, and proclaimed a general student strike. Principal Sloss, in a counter move, tried to generate support for his disciplinary measures from the university council governing board, so that a contest of wills was joined. Occurring as it did on the eve of the dreaded final examinations for the year, the excitement disrupted the study preparations of many students, especially members of University College; academic problems enhanced the appeal of the strike. Organizers shifted their headquarters to the Shwe Dagon pagoda, where they were fed and housed by public contributions, as had been done in 1920–1921. Strike promoters then penetrated university residence halls to advance their cause. Prostrate students blocked the main campus roads and the entrances to all examination halls on the University College side. Although Judson College initially was not affected by the disciplinary issue, all university examinations had to be cancelled. Meanwhile, strike promoters despatched agents to the various high school branches of the All Burma Student Movement, of which Aung San was president, in efforts to enlist student sympathy and cooperation throughout the province. When some thirty-two leading high schools were closed down by student action, the general tenth-standard examinations had to be postponed also.

The initial reaction of the secretary of education, functioning within Dr. Ba Maw's ministry assignment, was to denounce direct student action as irresponsible and completely inappropriate. The statement did concede that something needed to be done about changing the outmoded written examination system. Dr. Ba Maw himself, in a skillful maneuver, pointed out that the university council exercised exclusive authority over student disciplinary questions. The only appropriate action which the legislative council could take, therefore, was to reexamine the University Act itself. Raising this more general issue produced an almost unanimous response from the university student community. Ba Maw also pointed out that the university council was currently dominated by non-Burman faculty and official representatives, who were not interested in considering student grievances. The governor himself served as university chancellor.

When the issue was eventually debated in the legislative council on May 4, the final day of the annual session, political opponents of Dr. Ba Maw tried hard to embarrass him. They denounced his allegedly equivocal approach to the matter, especially his approval of the initial statement of his own educational secretary. A motion presented by U Saw was finally approved authorizing the participation of three designated members of the council in the pending official examination of causes for student discontent. Ba Maw refused to support the motion, but he did agree to convey to the chancellor-governor the expressed wishes of the council.

A prompt decision on the part of the governor's committee to accede to a number of student demands facilitated the conclusion of the strike, so that all postponed examinations were held in June. Both Nu and Aung San were readmitted to University College. The initial effort to amend the University Act was defeated in 1937. Aung San finally succeeded in such an effort in 1939, when he carried to the legislative council the basic student demand that a majority of the university council be composed of non-faculty and non-civil service personnel, and that the revised body be authorized to elect the chancellor. The new act also provided that the determination of examination procedures and results be subject to legislative review. In December 1939, U Tin Tut, the senior Burman member of the civil service, was elected as university chancellor. One factor contributing to the Thakin victory was the change in the political climate produced by outbreak of war in Europe in the late summer of 1939. For better or for worse, the university had become politicized.

The principal importance of the university strike of 1936 historically was to elevate a group of youthful leaders of the Dobama Asiayone to political prominence. Thakin spokesmen combined the audacity of U Ottama and Saya San with a more realistic and modern approach to national goals. Students still carried little weight in higher political circles, for they lacked financial resources and an influential constituency. They managed to elect only two members to the legislative council in 1936, and attained a third seat by appointment. Their popular influence was nevertheless destined to grow with time. As uncompromising champions of independence they enlisted wide national acclaim by opposing first British and then Japanese control. Virtually the entire roster of Burma's postwar nationalist leadership was drawn from participants in the university strike of 1936. Aung San and Than Tun led the independence struggle to 1947, while Nu, Kyaw Nyein, and Ba Swe took over the leadership of the new state in 1948. The military dictator who finally emerged in 1962 was a student associate named Thakin Shu Maung, who took the military title of Bo Ne Win.

The 1936 Election

The election contest of 1936 signalized the nearly complete fragmentation of the venerable General Council of Burmese Associations. The peasants had learned to distrust both U Ba Pe and Dr. Ba Maw, while the still respected U Chit Hlaing kept control of only one faction. The remnants of Ba Pe's People's Party allied with four upper Burma factions, ostensibly led by a distant scion of royalty, to form the Five-Groups Alliance. It enjoyed good financial backing and distributed its candidates judiciously to win 46 (reduced by defections to 42) of the 115 elected seats. The alliance delegates lacked a recognized leader and a unifying ideological commitment, so that they quickly fell to quarreling. The number of available offices to be distributed was too small to go around.

One of the leading politicians in the Ba Pe group was U Saw, who had been associated since 1932 with his mentor's newspaper, *Thuriya* (*The Sun*). After a visit to Japan in 1935, U Saw managed to find the funds to purchase the paper outright. He proceeded to use it for his own political ends and also for pro-Japan propaganda, probably subsidized from Tokyo. When U Ba Pe's coalition fell apart, U Saw formed his own Myochit (Patriotic) Party in 1938, with which he associated the Galon bird symbol which Saya San had exploited. Both his style and methods harked back to the ruthless standards of court intrigue prevailing during the nineteenth century. By 1938, he became a bitter and unscrupulous rival of Premier Ba Maw.

During the course of the election campaign, Dr. Ba Maw made strenuous, if futile, efforts to reenlist the backing of his onetime GCBA followers in the villages. He offered virtually everything that peasants were assumed to want, including the election of headmen, tax reductions, lower land rents and easier credits, repurchase of alienated lands, and free education. He also managed to enlist the aid of several friendly pongyi politicians. He formed the new Sinyetha (Proletarian) Party and outlined an approach which was vaguely socialistic. The mass of the voters generally discounted his labored identification with their needs. In the end the party ticket was made up of personal followers only, of whom a mere sixteen won election, to the temporary satisfaction of his political enemies. Other groups did less well. U Chit Hlaing's GCBA faction won only twelve seats, with independents garnering from thirteen to seventeen. Karens got their assigned twelve communal seats, the Europeans nine, and Indians eight. The remainder of the 135 was divided between tribal minorities, business organization representatives, and two for Burman labor. After Ba Pe's party fell apart, the clever Ba Maw succeeded in forming a coalition cabinet. It included two of his personal followers, one from the alliance group, one from Chit Hlaing's party, plus one Arakanese, a Karen, and several Europeans. He thus managed with difficulty to maintain assembly majority support for his government for almost two years, until February 1939. The political agility exhibited by Dr. Ba Maw from 1937 to 1939 was to be demonstrated repeatedly thereafter under widely differing circumstances. He eventually reached the end of his meandering political road, as will be seen, at the close of World War II.

The expanded opportunity for political expression afforded by the new constitution was at best a political gamble. Whatever chance of genuine success it might have enjoyed over a long-term period of time was cut short by world events beyond Burma's control.

VIII The New Constitution and the Japanese Occupation

During much of the period from 1937 to 1945 Dr. Ba Maw occupied the center of the political stage. As the country's first prime minister, from 1937 to 1939, he initiated a number of reform proposals covering long-neglected agricultural problems. He also had to deal with continuing student unrest and racial tensions that his political opponents used to discredit him. Even so, his troubled two-year performance as premier was probably the most creditable fragment of his political career. In addition to his agricultural reform proposals, he sponsored the preparation of a revealing bribery and corruption report. After being forced out of office in 1939 he reversed his political tactics, and joined hands with the ultra-nationalist Thakins to form the Freedom Bloc in September 1939, following the outbreak of war in Europe. The resulting political agitation was designed to take full political advantage of Britain's wartime involvement, in the interest of achieving complete independence. While Ba Maw's agents made early contact with the Japanese, most of the Thakins maintained their previous contacts with the Congress Party of India.

The agitation of the Freedom Bloc became increasingly subversive, with the result that Ba Maw and several of the Thakin leaders were sent to prison during the summer of 1940. Others, including Thakin Aung San and more than a score of associates made contact with the Japanese forces in China and Tokyo, with offers to assist in expelling the British from Burma. They returned with the Japanese army in 1942, serving mainly as interpreters and guides. Near the completion of the Japanese conquest, Dr. Ba Maw escaped from his upper Burma jail and established contact with the Japanese military authorities. They eventually selected him to head the Japanese-sponsored wartime government of Burma, which also included a number of the Thakin collaborators. Less than halfway through the war, the Thakin leaders lost confidence in Japan's proclaimed intention to accord independence to Burma and organized their Anti-Fascist League Army, which struck at the Japanese rear during the final retreat from India in the spring of 1945. Their courage and audacity enlisted the overwhelming support of Burman nationalists at the end of the war. Dr. Ba Maw was too Anglophobe to go along with the Thakins and elected to flee to Japan at the end of the war. He found it impossible on his return to Burma in 1946 to play any significant postwar political role.

Agricultural Reform Proposals

At the outset of Ba Maw's premiership in 1937, he took action to free political prisoners, to reduce postage rates and security deposits for newspapers, and to substitute state lotteries for unpopular household taxes. His first move in the direction of agricultural reform was to appoint a high level land and agricultural committee, including Burmese and British members, to prepare a series of detailed reform proposals designed to ameliorate rural poverty. The particular goals were to slow down the process of land alienation, to make a beginning of restoring cultivator ownership, and to attack evils associated with annual tenancy contracts. Such problems had been repeatedly investigated over the previous forty years, the last time in 1931–1934, but always under landlord and business auspices which virtually guaranteed that nothing would be done. The reports of 1938–1939 were more significant in their assessment of the scope of the several problems examined than in suggesting feasible solutions.

The subcommittee charged with investigating the progressive alienation of land ownership to non-agriculturalists reviewed previous unsuccessful efforts to correct the trend. It discounted the time-worn objections that the term "agriculturalist" could not be precisely defined, and that expansion of cultivation would be seriously retarded if access to moneylender credit were restricted. It argued in rejoinder that the persistent loss of cultivator ownership, greatly aggravated since 1930, was simply too high a price to pay socially for the desired maximum expansion of gross output. Cultivators would be better off in the long run if their borrowing capacity was limited to whatever security resources were available to them in terms of personal property and annual crops.

The resulting Land Alienation Act was a long time in gestation. It was finally approved in late 1941, just prior to the Japanese in-

vasion. It proposed to slow down the rate of land alienation to
absentee landlords by restricting future borrowings on the part of
owner-cultivators to loans based on current crops, livestock, or
jewelry securities rather than mortgage. Borrowing from other
Burman agriculturalists on mortgage security was theoretically
permissible, but such credit sources were very limited. The bill did
not interfere with mortgage liabilities already incurred to non-
cultivators. In the existing situation, where an estimated 85 percent
of lower Burma's rice lands were either already absentee-owned or
under heavy mortgage burdens, the proposed legislative cure was
not commensurate with the disease, constituting little more than an
ineffective holding operation.

The land and agricultural committee also attacked the staggering
task of reducing existing absentee landlordism. The proposed solution envisaged sweeping measures. The government should purchase
extensive compact blocs of land at market prices from non-agricul-
turalist owners that would then be distributed to cultivators in
family-sized units. The executive agency designated for the task was
the moribund government estates department, which had been
tried out on frontier areas in a limited way earlier in the century.
The plan also envisaged the expansion of cooperative agencies to
take care of credit needs, milling operations, marketing of output,
and the provision of consumer necessities. Consideration of such a
quasi-socialistic scheme would have been inconceivable a few years
earlier. The Land Purchase Act incorporating these measures also
passed the parliament in late 1941, but in full awareness that its
implementation depended on the accumulation of requisite funds,
not to mention the staggering problems of administering the
program.

The third task of improving conditions of tenancy focused mainly
on lower Burma, where annual rental contracts with absentee
owners had virtually displaced the earlier practices of cultivator
sharecropping. In upper Burma, by contrast, crop failure constituted
too heavy a risk for contract tenants to take, while sharecropper
landlords usually lived near enough to supervise the post-harvest
crop distribution. Another aspect of the problem peculiar to lower
Burma was that the availability of new land suitable for economic
development was rapidly diminishing, giving rise to increasing competition for access rights between rival renters. Lacking permanence
of tenure, lower Burma cultivator-tenants had no incentive to apply

fertilizers or otherwise to improve the land itself. Careless cultivation was the rule.

The basic fact of agricultural bankruptcy was incontestable. A banking inquiry report prepared in 1930 prior to the ravages of the depression had found, for example, that only one lower Burma family in four could actually pay the land rent (in paddy at harvest-time prices), plus interest obligations on loans incurred during the course of the crop year, and still have enough food to last until the next harvest. The inquiry also found that Chettyar moneylender-owners were usually more honest and efficient than were other credit sources, despite the larger holdings of the former. As of 1938, most cultivator tenants were clearly insolvent, saddled with a permanent debt. Unless the terms of tenancy could somehow be made less burdensome, any long-range prospect of promoting cultivator ownership was clearly out of the question.

Three legislative efforts were eventually initiated to ameliorate the tenancy problem. The first bill, which ran aground in 1937, provided that renters who had treated their owners fairly during the preceding year should enjoy the legal right to renew their contracts on the same terms. Others who abandoned their leases would, in any case, be compensated for improvements made to the land. While this bill was under reconsideration in early 1938, U Saw advanced a simplified alternative proposal. He suggested that annual land rentals be limited arbitrarily to not more than one-fourth of the gross output for a given year. Objections were immediately raised that such a simplified rule failed to take into account variable cost factors relating to land development, flood losses, and transportation expenses. The final revised version of the original proposal, as approved in May 1939, attempted to establish regular procedures for determining fair rentals, gave priority claim on the tenant's available resources for paying rental contracts and labor costs, and relegated to secondary status the repayment of loans advanced by landlords during the year for food and cattle hire.

The tenancy reform died aborning. The task of implementing the proposal immediately ran aground on the multitude of applications received for adjustment of rental contracts. It proved extremely difficult to determine fair rental levels under an enormous variety of circumstances, and the compensation due for land improvement was equally hard to estimate. Administrative machinery proved to be too corrupt and inefficient. Owners usually offered bribes, and overindulgent officials sometimes reduced rentals to levels below the landlord's tax assessments. For these and other reasons many official judgments affecting tenancy rights were disallowed by the courts. Efforts to revise the legislation to make it more workable were overtaken by the outbreak of war in 1941.

The overwhelming difficulties encountered by such efforts at agricultural reform were historically significant. They cast serious doubt on the possibility of accomplishing any substantial improvements within the existing legal framework of colonial rule. One should not, therefore, be surprised that arbitrary means were employed to liquidate Burma's landlord problem once independence was attained. The task of administering any massive reform effort was also complicated by continuance of racial and political feuding and by widespread distrust of police authorities, courts of law, and government officials generally.

Opposition to the Ba Maw Government

Far from supporting wholeheartedly the efforts of the Ba Maw government to initiate basic agricultural reform measures, the Burman opposition within the parliament conducted a persistent vendetta against the prime minister. He was accused of abandoning his leftist Sinyetha Party objectives, and his cabinet associates were burdened by the parliament with hundreds of time-consuming questions calculated to elicit damaging admissions of neglect of the public interest. Outside the chamber a hostile vernacular press, led by U Saw's *Thuriya* (*Sun*), joined forces with a radical Young Pongyis' Association to exploit opportunities to embarrass the government. In mid-1938 they seized upon the reprinting of a book on the Islamic faith, written by an Indian Muslim in 1931, which included some disparaging comments on Buddhism. In a deliberate effort to foment anti-Indian hysteria, U Saw's paper and his pongyi allies denounced the book as an insult to Burmese Buddhists and gratuitously condemned Ba Maw's government for connivance in the publication. Before the authorities could carry through a routine investigation of the charges, rioting broke out in Rangoon on July 26, 1938.

The basic objective of the instigators of the rioting was to bait the police and thus to embarrass the Ba Maw government. Following a rally on the Shwe Dagon pagoda platform, a pongyi-led mob invaded downtown Rangoon, overpowering the limited police force in its path. It then proceeded to victimize Indian residents in an orgy of fanatical violence and looting. In five days of disorder, nearly 200 Indians were killed and an additional 900 were injured. The Burman mob itself suffered 171 casualties, inflicted mainly by the police, who eventually placed some 4,300 participants under arrest. The rioting quickly spread to the provinces at the instigation of pongyi agitators. Major anti-government protests also developed in upper Burma where few Indians were in residence. Violence was particularly rampant in Mandalay-Sagaing, the oil fields areas, and the ancient dynastic center of Shwebo. Anti-Indian hatred was thus exploited for political ends.

Premier Ba Maw vigorously denounced the motivation of his political enemies and defended in parliament his use of police to restore order. With European support in the house of representatives, his government managed to survive U Saw's no-confidence motion by a narrow margin on August 26, 1938. This reversal for U Saw provided the signal for his instigation of another round of rioting, starting on September 2 and continuing for more than a week. In the second round the agitators were joined by Thakin elements, who introduced anti-imperialist posters and slogans. The governor was obliged to invoke the Rangoon Emergency Security Act permitting arbitrary arrest of suspected offenders, and he also banned the publication of U Saw's paper. A high level riot inquiry committee was eventually assigned to examine the causes of the disorders and the reasons for unforeseen police difficulties in coping with the situation.

The forthcoming riot committee report underscored the fact that anti-Indian sentiment in Burma was very strong. It had worsened since 1937, because Indian labor immigration was continuing despite separation, agricultural reform efforts had run aground in the legislature, and Indian landlord and moneylender domination persisted unchanged throughout lower Burma. Behind the ineffective role of the police in dealing with rioters were two important factors: sympathy for the disturbers of the peace from cultivators generally, including village headmen, and the almost universal popular distrust of the colonial government. The report pointed out that less than half of the arrested rioters were actually brought to trial, and that only 21 percent of those tried were convicted, mainly because of difficulty in obtaining supporting evidence. It was fairly obvious that qualified self-government, hemmed in as it was by constitutional and legal restrictions, was failing to contain the tide of national resentment, especially in situations where provocateurs were active.

Anti-government protests which persisted through 1938 and into 1939 operated within a larger political context than that of the racial violence instigated by U Saw and his pongyi friends. The activities of Thakin agitators, especially in the labor field, included overt collaboration with Congress Party agents from India. They endeavored to persuade Indian dock workers to strike at Rangoon port, along with the city's rickshaw pullers and renters of bazaar stalls, all of them Indian. Continuing Thakin efforts to organize Burman employees in the oil field areas and at the Syriam refinery near Rangoon ran aground in late 1938. An abortive attempt was made to stage a strikers' march to Rangoon. When two student leaders of the march, Thakins Ba Swe and Ba Hein, were arrested, the student movement demanded their release from jail. A new epidemic of school strikes was accompanied by an attempt to picket the secretariat headquarters at Rangoon. One university student died from clubbing at the hands of the police. A subsequent Thakin protest meeting displayed for the first time the communist hammer and sickle banner. U Saw tried to enter the act by getting himself arrested for leading a protest parade forbidden by the police. Violence at Mandalay reached such serious dimensions in February 1939, that the police had to use firearms to disperse a student and pongyi-led mob.

In the prevailing atmosphere of spreading disorder, the pivotal European bloc within the house of representatives decided to abandon its support of Premier Ba Maw in favor of a rival coalition cabinet led by U Pu, and including both U Ba Pe and U Saw. Three members of the Ba Maw cabinet carried over, along with two new appointees from the Ba Pe faction and Saw's Myochit (patriotic) Party, plus one Karen. The new government promptly suppressed the activities of the Thakins, penalized newspaper indiscretions, and banned the circulation of some thirty subversive (Marxist) books. U Pu also cooperated with allied efforts to keep open the shipment of war materials to Nationalist China via the Burma Road and refused any longer to tolerate Congress Party's anti-imperialist activities. The events of the final year of U Pu's ministry, from September 1939 to September 1940, related primarily to reactions to the developing European war which will be considered later. One more comment remains on a final episode connected with Dr. Ba Maw's efforts at political realism, namely the reform of village administration.

The long-considered proposal to make village administration more responsive to popular needs related to a basic problem of government. The proposed legislation recommended that village headmen should be elected locally for three-year terms, subject to recall for misconduct in office by the district deputy commissioners or by open-air hearings staged on petition by the villagers themselves. Committees to assist the headmen should be elected for five-year terms, and thugyi (headman) conduct would be subject to official review. The report also urged that designated village officials should be permitted to possess firearms, and that they should be more adequately compensated for their services. Like several of the other reform proposals, this one still awaited formal approval by the legislature when the East Asian war began.

The Bribery and Corruption Report

Closely related to the problems of local government was the significant report submitted by the bribery and corruption committee in 1940. It attempted to explain why the population generally had come to distrust not only the police but also government officials generally. Its refreshing candor owed much to the British chairman, B. W. Swithinbank, who insisted that both witnesses and indicated offenders remain anonymous. Swithinbank's purpose was diagnosis and inventory rather than to accumulate evidence for prosecution. All told, more than 300 witnesses volunteered to testify, ranging from public-spirited members of the legal profession down to numerous enthusiastic Thakin informants and villagers.

The evidence which the committee assembled indicated that governmental functions at lower levels of administration were involved in a mass of chicanery. Official rackets involved not only the police, courts, and revenue agencies, but also health and public works officials, land recorders, road and irrigation engineers, fishery and forestry officers. Payment of appropriate bribes and gratuities could obtain a reduction of a person's income tax liabilities, a favorable decision covering a land dispute claim, as well as the protection of gambling and brothel premises from police interference. Strategically placed revenue officers frequently defrauded both the recipients of government funds and the treasury itself, while contributions by interested parties influenced most of the "fair rent" decisions. Official reports covering the outcome of Buddhist scripture examinations were also influenced by bribery. Even if a substantial fraction of the accusations were discounted, the total indictment of official performance was staggering.

The explanations which were advanced by informers related only obliquely to the fact that recording clerks, constables, lesser magistrates, and deputy township officers were all grossly underpaid and not closely supervised. The more fundamental consideration related to the progressive deterioration, under the British type of bureaucratic rule, of the previously existing but ever-fragile harmony between people and local government agencies which had prevailed under traditional patterns of rule. Burmese opinion had always distrusted the rapacity of central government agencies, but local elders and myothugyi headmen had traditionally defended their clients from abuse by court officials. Under British administration, the office of myothugyi had been abolished, and the headmen themselves had become government officials. As such they had been baited and abused by Wunthanu athin leaders since the 1920s. Specialized governmental agencies had proliferated to provide a variety of new services, often unsolicited and misunderstood, which were not supervised effectively. Thus vaccinators regularly collected bribes for not doing their indicated jobs. The traditional Burmese administrative system had not been free from faults, but whereas payment of nominal gratuities had been tolerated by custom, gross injustices could be resisted. Under colonial rule, a host of officials had their hands out for bribes, and essential justice was often for sale without opportunity for any legal redress.

Correctional measures which were proposed seemed hardly commensurate with the problem. Some spokesmen counseled a return to open court (myoyon) proceedings, where a respected *Mahathera* (elder monk) pongyi administered a traditional Buddhist oath, and all the evidence was made public. They also recommended that arbitrary court adjournments should be prohibited during the course of particular trials, because such action was usually taken to facilitate dickering over the bribery terms. The conduct of all accused official bribe-takers should be scrutinized along with their cumulative bank accounts.

The Swithinbank report did not challenge the fact that the carefully selected and well paid India and Burma civil service provided
a dependable administrative superstructure. It held the government
together despite numerous bureaucratic weaknesses, especially when
supported by expanding economic output, increasing public
revenues, and private profits for business. The allegation of bankruptcy of the total situation, when viewed from the Burmese side,
was equally valid. It derived from the mass of irredeemable cultivator debt contracted under an alien legal system, and from the
destruction of traditional patterns of local responsibility and control. No easy remedy was available, for the abrupt removal of
British controls would jeopardize the stronger aspects of both the
administration and the economy, while doing nothing to improve
the demoralized lower levels of administration. The regeneration of
responsible indigenous controls would obviously require a long-
sustained effort.

The Changing Political Milieu of 1939–1941

Political developments within Burma immediately following Ba
Maw's retirement as premier in February 1939, were highly confused. The new U Pu cabinet was similar in personnel and political
tone to its predecessor, with the important exception that the chief
political troublemaker, U Saw, was now included within the
ministry and was therefore no longer interested in fomenting disorder. Thakin radicals persisted in their anti-imperialist and
Marxist-flavored attacks on colonial rule. They initiated new school
strikes, promoted labor unrest, and continued their affiliation with
the Congress Party program of India.

Dr. Ba Maw's Sinyetha group tried at first, with little success, to
reestablish relations with dissident pongyi elements and with his
erstwhile GCBA friends of 1932–1933. He also began to view the
prospective expansion of Japanese aggression southward from China
into Southeast Asia as a possible alternative for ending British rule
in Burma. Most moderate Burmese opinion seemed to prefer at this
time sending private good will delegations to Nationalist China
rather than alliance with Fascist Japan or with Indian Congress
Party radicalism. U Saw's Myochit Party retained its Galon bird
symbol borrowed from the Saya San movement and the allegiance
of a coterie of pongyi followers from the 1938 riots, while secretly

courting support from wealthy landlord elements, both Burman and Indian. As a member of the cabinet, U Saw was biding his time until the opportunity developed to take over full control of the government.

The equivocal political situation of early 1939 was clarified somewhat by the outbreak of war in Europe on September 1. The new developments provided a basis for *rapprochement* between the two most active opposition factions, the followers of Ba Maw and the Thakin Dobama Asiayone. Modulation was not easy, for the Marxist faction of the Thakin group, led by Ba Hein and Soe, denounced the cautious stance of the non-socialist Thakins, along with the equivocal Myochit and GCBA activities. The impact of the outbreak of war in Europe was twofold. It raised for many Burman nationalists the sobering prospect that Europe's fascist forces might take over control. At the same time, it offered an obvious opportunity for radicals to undertake serious political negotiations with a beleaguered British government to realize the goal of early independence.

Only a few weeks were required for Dr. Ba Maw to come to terms with the non-Marxist majority of Thakins led by Aung San. They agreed that student strikes, racial rioting, and labor union agitation had become largely irrelevant, and that socialist dreams of an idealized economic order would have to be deferred in favor of achieving early independence. The original Thakin nine-point program for national front collaboration was condensed by Dr. Ba Maw into a three-point demand which constituted the foundation of the Freedom Bloc. They would ask Britain to acknowledge Burma's right to independence, to initiate immediate steps for the convening of a constitutional convention, and to extend cabinet control over all powers which had been deferred constitutionally to the governor. The Freedom Bloc designated Ba Maw as its *Anashin* (dictator-king) and Aung San became the general secretary. Aung San himself agreed that ideological differences must be subordinated to broad national concerns and that political measures must be substituted for riotous bluster and superstitious magic. Freedom Bloc spokesmen thus urged all nationalists to unite and demanded that the U Pu government should surrender office if it refused to support the nationalist cause.

Behind the façade of such overt nationalist mobilization, Dr. Ba Maw's personal followers and several conservative Thakins (Ba

Sein and Tun Oke) made contacts locally with Japanese agents. While Ba Maw was touring the countryside to attract followers, his principal lieutenant and editor of the *New Burma,* Dr. Thein Maung, made a visit to Japan in November 1939. He spent a full month in Tokyo seeing the sights and conferring with Japanese officials. Thus the Freedom Bloc struggle gradually took on international dimensions. The full implications of Ba Maw's manipulations were nevertheless far from clear. Even when Aung San and his associate fled Burma to escape arrest in late 1940, communications broke down and the two nearly starved before they contacted Japanese agents on the China coast at Amoy.

Meanwhile, U Saw took advantage of Premier U Pu's political embarrassment following the arrest and conviction of Dr. Ba Maw in August 1940, to withdraw abruptly his Myochit Party support within the parliament, thus precipitating the downfall of the government. He was then asked in September to form his own cabinet. Approximately half of the new government was identical with that of U Pu, but U Saw's policies shifted farther to the right. He supported the British war effort, assisted in defense preparations, suppressed Freedom Bloc activities, and ceased publication of pro-Japanese articles in his own newspaper. He also outlawed private armies, including his own Galon supporters, silenced hostile newspapers, and even jailed his erstwhile mentor, U Ba Pe. Burma Road traffic was reopened, and British plans for an extension of the railway from Lashio to the China border were approved. In his attempt to appeal to the nationalist side, the opportunist premier advocated a Buddhist university and the Burmanization of the upper levels of the civil service as an economy measure. He also negotiated an agreement with the Indian government to limit Indian immigration. With British support, he might have continued as premier indefinitely along such lines, if the East Asian war had not intervened.

Premier U Saw finally was obliged to face the nationalist independence issue in the summer of 1941. Many Burmans took exception to the affirmation of the newly arrived governor, Sir Reginald Dorman-Smith in June 1941, that Burma's prospects for constitutional change would depend in large measure on the extent of its cooperation during the war. The issue came to a head in August 1941, following the issuance of the Roosevelt-Churchill Atlantic Charter, which affirmed among other things that a people had a right to choose their own form of government. When queried in the Rangoon parliament as to whether this statement applied to Burma, U Saw replied in the affirmative, to the considerable embarrassment of the governor. Since it was obviously desirable from the British point of view that the cooperative premier be permitted the opportunity to defend himself against mounting nationalist criticism, the governor proposed a delaying action. After agreeing to postpone the elections scheduled for November 1941, he persuaded London to invite the premier to visit Britain for "good will" talks with Mr. Amery, the secretary of state for India.

U Saw reached London on October 11 and made full use of the month's stay to air his views in the public press. But his talks with Secretary Amery and Prime Minister Churchill were equivocal and elicited no commitment as to Burma's postwar future. He began his homeward journey via the United States, where he spent several weeks giving secret vent to his bitterness toward London's negative response, and had reached Hawaii when Pearl Harbor was attacked. Reversing his course to the Atlantic route, he was detected by British agents in Lisbon while entering into seditious communications with Japanese legation officials. He was accordingly arrested in Egypt on January 19, 1942, and assigned to prison in Uganda for the duration of the war. In Rangoon, Sir Paw Tun, who had served successively in the governments of Ba Maw, Pu, and Saw, took over as premier, preliminary to shifting the exiled Burma government to its wartime base in Simla, India.

The Japanese Conquest

During the planning stages of the Japanese campaign in Southeast Asia, Tokyo's major concerns did not involve Burma in any essential fashion. One of Japan's immediate objectives was to conclude the China war by closing off trade through Tonkin, and denying the use of the Burma Road for supplying the military needs of the Nationalist Government of Chiang Kai-shek at Chungking. Tokyo also wanted to eliminate financial assistance to Chungking from overseas Chinese residents in Southeast Asia. Japan's long-range economic objective was to gain access to Southeast Asian markets and raw materials, particularly oil, coal, iron ore, rubber, tin, timber, rice, tobacco, and fibers. The ultimate political plan was to establish a kind of Japanese imperial dominion, which would integrate Southeast Asia into the Greater East Asia Co-prosperity Sphere.

For several reasons Burma did not constitute a necessary part of the overall plan: difficult to reach from Japan, located much closer to both India and China, it produced little that was not available elsewhere. The prospective German victory in Europe would presumably eliminate British rule in India. Tokyo naval authorities, furthermore, were not prepared to assume the task of patrolling the Indian Ocean until their domination of the Eastern Pacific was assured. Burma's initially peripheral status helps explain the somewhat confused character of Japanese policies during the course of the occupation.

Tokyo was not uninformed about political affairs in Burma. Civilian espionage had been carried on since the middle thirties by a popular Japanese dentist named Suzuki, who had adopted several Burmese orphans, and by a tennis-playing professional masseur named Kondo. Tokyo's official naval intelligence came from a fleet of fake fishing vessels operating off the Tenasserim coast, and through naval Lieutenant Kokubu, who proved indiscreet and was arrested in 1941. A more successful army intelligence officer, Colonel Keiji Suzuki (alias Matsuo Minami), posed successfully as a journalist and was able to establish secret contacts with Freedom Bloc personnel, particularly Dr. Ba Maw and Thakins Ba Sein and Soe. Marxist-inclined Thakins, particularly Ba Hein, Tun Oke, and Thein Pe, were strongly opposed to fascist Japan, and Thakin Aung San may have shared their distrust at the outset.

When Aung San and companion fled Burma in late 1940 to avoid arrest by U Saw's police, they obtained passage as Chinese crewmen aboard a Norwegian ship bound for China. Aung San's ostensible initial goal was to make contact with Chinese opponents of the Japanese, for he carried a letter of introduction from an Indian Communist Party leader to his counterpart in China. At the port of Amoy the two were long isolated and nearly starved. They were finally identified by Japanese agents on the basis of urgent solicitations drafted by Thakin Ba Sein and forwarded by Colonel Suzuki from Rangoon. The two then proceeded to Tokyo. After having satisfied themselves that Aung San was a *bona fide* member of the Burmese Freedom Bloc, the Japanese arranged his furtive ten-day return to Burma in mid-1941 to recruit thirty Thakin comrades who would assist in the Japanese conquest of Burma. Except for doctrinaire Marxists, most of the Dobama Asiayone and student movement leadership joined the conspiracy.

The "thirty heroes" who were associated with Aung San were trained for their roles on Hainan Island and later assembled at Bangkok. Most of them entered Burma in early 1942 by a little used route running from Tak and Rahaeng in Siam westward to Moulmein. Colonel Suzuki convinced his Burman associates within his project (*Minami Kikan*) that he was genuinely committed to freeing their country from colonial rule, and that Japan entertained no ulterior motives. He was accorded the Burmese title of *Bo Mogyo* (Colonel Thunderbolt), a name derived from the folklore tradition that a lightning bolt striking the palace would some day end alien rule.

Confusion developed within the Japanese ranks following a premature declaration by spokesmen for the Minami Kikan at Tavoy in January 1942, that Burma's independence was at hand. The Japanese army commanders were anxious to exploit whatever assistance the Burmese collaborators might be able to give, but they insisted that the conduct of the war was in no sense dependent on Burmese aid, and that military needs took precedence over political considerations. The Minami organization and its youthful supporters did little fighting during the course of the conquest, but they provided interpreters and useful jungle guides. The effort of the hurriedly recruited and undisciplined pro-Japanese Burma Independence Army to assume policing and governmental roles in the wake of the advancing Japanese army produced a number of serious crises, particularly in Karen-inhabited areas of the western Irrawaddy delta.

The Japanese conquest of Burma was a relentless affair, completed in conclusive fashion before the start of the monsoon rains in May. It left the population utterly stunned. The invaders first overran Tenasserim, then crossed the Salween river above Moulmein, where they encountered the first real resistance. By flanking attacks they forced repeated British withdrawals and finally the premature destruction of the only bridge across the lower Sittang River east of Pegu on February 23. This unfortunate action forced ten of the twelve defending battalions to abandon their heavy equipment on the left bank of the stream. Meanwhile, the demoralized dock workers at Rangoon, following successive Japanese bombing raids, were prevented from prompt unloading of arriving military supplies. When the advancing Japanese subsequently cut the road and railway facilities north of Pegu, the British-Indian forces around Rangoon, unable to evacuate by sea, had to move northward in retreat up the Irrawaddy valley, where the roads were already cluttered with tens of thousands of Indian refugees fleeing to India. The planes of the supporting American Flying Tiger Corps were destroyed on the ground above Prome, and no opportunity was afforded to make a stand.

The defense of the upper Sittang valley was undertaken belatedly in March by a Chinese army under the command of the American General Joseph Stilwell, but all his major decisions were subject to approval by distant Chungking. The Chinese fought well around Toungoo for a time, but when armored Japanese contingents managed to penetrate the Shan plateau and threatened to cut the road to China at Lashio, the army disintegrated into a demoralized and looting rabble. The defeated British-Indian forces and the remnant of Stilwell's command evacuated to India under the pouring monsoon rains.

The task of establishing some kind of a successor emergency government to fill the vacuum made by the British withdrawal was initially entrusted to Colonel Suzuki (Minami) and the Burma Independence Army (B.I.A.). Their earliest move was to despatch from the Tenasserim coast by sea across the Gulf of Martaban selected elements of the Minami Kikan Thakins to coastal areas of the Irrawaddy delta, where they were to take over from the departing colonial authorities. Following the British evacuation of Rangoon in early March, Colonel Suzuki designated his long-time collaborators, Thakins Tun Oke and Ba Sein, to head up the *Baho* (central) administration which was taking form throughout lower Burma. Coordination of the widely scattered B.I.A. units proved virtually impossible, and the Baho government functioned with increasingly unsatisfactory results over the ensuing three months, while the Japanese army pushed the conquest northward.

The overextended B.I.A. officials, including a number of political pongyis, were invariably officious, and often vindictive and predatory, particularly in their relations with the Karen inhabitants. In the end they made themselves thoroughly unpopular with both the Japanese conquerors and the Burmese people as a whole. In early June, the Japanese commander, General Iida, cancelled whatever

remained of the political and governmental role of the independence army, to the relief of everyone. In late July the B.I.A.
as a whole, which numbered 30,000 at one time, was assembled at
Rangoon and fully demobilized. The much smaller and highly
selected Burma Defense Army of 4,000 men was headed by the
newly elevated General Aung San.

Meanwhile, Dr. Ba Maw had managed to escape from jail in
northern Burma in late May, and made his way by a secret route to
the summer capital of Maymyo, where he made contact with
General Iida. Ba Maw was to become the key man in the Japanese
army plans. As an Anglophobe nationalist and former prime
minister, and as the acknowledged leader of the Freedom Bloc, his
credentials were superior to the already discredited independence
army of Colonel Suzuki and the Baho regime. He named a preparatory committee which included several of his personal followers,
plus leading Thakins who had been intimately associated with
Suzuki's Minami Kikan. The preparatory committee made plans
for an interim government.

Dr. Ba Maw as Wartime *Adipadi*

On August 2, 1942, Dr. Ba Maw was installed as head of the new
cabinet. Most of the members were his personal followers, but they
included also Thakins Tun Oke (forests), Ba Sein (labor), Than
Tun (agriculture), and Mya (without portfolio). Thakin Nu was
assigned the political role of amalgamating the new Dobama-
Sinyetha Party, while General Aung San headed the new Burma
Defense Army. Socialist Thakins cooperated hesitatingly, while the
more thoroughgoing Marxists refused to do so. Communist Thein
Pe fled to India and Soe sponsored a secret guerrilla operation in
the fastness of the delta. Ba Maw offended the rank and file of the
previous Baho organization when he actively solicited the assistance
of all available officials who had served in the prewar colonial administration. During the course of the ensuing year, the Tun Oke—
Ba Sein (Minami Kikan) faction broke with the regime. The two
were excluded from the "independent" Burma government set up in
August 1943, and were subsequently exiled to Malaya.

Colonel Suzuki's continuing efforts to generate popular faith in
Japan's alleged disinterested concern to promote Burma's early
independence met with diminishing success. His labored moves to

present the invaders as fellow Buddhists completely miscarried, especially after the Japanese troops began abusing Burma monks and desecrating sacred pagoda premises. He also sponsored an East Asian Youth League and endeavored to placate Christian Karens by utilizing Japanese Christians as liaisons. Suzuki was eventually pushed aside by the army command.

Throughout the countryside the Japanese military forces bullied village elders and appropriated whatever they needed in the way of food and transportation facilities, including the prized oxen of the peasants. They also required the Ba Maw regime to enlist forced labor on a grand scale. Probably as many Burmans died in the construction of the west end of the Railway of Death leading to Thailand as did European prisoners on the eastern projection of the line. Thakins Mya and Ba Hein were once despatched to the Tenasserim area to inspect conditions, but they could accomplish little. Although Japanese soldiers passing through the Burma countryside usually paid for what they took from the people, they used newly printed currency of dubious value, while Tokyo provided virtually no consumer goods imports to match the currency. Internal trade broke down. Lower Burma suffered from a glut of unsaleable rice while upper Burma was short of food. Several million acres of delta paddy land reverted to jungle, and cultivators had to take turns wearing their wornout clothing.

The most serious offenders were the infamous Japanese military police, or *Kempeitai*. Acting as a law to themselves, they employed brutal tactics to elicit desired information, while executing summarily those who refused to cooperate. One consideration which influenced the Thakin leaders to collaborate with the none-too-popular Ba Maw government was that it allowed them to escape Kempeitai surveillance and abuse. During the first year of the occupation, the Japanese wore out their early welcome and became increasingly distrusted and hated by the population. Some Japanese officers recognized the folly of treating the Burmese population like the conquered Koreans, Manchurians, or Chinese, but they made little headway countering the growing hostility. Resident Japanese army leaders came to hate the prideful Ba Maw, who refused to kowtow to them. They also opposed all suggestions that granting a larger measure of self-government might serve to mollify popular discontent.

The Ba Maw government had very little independent authority.

The 120 Japanese government experts sent by Tokyo to "assist" his administration were vastly outnumbered by the 800 to 900 representatives of Japanese business and manufacturing firms who came to manage the economy. The economic aides were all assigned to specific aspects of production and trade in an effort to contribute to Burma's self-sufficiency, since Japan could provide very little consumer goods during wartime. The assisting Japanese, whether in government or the economy, gave no indication whatever that Tokyo contemplated any early transfer of their own assigned responsibilities to Burmese control. Japan's plans were geared to serve Tokyo's long-range purposes of providing raw materials for Japan's industry and eventual markets for manufactured goods. For the time being, Burma's entire resources were to be exploited for the war effort.

Tokyo's moves to improve relations with the Burmese political leadership began in early 1943. The purpose was to enlist maximum cooperation from Burma as a base for eventual operations against India, and also to convince the resident Indian nationalists of Japan's *bona fide* intentions to liberate the subcontinent as well. The initial announcement Premier Tojo made in January 1943, that Burma would be granted independence within the year, was followed in March by his invitation to Dr. Ba Maw and party to visit Tokyo. Ba Maw was accompanied by Dr. Thein Maung and Thakins Mya and Aung San, with Thakin Kyaw Nyein acting as secretary. After being decorated by the Japanese, the members of the mission were informed that one of the conditions attending the grant of independence was that Burma must declare war on both Britain and the United States. Tojo's promises were not entirely convincing, nor did Ba Maw's own espousal of fascist principles on the occasion generate any Burmese enthusiasm for the new order. Upon his return from Tokyo, Ba Maw intensified his exortation that Burma's people should participate actively in the struggle for freedom in one or another of the state services: the blood army, nationalist agitation, political leadership, or the labor corps.

Despite popular distrust of Tokyo's designs, most Burman nationalists perceived no alternative at the time to going along with Japanese plans, especially since London advanced no counter offer of postwar independence. A widely representative independence preparatory committee, functioning under Ba Maw's chairmanship, finally convened in May 1943 to formulate plans, with the Japanese looking on. The emerging constitution made a limited commitment to the theory of popular sovereignty, but the proposed cabinet was to be responsible to Dr. Ba Maw alone, who occupied the dual role of prime minister and head of state. In a final preparatory move, which underscored the strategic aspects of Japan's policy, Dr. Ba Maw and Thakin Nu journeyed to Singapore in July to talk with Premier Tojo. There they also met the Indian Bengali revolutionary and former president of the Congress Party, Subhas Chandra Bose, who had been transported from Germany to the Indian Ocean by German submarine and reached Malaya in late June. With Ba Maw's consent, Bose later moved the headquarters of his Indian National Army to Burma in an effort to assist the Japanese invasion of India.

Burma's formal independence was recognized on August, 1943, in an elaborate ceremony staged at Rangoon. Baw Maw was accorded the pretentious title of *Nainggandaw Adipadi* (Head of State) and, in the Burman tradition, assumed the status of *Mingyi* (Great Prince). One of the first acts of the new government was to proclaim its alliance with Japan and to declare war on Britain and the United States. Both Ba Maw and Nu praised Tokyo on that occasion for Japan's allegedly disinterested intentions to free Burma from colonial rule. Significantly, however, the popular celebration of independence was deferred until some eight weeks later when Japan made good its earlier promise to recognize Burma's claim to most of the states of the Shan plateau.

Ba Maw's new cabinet was somewhat more representative than the previous one had been. It excluded Tun Oke and Ba Sein, who had been too closely tied to the Japanese generals who were still opposed to independence. He brought in Thakin Mya as deputy prime minister, Nu as minister of foreign affairs (with very little to do), Thakin Aung San as minister of defense, and three respected elder statesmen for finance, justice, commerce and industry. The selected twenty-member privy council included several ex-ministers, a former speaker of the house, five former senators and the same number of house members, two editors, and several businessmen. Ba Maw's closest confidant, Dr. Thein Maung, was eventually sent to Tokyo as the Burmese ambassador. The cabinet was on the whole an able group. The two exiled Thakins, Ba Sein and Tun Oke, protested vigorously their exclusion.

The Japanese high command in Burma, especially General Kawabe, was cynically opposed to the entire independence charade. He and his associates remembered too vividly the difficulties encountered previously with the supposed Chinese puppet ruler at Nanking, Wang Ching-wei, to whom they now compared Ba Maw. Kawabe discounted the prospect of realizing any possible assistance from Burmese nationalists such as Ba Maw or Nu. The gesture toward independence was clearly Tokyo's idea, not that of the local army command. For the army, as for the economic administrators' group, the realization of Japan's Greater East Asia Co-prosperity Sphere was apparently associated with the indefinite presence of Japan in Burma, as well as elsewhere in Southeast Asia.

Dr. Ba Maw's role as Burma's Adipadi was a difficult and frustrating assignment. His closest Thakin associates, Mya and Nu, appreciated his efforts to preserve the country's territorial integrity and protect the people from abuse by the Japanese. The Karen and Indian minorities in particular also were aware of Ba Maw's efforts to ward off abuse by the Burman majority. Yet his moves attracted limited support. He tried to qualify as a semiprincely successor to the defunct Konbaung dynasty by arranging to have a quantity of sacred earth transported from Shwebo to Rangoon for the ceremonial planting of a tree in the "soil of victory." His pose as a supporter of Buddhism was unconvincing, as was his studied deference to popular superstitions (numerology and astrology). Thakin Nu and other sincere Buddhists denounced the Adipadi's solicitation of undisciplined pongyi support for personal political ends as being an offense to the faith. He alienated all proponents of constitutional government by proclaiming the authoritarian doctrine of "One Party, One Blood, One Voice, One Command," and by his unconcealed contempt for "democratic bunk" and "political playacting."

Ba Maw's relations with the local Japanese command were generally bad. One one occasion in late 1944, the Japanese general in charge of relations with the government, Isamura, abruptly cancelled an elaborately planned ceremonial flag-raising. Face and protocol became heavily involved. Isamura later plotted Ba Maw's replacement, if not his assassination. Meanwhile, what little was left of routine governmental functions steadily deteriorated in an orgy of corruption, lawlessness, and abuse of power, with the Japanese army as a principal offender.

Rangoon's relations with Tokyo were far more friendly than with local Japanese commanders. A distinguished procession of Burmese were invited to visit Japan, including politicians, educators, newspapermen, and businessmen. Most visitors were impressed by Japan's dedication to the war effort and presumably to the goal of "Asia for the Asiatics." Scores of Burmese state scholars were also invited to Japan for carefully supervised training in banking, engineering, and industrial management. In May 1944 the elder brother of the Adipadi, Dr. Ba Han, was permitted to visit Korea and the Philippines as well as Japan. He raised some relevant questions about the actual character of the proposed Greater East Asia Co-prosperity Sphere in terms of the future relations between its component membership. Asia was to be for which Asiatics? He also flatly refused while in Tokyo to participate as a Christian in official Shinto religious ceremonies.

Following Ba Han's return, the Adipadi made his boldest bid for meaningful Japanese political concessions. His long-prepared *Burma's New Order Plan* was issued in June 1944, as the Japanese armies began to retreat from their abortive invasion of India. Ba Maw contended that Burmese must be accorded a substantial stake in the outcome of the war if they were expected to render effective assistance against the threat of British return. Administrative autonomy must therefore be expanded; Japanese political interference must be discontinued and a more effective Burmese liaison be established covering Japanese economic and military activities. He also asserted Burma's claim to all sequestered enemy property, whether Indian or British, and proposed that Japanese business operations in Burma be restricted to a modest 6 percent profit. These demands were not widely advertised, and no ultimatum was attached.

In November 1944 Ba Maw again visited Tokyo, where he supported the Kamikaze dedication to Japanese victory over the Americans. He also offered a discreet suggestion that if the Japanese army should be unable to hold Burma, it should consider voluntary evacuation of the country rather than force its people to endure the agony of a second prolonged military campaign. At no point, however, did Ba Maw waver in his preference for Japanese victory. Whether motivated mainly by his Anglophobia, by his close association with the Indian revolutionaries, or by his personal vanity and ambition, he lost touch with the Burmese people, and had cut too many bridges to be able to retrace his steps. His political career virtually ended with his postwar flight to refuge in Japan.

The attempted Japanese invasion of India via Manipur and Chittagong in early 1944 was a mad gamble. The invaders assumed that the growing allied threat from India could be countered by provoking a general rebellion in Bengal. That goal would be assisted by Subhas Chandra Bose, who was the head of *Azad Hind* (Free India) and of the Indian National Army, already mustered in Burma. The defending Indian forces might conceivably be influenced to mutiny, especially if a nationalist revolution should develop in their rear. The effort failed partly because the bulk of the Indian forces were well-trained Punjabi and Sikh soldiers, who were little moved by Bose's Bengali-oriented propaganda. Another substantial portion of the defending Commonwealth forces was made up of Africans who were used primarily in the Chittagong theater. The task of supplying the invading Japanese forces over poor mountain roads ran into difficulties when Imphal, capital of Manipur, refused to surrender after being cut off by land. The garrison was supplied for some time by American planes diverted from the Assam-China run. The invaders were overtaken in late May by the eruption of the summer monsoon rains, which disrupted road traffic and made their withdrawal unavoidable.

Even so, Japanese discipline held firm, so that the retreating army was able to regroup and make a vigorous stand in central Burma following the cessation of the rainy season in October. The American role in the Japanese defeat was confined to airpower and to the provision of massive lend-lease supplies, especially ground transportation. The Merrill's Marauders contingent, an American volunteer detachment operating under General Joseph Stilwell's command in north Burma, managed to capture Myitkyina, while a number of O.S.S. intelligence operations were carried out in the northern Irrawaddy valley and in the Arakan region. Virtually the full strength of available American airpower was diverted to central Burma during the ensuing dry-season campaign.

The Anti-Fascist People's Freedom League

The prewar Domaba Asiayone fragmented beyond recovery during the early phases of the war. As previously explained, the conservative leaders of the Baho regime, Tun Oke and Ba Sein, became thoroughly discredited and had been excluded in August 1943. The Marxist fringe of the Thakins—Soe, Thein Pe, and Ba Hein—did not credit Japanese promises, while Aung San and Than Tun quickly became disillusioned although continuing actively associated with the Ba Maw cabinet. A moderate group led by the able deputy premier Thakin Mya and foreign minister Nu was generally inclined to go along with Dr. Ba Maw.

Reintegration of the youthful nationalist leadership was largely the work of Aung San and Than Tun, close personal friends and brothers-in-law. By means of secret messenger service to and from India, they established contacts with Thakin Thein Pe, who in turn communicated in late 1943 with Lord Louis Mountbatten's Allied Southeast Asia Command in Ceylon. Than Tun turned communist during the course of the war, apparently convinced that Burma's freedom could be achieved only by means of Soviet aid. His positive contribution to the Anti-Fascist League owed much to the confidence generated by his dedicated performance first as minister of agriculture and later as minister of transportation under Premier Ba Maw, coupled with his ideological link with Marxist elements within the league.

Aung San occupied the strategic position. He maintained close contact with labor leaders of the old Dobama Asiayone and with subordinate commanders of the Burma National Army. He could also influence his former associates in the widespread student movement, plus the leaders of the several score chapters of the new East Asia Youth League. His immediate personal following was drawn from the Burma National Army, as set up in 1943. Aung San also won the confidence of minority groups, including the Karen Central Organization in the delta, which had developed its own separate contacts with the allied command in Ceylon. He was strongly secularist in his point of view, scorning the activities of the pongyi politicians. Personally Aung San favored constitutional government, political freedom, educational progress, and respect for minority rights. The league's leadership as a whole completely supplanted the older more Anglophile prewar Burman politicians who had fled the country with Governor Dorman-Smith. The younger group was committed to the daring task of striking the rear of the Japanese army when opportunity was afforded, hopefully in cooperation with allied forces.

Adipadi Ba Maw was by no means unaware that anti-Japanese plans were in secret preparation, but he preferred not to be told the details, of which he strongly disapproved. His personal pride as well as his Anglophobia ruled out any active collaboration with such plans. His contemptuous attitude toward the Anti-Fascist League organizers was clearly reflected in his autobiography, *Breakthrough in Burma* (1968). In it he denounced the Thakins generally as misguided turncoats and incompetent braggarts rather than genuine revolutionary leaders. They allegedly succeeded mainly in assimilating the poison of Japanese militarism, later exemplified by General Ne Win's army dictatorship in the 1960s. He scorned Aung San's reputation as a national hero, a role which Ba Maw himself obviously wanted to claim.

The exact contribution which the Anti-Fascist League and the Burma National Army made to allied military victory over the Japanese is difficult to evaluate. It related primarily to accelerating the rate of retreat southward by the Japanese forces at a time when it appeared very doubtful whether Commonwealth armies could reach Rangoon before the end of May 1945. The allies could be caught in the same supplies dilemma which the onset of the monsoon rains had produced for the Japanese forces the year before. In mid-March Rangoon was still far from the fighting line. The B.N.A. forces departed from Rangoon on March 17, ostensibly to reinforce the Japanese defenses. Eleven days later, widely dispersed Burmese units began attacking Japanese supply and communication services throughout lower Burma.

The most telling blow was levelled by the force led by Thakin Than Tun in the lower Sittang valley, where he achieved a prearranged rendezvous with the British-sponsored Force 136 (largely Karen) unit from Karenni. Whereas the allied advance had previously averaged some three hard-earned miles per day, the Japanese withdrawal rate accelerated sharply to some 20 miles per day. How much fighting Aung San's own forces did within the lower Irrawaddy valley is not clear, but the retreat in this western valley area during April became a veritable stampede. Instead of the Japanese being able to hold out at Rangoon and the delta area up to Pegu and Henzada until the start of the rains in late May, the high command was obliged to evacuate Rangoon on April 25, a fact which was promptly advertised to overflying allied aircraft on prominent roof tops by released prisoners. An accelerated British seaborne landing was accordingly made at the capital on May 5, in time to permit their participation in the wholesale destruction of Japanese forces exiting from the Irrawaddy valley via Pegu, which continued through July. The allied victory was devastatingly complete. B.N.A. contingents pursued the Japanese forces into the hill country east of the Sittang River through September, joining hands with Commonwealth forces.

However much the military claims of the anti-fascist B.N.A. forces may be discounted by Dr. Ba Maw and by British opponents of Mountbatten's policies, they cannot be dismissed as unimportant. It is historically significant that the supreme allied commander who was in a good position to evaluate Burmese assistance during the crucial concluding weeks of the campaign gave the claims full credence. At considerable risk to themselves, the anti-fascist Thakin leaders did organize an effective indigenous rejoinder to hated Japanese rule and made good their promises of cooperation transmitted through Thein Pe. Allied victory in any case would have been far more costly and less conclusive without the timely Burmese assistance. Lord Mountbatten was also convinced that the Anti-Fascist People's Freedom League (AFPFL), which expanded during May to include representatives of the older Myochit group, members of Ba Maw's own Mahabama Party, plus leaders of the Maha Sangha (monk) Association, represented the preponderance of Burmese nationalist sentiment. If the allied armies were to use Burma as an essential base for future military operations against the Japanese, who were still present in Siam and in Malaya, continued Burmese cooperation was essential. The Southeast Asian war at this juncture was still an allied affair, with virtually all overland transportation equipment being provided through American lend-lease sources, in addition to all air facilities.

When Mountbatten visited Rangoon in mid-June 1945, he showed particular regard to Aung San and Than Tun, by holding a special conference with the two aboard his ship in the harbor. Treating them as loyal allies, he refused to regard their assumed commitment to patriotic national concerns, whether made in 1942 or 1945, as a criminal offense. Neither London nor Dorman-Smith's government at Simla accepted such views, and the stage was thus set for an important British policy rift with respect to the future of Burma, which was not to be resolved until approximately a year later.

IX Burma After World War II

British governmental agencies responsible as of June 1945 for determining policy with respect to postwar Burma were not in full agreement among themselves. Governor Dorman-Smith's exiled government at Simla, India, initially entrusted with the problem, included a number of responsible Burman leaders who favored active popular participation in postwar planning, but regarded the Thakin leaders as inexperienced turncoats unworthy to be entrusted with major responsibilities. Prime Minister Churchill's Conservative government in London, acting under pressure from interested British firms represented in both Simla and London, adopted an extremely cautious position in its official White Paper of June 1945. It declared that Burma would have to revert to pre-dyarchy status for an indefinite period, in order to carry out essential economic recovery measures. But what man proposed, history disposed. Prime Minister Churchill gave way to Clement Attlee in July 1945, and the views of the military commander, Lord Louis Mountbatten, eventually prevailed over those of Simla and London.

As supreme allied commander for Southeast Asia, Mountbatten in early 1945 gave priority to military considerations. Burma had to be reconquered first and then transformed into a usable base for operations against Japanese forces which continued to occupy the rest of Southeast Asia. He therefore accepted the cooperation of the Burmese Anti-Fascist Army during the concluding months of the Burma campaign and accorded them standing as genuine nationalist representatives and allies against the common enemy. Following Japanese surrender, Mountbatten turned over his governing authority in Burma to returning Governor Dorman-Smith in October 1945, but he still retained command over the local Commonwealth armed forces, which were largely Indian and African. He objected to using such troops against a possible nationalist rising. A prolonged deadlock ensued. It was finally broken late in the spring of 1946 when London vetoed the governor's proposed arrest of Aung San, which would have precipitated violence. Sir Hubert Rance, a Mountbatten man, took over the governorship in August 1946, and worked out a cooperative relationship with Aung San. A crucial conference took place in London early in 1947. During the course of the subsequent preparation for independence, Aung San was assassinated on July 19, and his long-time associate, Thakin Nu, took over the unfinished task.

Independence plans were duly executed on schedule in January 1948, but in the face of growing disaffection on the part of thwarted communist partisans, supported by a group of disgruntled veterans. Rebellion broke out in March 1948, and by early 1949 Karen dissidents began a military operation of their own which threatened the capital of Rangoon. With some British help Nu's government recovered control by 1951. Burma was free from colonial control, but was far from economically viable, remained politically fragmented, and had an inexperienced government in charge.

The Exiled Government at Simla

The task of preparing postwar plans for Burma, which was assigned in August 1942, to Dorman-Smith's government-in-exile at Simla, India, ran into difficulties. The governor's entourage included ranking civil servants, both British and Burman, selected representatives of business firms, and premier Sir Paw Tun with other cabinet members. The governor himself did not lack sympathy for Burma's aspiration for freedom, and he was convinced that public opinion would welcome a temporary British reoccupation that was committed to early realization of full self-government. British members of his staff tended to stress the necessity of restoring the devastated economy before any resumption of progress toward independence could be seriously contemplated. They argued that the essential tasks could be accomplished most expeditiously with the assistance of representatives of prewar British firms, aided by public credits provided by London. An estimated five to seven years would be required to put Burma on its feet economically.

Burman members of the Simla staff, in cooperation with selected British members, insisted that the primary need was to find an effective basis for postwar cooperation. The Burmese, for example, must themselves share responsibility for formulating their future constitution, and they must also play an active role in determining economic policies. All large foreign business establishments must be subjected to governmental regulation, and the Chettyar money-lenders and landlords must not be permitted to return to Burma at all. The university should be nationalized, and divisive communal representation be abandoned. The exploitation of oil, timber, and mineral resources should be subjected to governmental control, together with electric power, transportation, and foreign trade. The gap between the two factions was wide. The essential issue, as explained by adviser John S. Furnivall, was whether economic restoration should take precedence, with primary concern for pro-duction, jobs, profits, and enforced order, or whether the main postwar emphasis should be on building a Burmese society capable of self-government and the exercise of economic controls.

Simla's policy deliberations ran aground in 1943 over the failure of London authorities to come to any clearcut decision on postwar policy. Burma's future was understandably a matter of low priority at that time. Following the formal recognition of Burma's in-dependence by Japan in August 1943, Governor Dorman-Smith made an extended visit to England to solicit a matching policy commitment. But Churchill saw little point in competing with Japan's dubious offer, since there was no early possibility of expel-ling the occupying forces. He did respond by appointing a parlia-mentary subcommittee to examine the problem of restoring and revitalizing Burma once the war was over. Its report was eventually published as a White Paper in May 1945. In the absence of any satisfactory British offer of postwar freedom, discouraged Simla observers who had accompanied Dorman-Smith to London, foresaw the forbidding prospect that the allegedly traitorous and inex-perienced Thakins might capture the national leadership.

The third agency concerned with determining British postwar policy for Burma was the allied command headquarters of Lord Louis Mountbatten in Kandy, Ceylon. Although pressed constantly by General Joseph Stilwell, Mountbatten's second in command, to initiate early measures to oust the Japanese from Burma and thus facilitate the delivery of war supplies to the beleagered Chungking government in China, the allied commander elected with good reason to bide his time until Commonwealth forces could be mobilized. As part of his preparations for reconquest in early 1944, he decided to encourage growing anti-Japanese sentiment, not only among the hill people and the delta Karens, but also within the anti-fascist movement that was emerging within the government of Adipadi Ba Maw. Soliciting the collaboration of the Burma National Army was only one of several British-sponsored projects. They included the sending of Orde Wingate's "Chindit" penetration unit into upper Burma, in 1943, and the preparation of a separate Karen detachment poised to attack the Japanese in the Irrawaddy delta at the propitious moment. Force 136 operations were organized to the east of the middle Sittang Valley ready to harass the Japanese flank and to cut off possible new reenforcements coming from Siam.

Mountbatten's primary responsibility as theater commander for the allied forces was to defeat the Japanese, and he accordingly gave secondary consideration to the possible effects of his actions on Simla's or London's still unformulated plans for the postwar period. On repeated occasions, he disregarded the protest of his own Command's Civil Affairs Section Burma, CAS (B). It was headed by General Pearce, an I.C.S. officer, and included a staff drawn in part from former employers of British firms operating in Burma. The conservative CAS (B) group denounced the AFPFL as a treasonable and communist-sponsored organization and therefore not sufficiently trustworthy to be provided with arms or to be given political recognition as a *de facto* British ally.

Twice during the early months of 1945 General Mountbatten overruled protests advanced by CAS (B). Both occasions followed urgent appeals from the local field commander, General Slim, that all available Burmese cooperation be solicited. Mountbatten's final decision of March 27 to grant allied status to Aung San's Burma National Army was understandably very unpopular at Simla. It was accorded London's reluctant approval on March 30, mainly as a *fait accompli*. Military need won out over political considerations. It was on May 16 that the victorious General Slim accorded formal recognition to the forces under Aung San's command as allies who would operate under Slim's overall command and be eligible for pay and food rations. The chiefs of staff in London approved the move on May 24. Thereupon the leadership of CAS (B) abruptly resigned, since its decision to arrest Aung San as both a war criminal and traitor was vetoed. General Pearce was belatedly replaced in mid-June by General Hubert Rance, a Mountbatten

protégé, who eventually set up a substitute civil affairs agency at
Rangoon, in August. It was not until October 1945, two months
after the total Japanese surrender, that Governor Dorman-Smith's
unhappy Simla government took over civilian governmental responsibilities at Rangoon, although still very much dependent on
the support of the military forces under Mountbatten's command.

Official British Postwar Plans

The Burma White Paper which was published on May 17 and
approved by Parliament in early June revealed among other things
how far out of touch wartime Britain had become with political
realities in Burma. The British authors accepted the bland optimism which Governor Dorman-Smith had expressed in 1942–1943
that a chastened Burma would welcome British deliverance from
Japanese oppression. But London ignored his essential condition
that the return must be accompanied by a convincing pledge of
early self-government.

According to the White Paper the first item of business would be
to restore order and economic facilities. The goal would be accomplished through requested cooperation of prewar British firms
and the Indian moneylenders. Recovery efforts must include utilities, industry, mining and oil extraction, agriculture, communications, and trade. Emergency rule by the governor under article 139
of the constitution of 1935 would probably have to continue for a
minimum of three years. Thereafter, elections could be planned and
constitutional government restored on the pre-1941 pattern. The
possibility of resuming constitutional progress would then be
determined in part by the degree of interim cooperation afforded
by the Burmese people in the total recovery program. Preliminary
to the preparation of any new constitution, proposed reforms would
have to be thoroughly examined to ascertain their suitability, to
be followed by subsequent negotiation of agreements with reference
to Britain's continuing obligations and claims. Meanwhile, the
Shan states and other tribal areas would remain under British
control until such time as the wishes of the inhabitants regarding
union with Burma were made manifest. The final goal of full self-
government within the Commonwealth would await subsequent
agreements covering administrative problems and treaty obligations.

The cold legalism of the May 17 document fell far short of the essential concessions advocated by Governor Dorman-Smith and his top-ranking Burman advisers, who had again accompanied him to London in April 1945. The governor had suggested a three-year maximum period of emergency rule, during which he might assemble *ad hoc* legislative and executive councils and initiate preparations for needed constitutional revision. Moderate Burman spokesmen in London, commenting in *The Times* in late May, advocated that constitutional government be restored promptly, with new elections staged within the first year. They also insisted that a general amnesty be declared covering political offenses and that a date be set for Burma's realization of dominion status.

A companion statement from AFPFL spokesmen in Rangoon, published by the London press on May 25, declared flatly that nothing short of political independence would satisfy Burma's postwar mood. The drafting of a new constitution should be entrusted to a popularly elected assembly as soon as war conditions permitted doing so. Meanwhile league spokesmen promised to continue to assist British authorities in expelling Japanese forces, restoring order, and rehabilitating the economy.

Parliamentary debate on the White Paper was brief and almost perfunctory. A few Labour Party spokesmen denounced the "wooden-headed imperialism" of Secretary Amery and Prime Minister Churchill, which denied the Burmese any political initiative until after colonial economic interests were again fully entrenched. They predicted that persistence in such a course would inevitably stimulate rebellion and arouse implacable Burmese hostility to British rule. Secretary Amery's personal comments on the White Paper tended to soften its harsh legalism. He pointed out that Governor Dorman-Smith would be free to seek advice from all strata of Burmese opinion, and would be permitted to accelerate governmental adjustments on the basis of permissory orders in council. London's primary economic concern would be to restore Burma's revenue resources, while taking Burman desires into account during the reconstruction program. Amery promised that no legal reprisals would be taken against persons who had obeyed Japanese demands in order to protect their own people and that the British authorities would continue to allow the overtly pro-Japanese leaders to "work their passage home" by cooperating with the recovery program.

Secretary Amery's qualifications were sufficient to mollify parliamentary misgivings, but they sounded extremely condescending to Burmans and operated to strengthen communist-inspired distrust within the AFPFL generally as to ultimate British intentions. Back in Simla in mid-June, the governor assured Burmese dinner guests that the holding of elections would not have to wait until 1948. Shortly thereafter, during a brief visit to Rangoon, he even consented to meet with Aung San and Than Tun, in addition to consultations with numerous older Burmese leaders of his acquaintance. The White Paper program was rendered somewhat less arbitrary as a result of the election victory by the Labour Party and Clement Attlee's displacement of Churchill as premier in July 1945, but the priority of economic recovery over political adjustments still held.

The CAS(B) Period

During the four months' incumbency of General Hubert Rance's CAS (B) agency in Burma, from June to October 1945, little could be accomplished to restore routine governmental operations. For one thing, fighting continued in lower Burma until early August over the attempted withdrawal of entrapped Japanese contingents. Strife continued along the Siamese border even following Tokyo's surrender. CAS (B)'s efforts to obtain and distribute desperately needed civilian supplies were hampered because of lack of staff and widespread thievery. New British currency was substituted for the cancelled Japanese money and used to pay for supplies and services rendered, but the shortage of consumer goods elevated prices by four to five times over pre-war levels.

Tens of thousands of peasant refugees fled to Rangoon and other cities to escape lawlessness in the countryside, increased by the availability of arms of all varieties. Feuding between Burmans and Karens in the delta flared up again. Early plans to demobilize the Burma National Army by some 60 percent were postponed because it was still pursuing the retreating Japanese forces east of the Sittang valley. Most of the B.N.A. partisans who eventually returned home kept their guns.

The quarrel between the Simla government and Mountbatten's command centered on whether AFPFL spokesmen should be regarded as genuine nationalist leaders, as Mountbatten maintained, or whether persons like Aung San should be arrested for treason, as was argued by General Pearce, who had meanwhile joined the Simla staff. CAS (B) authorities under Rance refused to regard political attitudes adopted during the course of the war as grounds for punishment, pointing out that AFPFL plans to resist the Japanese had long preceded any likely prospect of allied reconquest of the country. In September, Mountbatten offered Aung San a major general's commission in the British army. Now that the war was over, Mountbatten insisted that world confidence in Britain's good faith in promising fair treatment and restoration of self-government must not be betrayed. His decisions may have exceeded the bounds of his military prerogatives, but the stubborn fact had to be faced that the majority of African and Indian troops under his command might refuse to assume the onus of suppressing a Burmese rebellion.

The question of when the transfer of power from CAS (B) to civilian Simla authorities should be made was argued vigorously. Mountbatten contended that army control should continue until the end of 1945 in order to complete the essential tasks of rebuilding the port of Rangoon, providing water and electricity facilities, restoring railroad and river transportation, and preventing famine and epidemic disease. He pointed out that American lendlease supplies, including fuel, transport facilities, and arms would continue to be available to the army, but not (until formally declared surplus) to the civilian authorities. Meanwhile, he cancelled the army's wage contracts with imported Indian laborers, partly because inflated prices in Burma made such wage scales totally inadequate and partly because Burmese spokesmen were objecting strenuously to any resumption of Indian immigration. When the Simla authorities finally took over control on October 16, they were unable to command the labor of Indian coolies at previous contract levels and were also denied access to lendlease motor transport and other facilities abundantly available near the Rangoon airport. The ensuing seven months were filled with rising tensions and frustrations.

Role of the Returning Simla Authorities

The plenary authority theoretically enjoyed by the returning governor after October 1945 was qualified in a number of ways. For

one thing, he lacked an adequate police force equipped with necessary arms, transportation, and communication facilities. The main
law-enforcing agency was a largely non-British army commanded by
the governor's rival, the prestigious Lord Louis Mountbatten. In
mid-October, the governor was further embarrassed by Attlee's "Address from the Throne" delivered to the Parliament, acknowledging
the assistance which the Burmese had rendered in defeating the
Japanese and promising rapid progress in restoring the country's
prosperity and self-government within the Commonwealth. He indicated that as soon as orderly elections could be arranged, a
representative government responsible to the electorate would be
empowered to initiate plans for a new constitution.

Obviously chagrined over having his emergency powers thus
sharply curtailed, the governor on arrival tried to make the best of
the situation. He announced that he entertained no sentiments of
revenge against his country's opponents and proclaimed that Burma's
right to self-government was fully conceded, provided the transition
could be done in a gradual and orderly fashion with full opportunity afforded for expression of all shades of opinion. What he did
not explain was that the several "projects" for the recovery of various aspects of the economy to be financed by non-interest-bearing
London loans would be carried out by personnel drawn from prewar
business firms and banks, including the Chettyar moneylender caste.

The governor's initial efforts to reach agreement with AFPFL
leaders over their possible participation in an interim executive
council quickly ran aground. The League's spokesmen, U Ba Pe,
and Thakins Aung San and Than Tun asked that all council posts
except foreign affairs and defense be entrusted to Burman hands,
that the higher judiciary be entirely Burman, and that a Burmese
adviser be assigned to the London office of the secretary of state for
India and Burma. Accepting the governor's initial invitation to submit eleven names to be considered for the fifteen-member cabinet,
the league spokesmen added two provisos. The first was that the
home minister post be filled by one of their own nominees and not
by Sir Paw Tun, who had been responsible for jailing many Freedom Bloc members in 1940–1941 and was known to favor Aung
San's arrest. The second was that league cabinet members be permitted to report to their own group for instructions and then be
free to resign as a body if essential policies were not carried out. The

second proviso was designed to prevent individual council members from succumbing to the lure of the perquisites of power. They also asked that early revision of the official White Paper program be undertaken by London.

The governor replied by challenging the League's presumptuous claim to represent the whole of Burma. He would select his own appointee for home minister, and insist that unless council appointees were prepared to carry out the reconstruction program outlined by London, they could either protest or resign individually. Bargaining ceased abruptly and negotiations ran firmly aground.

The final council membership included none of the league nominees. Several European and Burman members of the Simla and prewar cabinet were selected, plus three Myochit Party members, one Karen, and renegade Thakins Ba Sein and Tun Oke, who were welcomed back from their wartime exile in early 1946. In February, Dorman-Smith's prewar friend U Saw was brought back from his Uganda prison in Africa in the mistaken hope that he might be able to assemble a rival nationalist faction. Instead, U Saw forced his Myochit followers to resign from the council when the governor refused to accept his own terms. The governor's administration thus failed to command Burmese support in competition with the AFPFL nationalist coalition.

Although the AFPFL leadership studiously avoided overt resistance, it was busy organizing cadres. The dispersed veterans of the original Burma Defense and National Armies were reorganized as units of the Patriotic Volunteer Organization. Ostensibly the PVO was dedicated to preserve order and to assist in the rehabilitation program. But together with the All Burma Youth League, which was a constituent element of the AFPFL, the younger nationalist leadership was capable of generating spirited guerrilla resistance, if a break should come.

At the peasant level, communist Thein Pe actively enlisted peasant support for his "no taxes, no rent" campaign, which was tantamount to challenging the authority of the government and the legal claims of landlords, Burman as well and Indian, especially in the prosperous Pyinmana area of the upper Sittang valley. Socialist Party leaders, such as Thakins Mya, Chit, and Tin, did not go quite as far as the communists. They were content to agitate for higher prices for government-purchased paddy surpluses (then up only

50 percent above 1941 levels whereas other prices were four times as high). The AFPFL advocated that cultivator occupants of Chettyar-owned land in lower Burma remain undisturbed until some comprehensive new land policy could be devised. Dorman-Smith had no power to enforce the legal honoring of landlord titles.

A final and significant focus of AFPFL propaganda was London itself, where Tom Driberg and other sympathetic Labour Party spokesmen championed the cause of Burma's economic and political freedom in Parliament. From December through February, the league sought in vain to obtain permission to send a delegation to London by air. The governor was understandably uncooperative, but he finally conceded that a two-member AFPFL delegation with a secretary might be permitted to accompany a larger private delegation drawn from other political parties, as soon as ship passage could be arranged.

In early 1946 a rift almost developed within the league in connection with a nationwide rally staged at the Shwe Dagon pagoda grounds in Rangoon. The principal resolutions approved at the rally condemned the pattern of the governor's recovery program, demanded the early election of a constituent assembly, and advocated nationalization of agricultural land with compensation to private owners. But the prevailing emphasis on attaining freedom by peaceful means was openly challenged by communist spokesmen, whose Marxist slogans and insignia were prominently displayed. Thakin Soe in particular tried to exploit rising popular anger to promote revolutionary ends. A bitter quarrel ensued when U Ba Pe denounced all totalitarian systems, including that of the Soviet Union, as enemies of freedom. More moderate communist leaders, Than Tun and even Thein Pe, were not prepared at this critical juncture to disrupt the nationalist front, and therefore refused to go along with Soe. When they later read Soe out of the Communist Party, he proceeded to form his own Red Flag Party and then resumed his underground wartime posture.

In early March, the governor and Sir Paw Tun moved to arrest Aung San on criminal charges based on accusations levelled by Tun Oke. The incident was connected with a reported court martial and execution of a Tenasserim headman at the start of the war in 1942. A month-long examination found the accused admitting freely that he did indeed participate in this particular court martial proceeding. Perturbed British army leaders protested that the proposed arrest of Aung San was in reality a political move which was almost sure to provoke widespread rebellion at a time when political conditions within India would virtually rule out the use of local Commonwealth troops, mainly Indian, against the Burmese. The initial authorization for Aung San's arrest issued by London in early April was countermanded shortly thereafter, presumably by Undersecretary Arthur Henderson.

News of the proposed arrest aroused a storm of public anger in Burma, ruling out any possibility of future popular accommodation with Dorman-Smith's government. During April and May, expressions of political disaffection and lawlessness increased throughout the Burma countryside at an alarming rate. Steamboat operations in the delta had to be suspended, while road and railway traffic proceeded only under the protection of armed guards. On May 16, the harried governor had to solicit military support for his outmanned police. Press reports predicted open rebellion.

Towards a Peaceful Settlement

Various considerations were working for a peaceful solution. Neither party wanted a renewal of warfare in a country which had already experienced two harrowing campaigns. London recognized by now that the White Paper plan was unworkable, and Premier Attlee's preparations to accord freedom to India made a new policy for Burma virtually mandatory. Burman communication with Driberg and other friends in Parliament convinced the Anti-Fascist League leaders that Dorman-Smith would be replaced and that political reforms would be accelerated under new leadership.

Moderate AFPFL leadership was determined to avoid revolutionary violence and proved this between May and July 1946. The League vetoed outright the provocative "no taxes, no rents" agitation of communist spokesmen. In July Than Tun resigned as secretary of the AFPFL, and two months later socialist U Kyaw Nyein managed a victory over Thein Pe in the election of a new secretary. In October the entire trouble-making Communist Party leadership, including Than Tun, was excluded from the counsels of the league. Than Tun, surprisingly, continued to cooperate, although he doubted that London would ever grant Burma's freedom and was preparing to escalate the inevitable anticolonial struggle into a full-scale social revolution. For a number of reasons, this crisis was postponed to 1948.

Belatedly, Governor Dorman-Smith himself undertook during the final weeks of his incumbency to advance reform proposals. On April 22, he suggested that new elections for a constituent assembly might properly precede the attempt to revive the 1935 constitution. On May 1, he proposed reconstituting the executive council by granting equal representation to the followers of Sir Paw Tun, U Saw, and U Aung San. Meanwhile, agents of several government-sponsored recovery "projects," particularly in agriculture, began objecting. Some resigned in protest against the assumed trend toward socialistic governmental interference. Undersecretary Henderson in London countered the protests by declaring flatly that the Labour government's policy was not to facilitate the reestablishment of monopoly capitalism in Burma.

As a final conciliatory move, the Rangoon government promulgated the Land Disputes Act of May 1946, which assigned to special land commissioners the power to reduce rental payments to twice the tax assessment, and to authorize continued tenant occupancy if taxes were paid plus a small additional fee. A new Tenancy Act was later promulgated in July 1946, guaranteeing three-year tenure rights with fair rental rates calculated at a fraction of the normal gross output, plus full compensation to departing tenants for land improvements they had made, and a twelve-rupee outright payment for each acre restored to cultivation. The requisite staff, funds, needed cattle, and the degree of order were not available for implementing such reform proposals, but they were historically sgnificant as admitted evidence of the existence of long neglected social problems.

On May 4 Prime Minister Attlee summoned Dorman-Smith to come to London for consultations on what was obviously his terminal leave. The governor's departure was delayed for more than a month to install an acting governor. During the delay, the governor contracted a serious dysentery illness which forced him to make the homeward journey by sea. He left Rangoon on July 14 and reached Britain in August. Meanwhile, London fashioned a face-saving official explanation, attributing the governor's difficulties to an inadequate staff and thanking him for his arduous labors in an admittedly difficult situation. Sir Reginald resigned on August 4, and the new governor, Sir Hubert Rance, proceeded to Rangoon to take over the unfinished task.

Preparations for Negotiations under Rance

Despite the fact that Sir Hubert Rance was very conciliatory, the sixteen months of his governorship featured political controversy that repeatedly threatened to explode into violence. Immediately following his arrival in Rangoon in September 1946, a strike for higher pay was initiated by the Rangoon police. Ten days later, the strike spread to other governmental employees, and subsequently to the railway and oil workers unions. Although the movement was apparently not politically motivated at the outset, various nationalist groups took advantage of the opportunity. In mid-September, the AFPFL staged a supporting protest march. When U Saw then amplified his own Myochit Party propaganda efforts in competition with the league, he was wounded in an attack by an unidentified terrorist.

The mounting crisis forced the resignation of the old executivce council, permitting Governor Rance to proceed to select a more representative group by September 27. Aung San became deputy chairman under Rance; Kyaw Nyein was the new home minister; Mya occupied a key economic role. To balance off the majority AFPFL control, U Saw was brought in after he recovered from his wound, and Communist Thein Pe was also included. Within a week after the new council took office, all of the strikes subsided. When the Communist Party decided not to accept the pacification terms, Thein Pe resigned his cabinet post, and the party was completely excluded from the AFPFL.

By early November, the new leadership had formulated a series of far-reaching proposals. They called for the election of a constituent assembly by April 1947, with representation for the frontier peoples as well. London must issue a proclamation before the end of January that full independence would be accorded Burma within the ensuing year. Finally, the program for economic recovery would have to be fully reexamined. Prime Minister Attlee's eventual parliamentary motion of December 20 to invite a delegation from Burma's executive council to visit London for the purpose of discussing constitutional reform and revision of the White Paper aroused some caustic British comment. Winston Churchill denounced such scuttling of the empire and the betrayal of Britain's loyal Karen friends in Burma, but to no avail.

London's invitation was seconded by the visiting undersecretary of state for Burma, and was accepted by the AFPFL following a thorough discussion. The six-member delegation which arrived in the British capital on January 9 included Aung San, Mya, and Ba Pe of the AFPFL, with Ba Sein, U Saw, and a distinguished I.C.S. diplomat politician, U Tin Tut. Meanwhile in Burma, preparations for a wide-scale nationalist rebellion proceeded apace just in case essential demands were not met. Communist agitators, PVO veteran groups, and students took the lead.

The conclusions of the London talks announced on January 27 were far-reaching. They conceded eventual independence to Burma, with constitutional assembly election scheduled for April. A selected portion of the elected body would later serve as an interim legislative assembly. Britain also agreed to meet a portion of the current revenue deficit, and to make an additional cash loan. A joint British-Burman mission would strive to realize the agreed objective of early unification of the peripheral frontier areas with ministerial Burma. The minority tribal peoples themselves would be represented on the final frontier areas committee.

Execution of the London Agreement

Two factors complicated Burman approval of Premier Attlee's generous offer. One was the incipient rebellion, largely promoted by the communists, which persisted in central Burma and in the Arakan. The other was the irresponsible decision of U Saw and Thakin Ba Sein to refuse to sign the London agreement and to resign from the council. The two joined with Dr. Ba Maw shortly after their return to form the Democratic Nationalist Opposition Front. This threat from the right had the counter effect of influencing the responsible Communist Party secretary, Than Tun, to cooperate with Aung San in quieting worker and peasant unrest. Than Tun was not a gratuitous troublemaker.

As soon as the London agreement had been officially approved, Aung San and a ranking British official for dominion affairs proceeded to Panglong in the southern Shan states to attend a conference of representatives of the Shan, Kachin, and Chin leaders. An understanding was reached that the three minority groups would be represented in executive council sessions whenever frontier matters were being considered. One representative from the three would occupy a permanent seat in the council. It was also agreed that the frontier areas would be assisted financially by the center. Shortly thereafter the wartime Shan States Frontier Congress was revived as an ally of the AFPFL. Subsequently the frontier areas committee of enquiry was set up under a British chairman to work out operational details.

The important minority problem not covered by the Panglong agreement concerned the future status of Karen-inhabited areas in portions of the delta and in the watershed areas between the lower Sittang and Salween valleys. Apart from the Karen Youth Organization, which had been directly affiliated with the league since 1944, the more representative Karen National Union was too distrustful of Burman rule to accept the emerging independent state. They made no secret of their preference for British rule. An enquiry committee itself uncovered the disturbing fact that radical Karen Youth Organization leaders from the delta had been promised personal favors in administering the Salween district in return for their support of AFPFL proposals. The three small Karenni states to the east of Toungoo flatly rejected membership in the proposed union, to the annoyance of the AFPFL. The most reassuring offer which Burman spokesmen made was to designate the senior Karen army officer, the British-trained General Smith-Dun, to head the emerging Burma army. Chin tribesmen located along the borders of India rejected separate statehood, but they demanded full autonomy and preservation of Chin customs. They wanted Britain to guarantee any future agreements covering assistance from Burma proper in matters of health, education, and other government services.

As independence planning proceeded, Burman-Karen relations tended to grow worse rather than better. The basic disagreement concerned the demand for a separate Karen state. The Karen Youth Organization representative whom Aung San had appointed to the executive council, Saw Ba U Gyi, resigned his post in February 1947, following a general protest of the Karen National Union in Rangoon. He was replaced by the more pliable Mahn Ba Khaing, who agreed to accept the eventual findings of the official boundary commission. The AFPFL flatly rejected the basic demand for an eventual Karen seaboard state. Thereupon the Karen National Union voted to boycott the constituent assembly elections of April.

As a consequence, all of the twenty-four Karen delegates were chosen from the Youth Organization candidates or from pro-AFPFL independents. Since the conservative "independence first" alliance sponsored by Dr. Ba Maw, U Saw, and Thakin Ba Sein also decided to boycott the election, the result was a landslide AFPFL victory: 170 of the 180-odd noncommunal seats. The communists scored only seven victories in the 29 seats contested. The most ominous result was the decision of the Karen union to sponsor its own veterans' Parliamentary Defense Organization to parallel the Burman PVO, which was heavily represented in the elected assembly.

The key leaders in the preparations for Burma's independence were U Aung San in the political field and U Mya in the area of economic affairs. U Nu was vice-president of the AFPFL, but remained in the background. He was not even a candidate in the original constituent assembly election, and obtained a seat in a by-election held following the death of an elected member. Aung San's role was crucial because he was uniquely able to command public confidence and particularly the allegiance of the restive PVO constituency. Mya negotiated the financial agreements with London, and also served as chairman of the new economic planning board. He acknowledged Burma's responsibility for repayment of British loans, for meeting interim troop expenses, and for turning over to Britain the receipts realized from the sale of CAS (B) stores. Income from the sale of lend-lease surpluses was allocated to the American-sponsored Fulbright Foundation. The initial draft of the new constitution was prepared under Mya's leadership. When the plenary constituent assembly convened in June, Nu took over the chairmanship, but at no time did he approximate the importance of Aung San or Mya.

The crucial Burmese decision to opt for complete independence from the Commonwealth was more the inexorable byproduct of events than the overt decision of leaders, who might have wished to avoid it. Ingrained popular distrust as well as immediate political factors were important. The considerations advanced by the British-controlled Rangoon Chamber of Commerce in February, questioning the wisdom of eliminating the participation of prewar firms in Burma's economic recovery program, provoked an emotionally negative response to the idea of dominion status. Any conciliation of alien economic interests at the time would have played into the hands of communist agitators, who insisted that imperialism could never be liquidated except by armed struggle. The leftward drift of opinion within the AFPFL was evidenced by the forced resignation of anti-Marxist U Ba Pe from the executive council in mid-May, and by the decision of the 800-member league convention, which met on May 17, to approve the goal of complete independence.

While the final draft of the constitution was under preparation at Rangoon, U Tin Tut, later joined by U Nu, proceeded to London to arrange the terms of provisional agreements with the British on defense arrangements, finances, definition of nationality, and commercial relations. Resentful British Conservatives in Parliament tried to cancel the promises of financial assistance to the Burmese government, but they were thwarted by Undersecretary Arthur Henderson. However inescapable politically the decision to withdraw from the Commonwealth may have been, the action did deny the new state much-needed private firm assistance in economic recovery. Meanwhile U Soe's communist rebellion persisted in the Arakan district and in the delta, while Kachin and Karen disaffection threatened trouble from the opposite side of the political spectrum. The road ahead for independent Burma was filled with serious hazards.

Tragedy struck on the morning of July 19, 1947, when two assassins forced their way into the cabinet chamber at the secretariat building at Rangoon and turned their automatic weapons on those seated around the table. Among the eight killed were Aung San and Mya, the venerable scholar-artist U Ba Choe, the Muslim, Karen, and Shan members on the Council, and the elder brother of Aung San. The assassins were traced to U Saw's political headquarters, where other guns were found. The unscrupulous U Saw himself spread the rumor that the British had been responsible for the crime, in his efforts to precipitate a general revolution which his Myochit faction was prepared to exploit. His trial, conducted from October to December, revealed that the murderous episode had been planned months in advance.

The immediate request by Governor Rance on July 19 that U Nu form a new government, and the support which the communist Than Tun gave to the pacification effort at this juncture prevented any rightwing coup. The conviction and execution of the vengeful

U Saw did little to repair the disastrous loss suffered by Burma at so crucial a time. Perhaps the most serious problem was the ensuing demoralization of the PVO faction, both within and outside the constituent assembly, now that the influence of Aung San was removed. In the longer run, the absence of the able and steadying influence of the moderate socialist U Mya would also be sorely missed, especially in the economic sphere. However much the Burmese respected U Nu's sincerity and dedication as a nationalist, he was not a dynamic political personality and was destined in time to prove woefully lacking in administrative ability.

Burma's Constitution and Its Policy Implications

The 1947 constitution for the Burma Union, which was approved in late September, borrowed substantially from a variety of sources. The British principle that the cabinet should be responsible to a majority of the elected parliament was incorporated as were the basic legal principles and court procedures developed during the colonial period. The office of symbolic president followed the French pattern. He was to be elected for a five-year term by vote of the whole parliament, but he lacked political influence or power. From American sources came the affirmation of popular sovereignty, a high court competent to determine the constitutionality of legislative enactments, and a modified federal system for the five-member Union. The comprehensive but heavily qualified statement of the bill of rights and specific freedom quarantees also followed the American pattern. A number of socialistic provisions were borrowed from the Yugoslav constitution, and the proposed chamber of nationalities, in which minority peoples and states were represented, was Soviet in origin.

Hidden behind this formal façade were numerous qualifications which greatly modified liberal aspects of the system. Enjoyment of the terms of the bill of rights, for example, including legal equality of property holding and for employment, was limited to citizens of the Union. By definition, the latter would include only persons with at least one indigenous grandparent, and other British subjects who had been resident in the country through eight of the ten years preceding January 1, 1942. The ostensibly forthright guarantees of the right of ownership of private property and exercise of free initiative in the economic sphere were sharply qualified wherever the public interest was allegedly involved. Monopoly control and price dictation were explicitly prohibited, and the state reserved the plenary authority to nationalize the means of production in the public interest. Legislation appropriating private property whether in single industries or in larger branches of the economy would specify the extent of compensation to be granted to the previous owners.

The constitution also included statements of the general policy which would be followed. It flatly outlawed large land holdings such as the Chettyar claims and asserted the authority of the state, as the ultimate owner, to alter or to abolish existing tenure regulations and to redistribute land to individual tenants or to cooperative cultivator agencies. Legislative authority would also encompass worker organization and protection, housing needs, and social insurance. A special section of the constitution entitled "Directive Principles of State Policy" espoused such generalized objectives as economic and cultural progress, the right of all citizens to jobs, broadened educational opportunity, old age and disabled veteran care. Public utilities and natural resources development projects which were not publicly operated (the general expectation) would be reserved to private companies in which 60 percent of the stock was citizen-owned.

Economic plans were spelled out more explicitly in a statement prepared by U Mya prior to his death, but published in 1948. Mya affirmed that the government's primary concern was to prevent any return to the prewar *laissez faire* system under which foreign capital and entrepreneurs had been able to deny to Burmese citizens a fair share in the advantages of expanding production. Mya's declared immediate objectives were to speed up the recovery of industrial output and agriculture, while laying a longterm foundation for a progressively socialized economy devoid of worker and peasant exploitation. Utopian socialist euphoria permeated the entire document, leaving many options open.

The special councils of the several minority-people states of the Burma Union were to include all members of particular groups present in both chambers of parliament. Such separate state councils could be convened by the respective cabinet ministers of each group, who acted as chairmen. Seventy-two of the 125 members of the

chamber of nationalities were to be non-Burmans. The body shared
legislative responsibility with the chamber of deputies except for
money bills. The Karen affairs council would include the twenty
communal members of the chamber of deputies, to which could be
added five Karens from the nationalities chamber. A Karen state was
promised for the future, to be combined with Karenni and centering
in the Salween district watershed. Its establishment would be contingent on the expressed approval of the inhabitants of the region
and fall within boundaries to be fixed by a special commission
appointed by the president of the union. For the time being, a
special Kawthulay Karen district was set apart. In the new proposed
Kachin state, Burman and Shan residents were accorded equal
minority representation in the state council. Karen minority participation was destined to become a perennial problem in the
emerging Union.

The Shan state explicitly and the Kayah state (Karenni) by implication were accorded a qualified right to secede from the Union
after ten years' time, but since the center controlled both finances
and trade their complete secession was not realistically feasible. The
Karen state of 1951 was denied any right of secession, as the Karen
rebels had demanded in 1949. All decisions authorizing the exploitation of forests, minerals, and oil fields located within the boundaries
of the border states were valid only if supported by the state minister
concerned, but he was himself subject to cabinet control. State laws
which trespassed the authority of the central government could be
rendered inoperative by action of the supreme court.

Except for the twenty Karen communal members, all deputies
were to be elected from general constituencies for a four-year term.
All citizens twenty-one years and over could vote except the pongyi
monks, who were also barred from membership in parliament. Only
the Union parliament could maintain an armed establishment.
Until regular elections could be held, the constituent assembly itself
would function as an interim parliament. Karens were accorded
special rights in the control of their own schools, largely Christian,
and in the preservation of their religious and cultural practices. In
this connection, American missionary authorities moved as rapidly
as circumstances would permit to transfer titles of all real property
to the respective indigenous church bodies, Burmese, Karen, Shan,
Kachin, and Chin. The Baptist Mission's Judson College had been
sold to the government in 1946–1947.

Implementation of Independence

The final months of 1947 witnessed a concerted effort by Rangoon
and London authorities to agree on the terms of separation. A secret
defense agreement was signed on August 29 providing for the early
evacuation of British military forces and London's waiver of payment
for equipment and installations left behind. At Rangoon's request,
the United Kingdom agreed to assist in the military training of
officer personnel, with facilities to be provided for three years, covering all three branches of Burma's armed services. London also
agreed to assist in the operation of airports at Mingaladon (near
Rangoon), at Akyab, and at Mergui, and to provide war materials
on reasonable terms. Military aid would be solicited only from
Commonwealth countries, which would be accorded in return ready
access to Burma by sea and air. This agreement was subsequently
incorporated in the Nu-Attlee Treaty of October 17.

Concrete plans for restructuring of the economy were based on
the *Two-Year Plan of Economic Development,* published in 1948,
which had been drafted by Thakin Mya prior to his assassination
and revised by his successor U Kyaw Nyein. It was a pragmatic
project, moderate in tone and devoid of vindictiveness. It proposed
that the government should assist in early restoration of rice production by providing tenant cultivators with credits needed during the
ensuing paddy season. The government would also collect rentals on
lands not under landlord control at the rate of twice the tax assessment, and act to protect cultivators against market fluctuations.
Domestic purchases for overseas sales at twice the prewar price would
continue to be managed by the state agricultural marketing board,
one of the continuing CAS (B) projects.

The agricultural plan anticipated that the two million acres of
paddy land abandoned to jungle during the course of the war would
be restored to cultivation within four years, plus a possible one
million new acres to be brought under cultivation during the same
period. The state would acquire title to some two-thirds of the
noncultivator-owned land, which would subsequently be distributed
in a fashion designed to eliminate landlordism and to prevent
future alienation of cultivator titles. Prior to the contemplated
opening of the central state agricultural bank in 1949, the government itself would regulate private moneylender operations. Once
established, the bank's policy would be to give preferential con-

sideration to cooperative societies and to state-colony units. Other agriculture (sugar, onions, cooking oil, pepper) would hopefully become self-sufficient by 1952. The plan was a far cry from any thoroughgoing communist-type regimentation of agriculture.

Similar moderation was apparent in other aspects of initial economic planning. Existing longterm timber leases would be honored, but they would not be renewable. During the first year, the state planned to take over around one-third of the timber opera- tions and would acquire the remainder as leases expired. Meanwhile, foreign experts would be asked to assist in the extraction, processing, and marketing of the output. The plan also left open a fairly wide field for private activity in industry, with the state assisting in labor mobilization, and in meeting housing and welfare needs. Priority in the nationalization program would be accorded in order of pref- erence to banking services, public utilities, and development of nonagricultural resources (minerals and oil), with handicrafts and agriculture ranking lowest on the scale. The ministry of planning would include an advisory board over which the prime minister himself would preside. The proposal was very optimistic, almost utopian, but it did give a valid idea of the intentions of the govern- ment at the time.

The obvious contradiction between the studied moderation ex- hibited in the official two-year plan, as compared with the PVO- sponsored constitutional declarations and the more revolutionary approach advocated by communists, helps to explain the outbreak of the revolution in the spring of 1948. The same contradictions were apparent to a lesser degree in the terms of the Nu-Attlee Treaty itself in October. Nu agreed that Burma would pay the pensions and leave salaries for discharged British civil servants previously serving in the country and would consult London in advance if any action was contemplated prejudicial to the economic interests of United Kingdom interests. Burma would also cover most of the CAS (B) costs, including repayment of moneys advanced by London on the various economic recovery project operations initiated by CAS (B). The government would honor all valid contracts held by British companies at the time of political separation. Premier Nu qualified these pledges by calling attention to the constitutional provisions committing his government to the policy of state so- cialism, albeit with equitable compensation to United Kingdom interests involved. The documents nowhere undertake to explain precisely what was meant by "state socialism." Trouble developed when the less moderate PVO faction within the assembly challenged Nu's treaty commitments. Both the two-year plan and the Nu-Attlee Treaty terms appeared to lend limited credence to the communist contention that real political and economic independence could be attained only by armed struggle.

The Nu-Attlee Treaty was ratified by the British Parliament as a *fait accompli,* but not without sharp challenge from Winston Churchill. He argued that Mountbatten had never been authorized to elevate the antifascist leadership to the level of plenipotentiaries competent to speak for all of Burma's people, and that a firm show of force in 1945–1946 would have afforded opportunity to carry out the original White Paper policies. Britain was abandoning its friends in Burma, and the Labour government would have to accept responsibility for the bloodbath rebellion which was sure to follow. Premier Attlee's rejoinder was that any British attempt in 1945–1946 to subdue the Burmese nationalists without the aid of withdrawing Indian troops, would have been a highly risky military venture and would have closed the door to any future conciliation. Arthur Henderson concluded the debate by affirming that the treaty under consideration was an expression of British good faith in proclaiming the world charter of freedom, friendship, and peace to replace imperialism and economic exploitation. Parliamentary approval came on November 14.

Sharp criticism of the terms of the Nu-Attlee Treaty in Burma tended to exacerbate political rifts already present. Karen partisans were more angry with Britain than with the Nu government, accusing London of betraying traditional Karen cooperation and friendship. The ultimate Karen contest, of course, would have to be waged with the distrusted Burman majority. The Communist Party leader, Than Tun, denounced the special position which Nu had accorded to the British military. He also objected strongly to promised payment of cumulative debts and pension obligations and to Nu's promised compensation for nationalized British property holdings. Than Tun favored the immediate and arbitrary expropriation of all landlord holdings by people's courts and local agricultural committees. The communists also contested socialist control over emerging peasant (Tin) and labor organizations (Ba Swe). Than Tun had been prepared to exploit the anticipated revolutionary struggle against imperialism for his own communist political ends, but Nu's treaty had closed the door to such a prospect. Late 1947 and early 1948 witnessed the spread of communist-instigated popular unrest, based largely on economic grievances. Government leaders countered such communist threats by the use of government patronage and bribery.

The third element of discontent, that of the PVO veterans, was based essentially on political rather than on ideological considerations. Although the PVO faction was much the strongest element within the assembly, it was accorded no representation in the cabinet of Premier Nu. Aung San had filled such a role prior to his assassination. Few PVO leaders possessed the training and experience needed to take over important roles within the government, while disorderly elements at the lower levels posing as national heroes flatly refused to revert to the level of paddy farmers. Socialist leaders within the AFPFL tried to amalgamate the veterans' groups with the league's own apparatus for mass control, so that the PVO would lose political influence and become a kind of local militia element within the total league organization. The PVO rank and file cared little about the terms of the Nu-Attlee Treaty, but they refused to become a mere addendum to the League's anti-communist program. Thus, for a considerable fraction of the veterans' group, as for the communists, the Nu government became an object of hostility.

The popular acclaim which the Nu government attracted in its role as the author of Burma's independence was an invaluable asset at the beginning, but it was subject to erosion in time. The government's major problem was that the youthful political leadership on which it depended in large measure lacked experience and administrative competence. Virtually all non-Burmese officials (British and Indian) were being eliminated from the service at a time when governmental responsibilities were being extended far beyond the traditional and routine services. The new duties included the operation of banking and credit facilities, rice purchasing and processing, monopoly of exports, purchasing missions sent abroad, in addition to the rehabilitation of transportation, mineral and oil extraction, and timber facilities. Popular expectations were far too high for government agency performance to approximate even within their routine administrative chores, quite apart from the implementation of the planned socialization process. All of this must be accomplished in a context of ineffective police control and threatened revolution.

In a very real sense, Premier Nu himself epitomized the problems of the administration. Despite his personal charisma, his skill as an orator, and his acknowledged sincerity of purpose, Nu lacked intellectual stature and the capacity to carry through to realization declared policies and commitments. As a person completely devoid of military experience, Nu exercised no influence over the PVO veteran group, and he also generated no organized political following of his own. He lacked any appreciation of the inherent contradictions in his combined espousal of liberal democratic ideals and utopian socialism, along with his concern for religious revival. Nu's closest associates within the government (Kyaw Nyein, Ba Swe, and Bo Let Ya) had been his personal friends since the student strike of 1936, and not one of the group was really capable of taking charge. All high officials of the government, furthermore, were overburdened with minor responsibilities, which should have been handled by subordinates. The ministers had little opportunity to develop the detachment needed for effective administrative direction. One can admire Nu's rhetoric on the early morning of January 4, 1948, when independence was acclaimed, while still appreciating subsequent popular concern that he may not have selected the best astrologer to designate the most propitious time (4:20 A.M.) for launching the new state. He said: "We lost our independence without losing our self-respect; we clung to our culture and our traditions, and these we now hold to cherish and develop . . . We part without rancour and in friendship from the Great British Nation which held us in fee."

X The Ordeal of Independence

Although Premier Nu's government survived the rebellions which erupted in 1948 and 1949 and dominated the elections held in 1951, it accomplished little in improving administrative efficiency and economic recovery. An overly-optimistic economic development program, designed with the aid of American counseling agencies, was rendered more impractical by Nu's own utopian *Pyidawtha* (happy country) plans of 1952, which were designed to end all worker exploitation and provide for the needs of all people. The American-conceived program took too little account of such problems as continuing disorder and faltering governmental performance. It also failed to anticipate the collapse of the world rice market following the end of the Korean war. Meanwhile, Premier Nu became involved in a diversionary Buddhist revival effort, which related more to national prestige and nostalgia than to tangible economic and social objectives. Following the generally corrupt elections of 1956, the discouraged premier withdrew into an eight-months retirement period, which witnessed increasing recrimination among leaders of the disintegrating AFPFL coalition. The split widened following Nu's return in early 1957, reaching the point in mid-1958 of threatened civil war. The rival factions thereupon agreed to institute temporary army caretaker rule under General Ne Win, starting in October 1958. The army restored order, cleaned up Rangoon, got rid of the foreign advisors, reverted to more traditional economic objectives, and eventually retired after arranging for new elections in early 1960. Nu's Union Party coalition won the election by appealing for religious and minority group support, and was thus afforded a second chance to implement democratic rule.

Cominform-Instigated Revolution

The travail of revolutionary violence which the Burma Union endured during its early years was attributable in part to deliberate

Cominform instigation. Rebellion was precipitated in March 1948 by Burma's orthodox Stalinists Than Tun and Goshal, shortly after their return from the Calcutta sessions of Congress of Southeast Asian Youth and from meetings with European and Indian communist spokesmen. The new Cominform policy of fomenting overt revolutionary action was approved at Moscow in September 1947, and transmitted to India by ambassador Novikov, who arrived at New Delhi in November. Soviet directions to Communist Party leaders in India and Southeast Asia had previously been cautious in view of the need to avoid giving political embarrassment to European party units by gratuitous interference in colonial matters and the consequent alienation of Western European nationalist opinion. The early Soviet hope was that the possible collapse of Western European economies would precipitate political confusion which could be exploited effectively by local Communist Parties. This situation was altered in late 1947, when America's Marshall Plan aid program began to put the European economies back on their feet. Moscow thereupon shifted the principal focus of its world revolutionary tactics to the colonial areas of Asia. The result was a deliberate attempt to exploit the Hobson-Leninist theory that imperialism was essentially a projection of capitalism, and that the latter might be overthrown by destroying the props of colonial markets and investment opportunities which supported the faltering Western economies.

The attempted implementation of the new policy of overt revolution in India and Burma, where newly independent governments had already emerged under Premiers Nehru and Nu was posited on dubious premises. The communist line affirmed that full independence could be achieved only by armed struggle regardless of the particular setting. Ambassador Novikov's efforts in India from November to early March succeeded in driving out the able Communist Party Secretary, P. C. Joshi, in favor of the far less effective Ranadive, thus seriously weakening the party's role. Joshi flatly refused Novikov's demand to denounce Nehru as a renegade colonialist stooge, thereby losing his editorship of *People's Age*, his party secretaryship, and even his place in the Politbureau.

Cominform spokesmen at the Calcutta conference made direct contact with the Burma party representatives in January 1948. The latter already disagreed with Nu's policy of accepting London's continuing military and economic role in independent Burma. An attack on Nu's "sham independence" would afford them opportunity to launch a revolutionary rising to serve Marxist ends. The final decision to initiate such a struggle was reached at sessions of the All Burma Peasants Union held at Pyinmana in mid-March, with at least two Cominform representatives present. The overt rising began on March 28 in central Burma, following an abortive effort at Rangoon to foment a trade union strike. Similar efforts were made in Rangoon to enlist the cooperation of malcontent PVO elements within the AFPFL.

The communist rebellion itself was a limited operation confined to the upper valley of the Sittang River (from Toungoo to Yamethin) and extending westward around the north rim of the Pegu Yoma mountains into the oil field areas along the Irrawaddy valley. The rising disrupted transportation and economic recovery efforts, but posed no immediately serious threat to the nationalist government of Nu. Except among the PVO malcontents, Communist Party agitators enlisted little popular support even among the dissident elements in the delta and Arakan. The armed communist forces numbered less than 25,000 men. Even the communist leader Thein Pe, in many respects more radical than Than Tun, had no stomach for the rigors and risks of rebellion; he remained in Rangoon.

Other Sources of Disaffection

Premier Nu's principal concern following the break with the communists was to prevent the threatened defection of restive PVO elements within the AFPFL. At stake was the establishment or the repudiation of the very basis of the authority of the government. The allegations of opponents that his treaty with Premier Attlee had betrayed the national cause and the socialistic principles of the constitution found limited confirmation in the possible shortcomings of the *Two Year Plan*. At the time of its publication in May 1948, the co-author of the plan and minister of economic development, U Kyaw Nyein, was ill and unable to defend its proposals. Nu's confused defense of the plan included the frank admission that the AFPFL was itself corrupt and privilege-seeking. To regain credence, he made an official move to implement, without promised consultation, the arbitrary nationalization of the Irrawaddy Flotilla Company and a major segment of the British-held timber concessions. Compensation was to be paid in nonconvertible bonds covering a small fraction of the estimated worth of the facilities. Nu also elevated the goal of nationalization of land titles (especially Chettyar holdings) from low priority under the *Two Year Plan* to the top level. He ended his frantic political maneuvering of early June with the disturbing announcement that he planned to withdraw to a monastery in July preparatory to full retirement from politics.

In a kind of final desperate effort to reach accommodation with the majority faction of the PVO, Nu solicited the aid of Thein Pe in drafting a fifteen-point Leftist Unity Program, which he also released in early June. The initial version of the program advocated entering into political and economic relations with communist Europe and the active propagation of communist doctrine through a government-sponsored Marxist league. Burma's national army would be transformed into a "people's democratic force," while "democratic" village committees (people's courts) would be entrusted with local police, judicial, and fiscal powers. Finally, he proposed that Burma's economic and military independence would be preserved by rejecting all outside aid which might compromise accepted Marxist objectives.

This seeming ideological surrender on Nu's part created consternation among anti-communist elements throughout Burma. The unity plan actually served Thein Pe's intended purpose of intensifying PVO demands to appease communists. The program and associated nationalization moves became the subject of worried diplomatic inquiries from London. Although most of Thein Pe's program was approved by the supreme council of the AFPFL in early July, the dissident PVO majority, despite such concessions, proceeded to join the rebellion. The move was accompanied by the mutiny of two of the five battalions of the Burma Rifles, leaving the government dependent in large measure on non-Burman Karen, Kachin, and Chin regiments, commanded by General Smith-Dun, himself a Karen. Fortunately the two mutinous battalions were widely separated geographically, while the PVO strength was narrowly concentrated in the lower Irrawaddy valley from Bassein to Prome. Nor were the disparate rebel elements (communist and PVO) capable of genuine cooperation militarily even when adjacent.

The political crisis worsened steadily. In mid-July Nu's entire cabinet resigned, and the premier himself agreed to stay on only to thwart the alternative bid for power made by Dr. Ba Maw and the renegade Thakin Ba Sein. Nu finally agreed on September 14 to

head a new cabinet including a number of competent conservative
leaders, including E Maung and Tin Tut. Five days later Tin Tut
was killed when a bomb exploded in his car. During the remaining
months of 1949, a mediating mission headed by the banker Thwin,
tried in vain to find some basis for peace with the PVO rebels. But
the regime's darkest hours were still ahead.

Governmental efforts during the latter half of 1948 to prevent an
armed break with the Karen nationalists proved equally ineffective.
General Smith-Dun was able throughout most of the year to keep
the Karen army detachments under effective discipline. Even so,
they twice seized Moulmein and staged temporary risings in
Toungoo and Karenni, and the southern Shan states. But the pledge
given by the moderate Karen leaders in July to seek their desired
separate state by peaceful and democratic means could not be indefinitely maintained. Younger Karen radicals were being encouraged by non-official British friends in their demands for an
enlarged state. In October, Karen leaders agreed to participate in a
regional autonomy enquiry commission, headed by Justice Ba U,
which was designed to consider Arakanese and Mon claims as well
as those of the Karens. A month later, the Karen National Union,
acting quite independently, raised the impossible demand for the
inclusion of virtually all of the Irrawaddy delta in the proposed
Karen state. The fact that the government was under serious attack
from its own Burman malcontents presented an opportunity which
the partisan Karen leaders refused to forego.

Relations deteriorated between regular army Karen units and the
poorly disciplined Burman recruits. When strife erupted in January
1949, Karen regiments in widely dispersed areas all turned against
the government. They occupied Bassein and Prome in the lower
Irrawaddy, the city of Insein only fifteen miles from Rangoon, and
Toungoo in the Sittang valley, where they collaborated marginally
with the communist rebels. Other risings took place in the summer
capital of Maymyo in the northern Shan states and in Taunggyi to
the south. The Karen position at Insein was particularly threatening, for the rebels raided the nearby Mingaladon cantonment to
acquire arms and munitions. They then waited in vain for other
contingents to join them, whereas an early Karen attack on Rangoon
might have captured the capital.

The government used semi-loyal Kachin and Chin regiments to

prevent the Karens from concentrating their power against Rangoon, while Burman regiments and volunteers took over the actual defense of the city. Some of the PVO dissidents and army mutineers, when faced with the possibility of Karen victory, shifted back to the government side. As if widespread rebellion was not enough, a strike of civil servants developed in February 1949, protesting an imposed salary cut. The action came near paralyzing governmental operations for a time. In April 1949, the leaders of the loyal minority faction of the PVO also withdrew from the government. Shortly thereafter, important Socialist Party ministers, as if fleeing the sinking ship, asked to be released from their ministerial duties in order to be free to mend their political fences. Most of them did not return until 1950.

Nu's cabinet during the interim period thus included a large number of non-Burmans, plus non-AFPFL judges and older conservative former civil servants. Rangoon authorities managed to maintain contact with regional administrative centers only by air. With the start of the Karen rebellion, General Smith-Dun was succeeded by General Ne Win (Thakin Shu Maung) as top army commander. The minister of foreign affairs, Justice E Maung, took a leading role. He negotiated a Commonwealth loan of some 350 million rupees in December 1949, which insured a steady flow of essential military supplies.

Recovery Measures

Once Premier Nu recovered from his initial panic and became reconciled to enlisting conservative nationalist backing for his government (Ba Maw and Ba Sein excepted), the situation began to improve. Disdaining the threats of rebel groups, Nu raised a democratic standard which attracted all of the older educated elite. He preserved the loyalty of Kachin and Chin regiments, and also intervened to protect nonbelligerent Karen communities in the delta from Burman abuse. Nu's personality also provided a valuable link with the peasant Buddhist majority, whose traditions he widely shared. In the face of spreading corruption and abuse of power, the premier's recognized concern for honest administration and an end of political chicanery carried a note of much needed reassurance. London's Labour government was particularly helpful, refusing to heed the representations of British friends of the Karens expressed in both press and parliament, and mobilizing Commonwealth assistance for the Rangoon authorities.

The rebellion dragged on at a slower pace through 1950 and into 1951. Denied regular replacement of military supplies and unable to cooperate because of disparate objectives and personal rivalries, the rebels offered no real alternative to the legal government headed by Nu. Neither the United States embassy nor the American Baptist Mission afforded encouragement to the Karen rebellion. Its leadership was Christian, but the movement included few of the older leaders of the community. The Karen detachment finally abandoned Insein, crossing the river into the delta, where it disbanded. Rebel remnants survived for a time in Tenasserim and in the Salween district watershed region. PVO political and military influence also eroded in favor of mass organizations of laborers and peasants mobilized by the socialist leaders within the AFPFL. The Than Tun communists managed to hold on to their well-defended bastions around the northern extensions of the Pegu Yomas.

At the end of 1949 and early in 1950 a kind of counter revolution took place. Socialist politicians returned to their government posts, driving E Maung and his sympathizers from power and vetoing many of their projects. These included possible Burmese participation in a proposed Commonwealth security pact aimed at China and also Nu's contemplated participation in a Commonwealth conference scheduled to convene in Ceylon. E Maung had even proposed the enlistment of British business interests in restoring the Burmese economy. Anti-British sentiment was too strong within the AFPFL to acquiesce in any such reversal of policy, especially after Nu himself refused to support his conservative advisers. E Maung resigned from the cabinet at the end of 1949, and Burma became the first non-communist government in the world to recognize the independence of the emerging People's Republic of China in early 1950.

Other significant actions taken by the Nu government reflected a continuing drift in an anti-Marxist direction. He accepted from Washington an assistance offer of $8 million from the Technical Cooperation Administration in September, 1950, to hire an economic planning team of Rangoon's own selection. In the same month, Premier Nu persuaded his parliament to approve the United Nations resolution challenging the communist assault against South Korea. The move was conceived as providing Burma future insurance

against such an attack. In 1951, Nu invited the pre-war British-
Burma Corporation to participate in a fifty-fifty joint undertaking
to revive mining operations in silver, lead, and zinc in the northern
Shan states, and to reactivate adjacent refineries. A similar arrangement was concluded with three British oil firms, to be initiated as
soon as the communist insurgency in the oil field area had waned.
The government's one-third contribution to the revival of oil production would be financed by a London loan.

This initial anti-communist orientation was sharply challenged
by a number of Marxist partisans operating at lower levels of
leadership within the Trade Union Congress (Burma) of the
Socialist Party. The TUC (B) at the time favored direct affiliation
with the Cominform-sponsored World Federation of Trade Unions
as well as participation in the World Peace Congress. The instigator
of this agitation was the devious Thein Pe Myint (as he now
preferred to be called), whose newspaper, *Voice of the Union*,
denounced American intervention in Korea, calling President
Truman a second Hitler and the *New York Times* an organ of the
capitalist warmongers. Thein Pe also made an unsuccessful effort
to base much of the university curriculum on Marxism. The pro-
communist spokesmen for the TUC (B) were eventually expelled,
thus elevating the socialist U Ba Swe to head the organization. He
continued to exploit the hammer and sickle symbols of the organization, while making persistent efforts to reconcile communism and
Buddhism.

The Marxist leadership of the All Burma Peasants Organization
was similarly purged in favor of responsible AFPFL supporters,
with Thakin Tin heading the peasant movement. The two excluded
pro-communist factions later joined under the banner of the Burma
Workers and Peasants Party, which was permitted to criticize governmental policies as the reward for non-affiliation with the rebellion. Most of the important AFPFL leaders, especially Ba Swe, Tin,
and Kyaw Nyein, continued to be socialistically inclined, rejecting
all proposals of the conservative press to halt the nationalization
program or to accept additional Anglo-American assistance.

There was little overt opposition to several legislative proposals
made by Premier Nu for religious revival and reform. His first
recommendation was to set up two ecclesiastical courts, one at
Rangoon and the other at Mandalay, in an effort to restore discipline to the disorderly Sangha monastic community. A second

law provided for a Pali (language) university authority to regu-
larize accreditation standards for teachers of the Buddhist scriptures
trained in qualified monastic institutions, the program to be
financed by limited state funds. Nu's third move was to establish a
Buddha Sasana (religion) organization designed to promote the
faith among all the peoples of Burma. It was charged to provide
translations in simplified Burmese of Pali scripture passages containing ethical teachings, intended for use in government elementary schools. The program was designed to replace the faltering
monastic schools. Even the most pro-Marxist agitators made no
effective rejoiner to Premier Nu's supporting affirmation that the
wisdom of the Buddha far surpassed that of Karl Marx, including
the particular aphorism that enmity could never be overcome by
enmity. Nu's policies appealed strongly to Burmese Buddhist tradition.

Even so, many of the secularist leaders within the AFPFL,
followers of the revered Aung San, were wary lest religious revival
emphasis might encourage the irresponsible political activities of
pongyi dissidents. The doubters did not have long to wait. By mid-
1951 a body of disgruntled monks, whose religious credentials were
being questioned, set up their own Burma Sangha Party. They
started attacking the AFPFL for interfering in religious matters
and loudly demanded official recognition of Buddhism as the state
religion. They defied control by the high level Sayadaw operated
ecclesiastical courts and also denounced the government's legislation.

Premier Nu's most important move in a democratic direction was
to stage general elections during the latter half of 1951. The political
situation favored the prestigious AFPFL coalition. It was pledged to
the peaceful establishment of a socialist state, the rejection of anti-
religious ideologies, neutrality in the cold war but opposition to
aggression, fair treatment of minorities, land nationalization, aid
to cultivators, and a planned program of economic development in
the people's interest. Posing as the saviour of the infant Burma
Union, Nu challenged his opponents to submit their counter-
proposals to the decision of the people. The government elicited
additional support by restoring salary cuts to civil servants and by
increased budgetary allocations for educational and health services.

By comparison, the opposition was badly fragmented. On the
extreme left was the overtly pro-communist People's Democratic

Front, the slightly less extreme PVO People's Party and the Peace
Unity Front, and finally the Burma Workers and People's Party. All
of them represented distinct factions, although they entertained
similar ideologies. To the right of the AFPFL were Ba Sein's Burma
Democratic Front, which catered to Karen and pongyi malcontents,
Dr. Ba Maw's feeble Mahabama faction seeking Anglo-American
aid, and Ba Pe's Burma Union League. The latter enjoyed support
from landlord and employer groups who favored rejoining the Commonwealth.

The voting started in the fully pacified areas (30 percent of the
districts) as early as June 1951, with a second round of voting in
August, and a third in October, as soon as additional regions were
pacified. The respected high court justices who headed the commission to supervise the voting, E Maung and Ba U, helped to
ensure that the balloting was honestly conducted. AFPFL candidates
won some 85 percent of all the seats. AFPFL strength lay not only in
the mass-organization peasant and workers groups sponsored by the
Socialist Party leaders but also in such minority groups as the
Muslim Congress, the moderate Union Karen League, and the
Chinese chambers of commerce. Opposition elements fragmented
badly. The refashioned cabinet of March 1952, which reflected the
election returns, was still largely controlled by socialists, with Ba
Swe, Kyaw Nyein, and Tin strategically placed in both the government and the party. Nu was the popular symbol of the government,
but he had cultivated no organized personal following. Local chiefs
dominated the elections in the Shan and Kachin states.

The Task of Economic Rehabilitation

The problems of economic recovery which the government faced
following the elections of 1951 were formidable. Many of the material losses sustained during the course of the Japanese occupation
had not been made good by 1948, when the multiple rebellions had
halted all recovery efforts. Millions of acres of lower Burma paddy
land continued under jungle growth, while many thousands of
peasant refugees lived precariously as squatters in Rangoon and
other cities. The cattle lost during the war were not replaced, and
the human death rate continued inordinately high. Prewar British
industries were largely inoperative, including mining, timber, and
oil, along with banking and overseas trading facilities. During the

rebellion internal transportation, except by air, had been paralyzed. River steamers still operated spasmodically; highway and railway bridges awaited permanent replacement, along with the restoration of rolling stock and damaged trackage.

Recovery efforts were also hampered by the continued absence of important segments of the prewar Indian population, which had fled before the Japanese invasion. In prewar times Anglo-Indians operated the railway trains, and Chittagong boatmen ran the Irrawaddy river steamers. There were now no Indian coolie freight handlers at the Rangoon docks and railway yards, and no one at all volunteered to take over garbage collection formerly performed by outcaste labor. Absent also were the trained Indian artisans and craftsmen, operators of bazaar shops, or moneylenders, lawyers, teachers, and civil servants. Chettyar land titles had been voided by the Land Nationalization Act of 1948, which had also abolished all landlord holdings in excess of fifty acres, but no final allocation of title claims had been achieved. Burmese hostility to all business activities of alien groups, including the British and Chinese as well as Indians, was based in part on strong ethnic prejudices which had no relevance to economic recovery needs. Few Burmans had acquired experience in conducting business affairs, and government personnel was ill-equipped to assume economic responsibilities generally.

And yet the demand for economic development was insistent. The dire privations which the nation had suffered during the war period from the shortage of consumer goods (clothing, hardware, construction materials, drugs, canned goods) exposed the vulnerability of any economic system limited to agriculture and the processing of locally produced raw materials for export purposes. Burma's youthful postwar leadership was determined to strive for industrialization despite formidable handicaps. Material deficiencies were many. Burma lacked essential coal and iron deposits, long staple cotton, a disciplined labor supply, not to mention risk capital and technical competence. Even in those areas of industrial production which would be feasible in terms of available resources, comparable manufactured imports from India, Japan, and Europe would usually be better and cheaper. Wage incentives would be required to persuade farmers to abandon familiar cultivation routines, coupled with family and community ties. Thrift and acquisitive effort were generally discounted within traditional Burmese

culture, not so much by reason of Buddhism's exhortation to conquer "desire" and to appreciate the unreality (*maya*) of the physical world, but rather because of climate, geography, and ingrained
social tradition.

Leaders of government were convinced that if a return to alien
domination of the economy was to be avoided, the contemplated
industrial development program would have to be state-sponsored.
State socialism was accordingly idealized as the alternative to exploitive capitalism which had characterized the colonial economy.
A truly socialist society would theoretically be free of employer
exploitation and other forms of social injustice. It would also
provide educational and health services and promote the general
happiness of all. If Burmans were to learn how to provide things
for themselves, the state itself at the outset must generate the
required capital resources through control of all export activities.
It must then direct the utilization of available funds for capital
equipment according to planned, officially sponsored development
programs.

In retrospect, it is easy to see that a more feasible approach
would have been to concentrate at the outset on a revival of the
prewar economic program until order had been fully restored,
refugees resettled on the land, land ownership patterns clarified,
and governmental routines established, including the collection of
essential statistical data. The postwar government was handicapped
because it lacked most of the traditional symbols of power (a palace
in the Mount Meru tradition, the White Umbrella of divine kingship, the Sacred Sword, and the prestige of Buddhist patronage),
but only the exercise of full governmental authority could undertake a massive restructuring of the economic sphere. Thus it was
one thing for the daring Thakins to capture popular imagination
by championing the nationalist cause; it was quite another for persons inexperienced in both governmental and business administration to carry out a program of forced industrial development.

Early Development Plans

By a kind of ironic twist of fate, Burma's initial development
plans were fashioned by the American engineering firm of Knappen,
Tippetts, and Abbot, assisted by Pierce Mining Engineers and by
Robert Nathan Associates serving as general economic consultants.

The costs of the initial contracts for the three American firms were covered in large measure by Washington's Technical Cooperation Administration contribution made in 1950. The firms involved were competent in the technical sense, but they were completely unfamiliar with the local situation and were very much concerned to please. In a deliberate effort to dispel the distrust of socialist members of the government, the initial American report which was submitted in early 1952 accorded full support for Burma's economic aspirations. To encourage maximum response the authors affirmed the definite possibility of Burma's recovering, during the contemplated eight-year period of the plan, from the 1952 level of per capita income some 40 percent below that of 1938 to more than full parity with prewar standards. Furthermore, the feat could allegedly be accomplished in large measure by savings generated locally, with two-thirds of the needed amount derived from government sources. The prerequisites were: (a) restoration of order by 1954, (b) doubling of total agricultural output to sustain an annual two-million-ton rice export trade at the expected average price of £50 per ton, (c) reorganization and remotivation of governmental agencies to perform essential duties, and (d) improvement of transportation facilities and the establishment of selected new industries.

The report attempted in labored fashion to blame the lack of all-round development of economic potential on the allegedly debilitating character of the colonial administration of prewar times. Actually, Burma's inexperienced administrative structure, already struggling to take over routine government functions, was being called on to assume the much more exacting responsibilities of state-planned economic development with no assurance that the specified conditions could be met.

The initial Burman response to the encouraging report was cautiously skeptical. In March 1952 a spokesman for the ministry of national planning exhorted the people to expand their economic horizons and rise to the challenge. At the same time, he admitted that the rate of capital formation accomplished in the past afforded no realistic hope of attaining the objectives indicated. He also pointed out that bureaucratic and administrative problems would have to be solved, and the four proposed autonomous development corporations (for industry, mining, agriculture, and transportation) would have to operate on efficient business principles.

The Pyidawtha Program of 1952

At the widely attended Pyidawtha conference at Rangoon in August 1952, Premier Nu and other government spokesmen proclaimed the launching of the socialist welfare state. Discarding dependence on the cautious bureaucratic routine inherited from colonial administration, Nu argued that the government must prepare to move boldly in order to end class exploitation and crime and also to meet the needs of the people, including livelihood, health, and education. Nine million acres of land would be redistributed to actual cultivators and three million additional acres would be developed. The Pyidawtha system would also provide lending services for crop cultivation, housing needs, electricity, and transportation. Finally each Burmese township unit was allocated the sum of 50,000 kyats (around $10,500) to be spent on improvements as determined by locally elected councils.

Except for health and educational programs, which had been outlined in some detail with World Health Organization and UNESCO assistance, the blueprint for the welfare state was only vaguely defined and essentially exhortive and promotional in character. Its purpose was to enlist public understanding and enthusiastic response by stressing positive objectives which the people could appreciate. The conference agenda included no detailed references to such favorite socialist projects as manufacturing industries, mining and forestry expansion, and new facilities to generate electric power. Premier Nu gave the welfare program a strongly conservative cultural tone by again proclaiming the superiority of the teachings of the Lord Buddha over the doctrines of Karl Marx and by stressing the need for religious revival.

The final report of the American advisory group, submitted in 1953, did nothing to curb the excessive optimism of the sponsors of Pyidawtha. The report even predicted on the basis of current prices for exported rice (some £60 per ton), that the entire cost of the economic development program might be financed without foreign borrowings. The document anticipated that the possible annual sale of some 2.3 million tons of rice, even at a price of £50 per ton, would be adequate, since foreign sales would not have to carry the 7 percent dividend burdens payable to export company shareholders in colonial times. The report did call attention to the advantages to be realized, in such competitive areas as housing construction and industrial operations, from the greater efficiency obtainable through private enterprise. It also continued to stress the importance of improved management standards, the reorganization of governmental agencies to expedite decision implementation, and the need for early restoration of law and order in the countryside.

The basic thrust of the report was to move boldly forward in the development of state owned industries which could become a source of needed earning for the treasury. There was no suggestion that the desired restoration of timber, oil, and mining production would be most quickly realized by enlisting the cooperation of experienced British personnel drawn from prewar firms, even though Burma's parliament had authorized in 1950 the possible approval of selected joint-venture projects on the basis of 60 percent government ownership.

Delays in Implementation

Before the proposed economic program could be implemented in any serious fashion, Premier Nu launched his religious revival program mentioned at the Pyidawtha conference. It was designed ostensibly to correct manifold ethical and social deficiencies carried over from the past. Not only were governmental officials admittedly inefficient and corrupt; many officials at lower levels of the administration were frequently intimidated by local political leaders who threw their weight around. To the correction of such deficiencies, according to the premier, it was necessary to carry through a massive effort at Buddhist ethical revival comparable to that staged by King Mindon in 1871.

Accordingly, in early 1953 he authorized the convening of the Sixth Great Buddhist Council, where the Pali scriptures would be reviewed by distinguished scholars invited from all Theravada Buddhist countries, especially Ceylon and Thailand. Simulating the cave setting used by the First Great Council held in India, Nu sponsored the construction of an artificial cave assembly hall, supported by massive steel girders and capable of seating some 10,000 spectator participants. The initial appropriation of some 5.5 million kyats ($1.1. million) had to be sextupled by 1956, an expenditure which the beleaguered treasury could ill afford. Adjacent to the cave structure, Nu erected a gold-covered Peace Pagoda, in which he enshrined an alleged Buddha tooth provided by China. The ceremonies continued into 1956. However much the council may have contributed to authenticate Premier Nu's role as a modern patron of Buddhism, it contributed little to ending official ineptitude and diverted both resources and attention from the goal of economic development.

Meanwhile, Rangoon-Washington relations were fouled by America's failure to stop Taiwan's support of anti-communist refugees from Yunnan, China, who had moved into Burma's easternmost Shan states in 1949. Burmese suspicions of American involvement were aroused initially in 1951, when several representatives of the refugee group showed up unexpectedly at the U.S. Information Center at Mandalay. The KMT refugees eventually established a headquarters near the northern border of Thailand, where they began trafficking in opium. When Burmese forces attempted to assert control over the region, the opposing KMT forces were found to be in possession of American-made arms of recent serial number, delivered to them by American planes and pilots, presumably from Taiwan via Thailand. Both the State Department and the Rangoon embassy denied any knowledge of the arms transfer, and Washington authorities took no effective action to force Chaing Kai-shek to halt the arms traffic. Burma's leaders also came to distrust the motives underlying the current American aid undertaking to contruct a modern road leading northward up Burma's central valley toward the China border, still undemarcated. They became convinced that any tolerance of the presence of enemies of the People's Republic of China along Burma's border would afford a ready excuse for Peking to intervene. The prospect that Burma like Korea might again become a battlefield in a worldwide struggle had to be avoided at all costs. The problem was aggravated in early 1953 when KMT agents began bartering American weapons to Karen and other rebel groups within the southern Shan states in return for needed food and consumer supplies. In March 1953, Burma's authorities abruptly cancelled all American aid services and then appealed to the United Nations to halt Taiwan's alleged acts of aggression against Burma. Even after the United States, in the late fifties, undertook to transfer to Taiwan a substantial portion of the Yunnan refugee forces, the border situation and arms traffic persisted as a stumbling block in Burma-American relations.

Collapse of the Development Program

The first serious effort to initiate the state-sponsored industrialization program came in the projected budget for 1954–1955. Some sixty-five areas of economic development were designated. The suggested initial capital expenditure of 10.7 million kyats exceeded the previously proposed maximum estimates of Nathan Associates by some 50 percent. The subsequently revised figure was still one-third more than the recommended sum. The firm's director commented later as follows: "Having worked for . . . two years to persuade the government to adopt an ambitious and aggressive approach, the economic consultants were now obliged to try to persuade it not to go too fast." A visiting World Bank investigator reported at the time that Burma's development program was badly managed, being overambitious in its industrial objectives and neglectful of more feasible projects in agriculture, forestry, and mining. By 1955, the twenty-odd Nathan Associates advisors in Burma were being paid salaries and allowances averaging $45,000 per person, which was more than ten times the pay of top-level Burma cabinet ministers. In 1955 Washington refused a Burmese request that it purchase ten million tons of surplus Burmese rice to help meet such costs. The American advisory role had clearly reached the point of diminishing returns.

The financial collapse of Burma's development plan came with the decline of world prices for exported rice, following the ending of the Korean war in 1953. From the early price of £60 per ton in 1954, the price fell to £44 in 1955, 36 in 1956, and down to 32 by 1959. Unprepared for such an emergency, the state agriculture marketing board rejected the new low prices and failed to assemble and market the carryovers. The unsold rice for 1955 was 1.5 million tons and that of 1956 some 1.8 million additional tons, which far exceeded storage facilities. Much of the exposed surplus spoiled during the successive monsoon rains. The situation forced the cancellation of incentives for increased peasant output, so that the acreage declined sharply. During the course of the Khrushchev-Bulganin visit in early 1956 the Russians agreed to accept on a barter basis some 150,000 tons of Burma rice, which was promptly forwarded to then famine-stricken North Vietnam.

Most of the rice surplus became weevil-infested and unsaleable at any price. The several Burmese purchasing missions sent to

Eastern Europe seeking imports in return for Soviet barter credits ended up by contracting for 100,000 tons of Soviet cement. Much of it reached the port of Rangoon in May 1956, on the eve of the summer rains. With storage facilities inadequate for such a volume, the losses sustained on the Rangoon docks were substantial. Meanwhile the prices of cloth and other consumer imports rose rapidly due to short supply and to the falling value of the kyat.

In 1956 Nathan Associates seriously pondered the question of whether to advise any further substantial investments in state industry unless and until order was fully restored and administrative standards were improved. In the end they again advocated, in rather equivocal terms, continued pursuit of the second four-year plan as previously projected, provided essential reforms were made. They recommended in particular the encouragement of private investment and the generation of increased tax revenues to reduce growing deficits. The most practical suggestion, later adopted, was that the government offer price incentives to both peasants and millers for the delivery of superior quality paddy and milled rice suitable for export.

The concluding report prepared by the Nathan Associates when they were finally dismissed in late 1958 admitted important mistakes. It would have been better from the outset to have posited an alternative development schedule of more moderate dimensions to be followed if the essential conditions for accomplishing the larger scheme could not be realized. Meanwhile, the Russians made good Khrushchev's promises to build a modern tourist hotel on Inya Lake opposite the university campus and a technical institute located at Insein. A new sports stadium followed.

The Elections of 1956

The constitution of the Burma Union followed the British pattern of vesting the supreme executive authority in a prime minister responsible to majority support in the chamber of deputies. The president of the union was elected periodically by the combined action of the two houses of parliament, with the understanding that the choice would rotate between the major ethnic groups—a Shan, a Karen, a Burman, or a Kachin. The president would exercise residual authority during interim periods between cabinets, but the office was to be completely divorced from policy considerations. The various ethnic groups were also represented in the chamber of nationalities, in which the membership was allocated roughly in proportion to population size: two-fifths Burman, one-fifth Karen, one-fifth Shan, with the remainder shared between Kachins, Chins, and Karenni Kayahs. The constitution also followed the centuries-old British pattern of subordinating the military establishment to the civilian authorities.

The constitution was ostensibly federal in character. Three subordinate states were indicated for the Karenni, Shans, and Kachins, with a fourth promised for the lower Burma Karens. Chin areas were designated a special division. Membership within the several "state councils" was to include the ethnic group representatives elected to the chamber of deputies. But the chairmen of such councils were all appointed by the prime minister and were responsible to him. Any legislative actions by the several state councils were subject to suspensive veto by the president of the Union and to review on constitutional grounds by the supreme court of the Union. Except for revenues collected locally, the state budgets were controlled by the central authorities. The subordinate states were thus amenable to fairly strict financial control. But with all of its difficulties and qualifications, the Burman commitment to parliamentary democracy was for many a matter of genuine sincerity and concern.

The first real test of democracy came with the second general election, held in April of 1956. The AFPFL coalition still appeared to be in an unassailably strong position, due to its well developed nationwide political organization and its control over government services and funds. This surface appearance of strength was nevertheless deceptive because the ruling league hierarchy was split by rivalries both personal and organizational. Thakin Tin's All Burma Peasants Organization (ABPO) tended to overshadow the Trade Union Council (Burma) headed by U Ba Swe. The party leaders also differed with respect to policy alternatives and priorities, which actually involved control over the AFPFL organization itself. During the previous four years popular discontent had become widespread, but it was not organized and articulate. It related primarily to rising consumer prices alongside the glut of unsalable rice, buttressed by dissatisfaction with the government's fumbling performance generally. The countryside had not returned to orderly control, and exaggerated promises of welfare objectives were unrealized.

The only potent political opposition was the newly formed coalition known as the Nationalist Unity Front (NUF), sponsored by the leftist Burma Workers and People's Party. In the absence of any feasible alternative, the NUF attracted the support of a number of moderate opposition leaders, such as E Maung, who had held office briefly in 1949, and the popular brother of the deceased Aung San, Aung Than. The voting in 1956 was much less orderly than in 1951, with both the AFPFL and the opposition resorting to irregular tactics. Official intimidation was rife in the crowded urban areas, where the AFPFL candidates won overwhelmingly. But in central Burma opposition elements generated strong resistance. The NUF elected forty-seven of its own candidates, including E Maung, and commanded the allegiance of seven other elected members.

The 155 member AFPFL majority, plus their 28 allies, was more impressive in appearance than in actuality. For one thing, the majority was far from unified, and the popular vote was much closer than the total election victories indicated. The NUF alone registered two-thirds of the vote obtained by the AFPFL candidates, while the combined opposition vote amounted to 46 percent of the total. Embarrassed government apologists argued unconvincingly that the outcome had been influenced by intimidation and by foreign interference, presumably from the communist bloc. The government party had clearly lost face, a factor which served to exacerbate its own internal dissensions.

Premier Nu in particular was profoundly discouraged. The depressing election experience was added to the country's complete disarray in the economic field. He was personally vulnerable to charges that exaggerated efforts at religious revival, presumably calculated to establish the premier's personal reputation as a patron of Buddhism, had diverted both resources and energies from more basic considerations. The irregularities of the election campaign itself implied the almost complete repudiation of the high ethical and social standards which the Buddhist revival was supposed to help reestablish. The principal offenders were undisciplined local cadres of the AFPFL itself. Equally discouraging to the premier was the evident erosion of popular confidence in the ideals of democracy and socialism which he had so ardently championed. The Pyidawtha program had become the butt of popular derision. Apparently convinced that the deteriorating situation was headed for disaster unless drastic improvements were made in the performance of the AFPFL, Nu

decided in June to take leave for an indefinite period for the purpose
of instituting a political housecleaning. He spent much of the
ensuing eight months in his monastery retreat.

The particular target of U Nu's attack was the Socialist Party
headed by Kyaw Nyein, who was also minister of economic development and secretary of the AFPFL. In their initial private exchanges
in July 1956, Nu charged that the AFPFL was full of thieves and
that its very survival depended on the speedy elimination of corrupt
elements. He then engineered the replacement of Kyaw Nyein as the
league's secretary by Kyaw Dun, the new minister of agriculture,
while the latter's mentor, Tin, became deputy premier as well as
head of the peasants organization, or ABPO. Most of Nu's purge
victims were members of the socialist party faction. In rejoinder,
Kyaw Nyein accused Nu of being susceptible to flattery by wealthy
sycophants who had solicited political and other favors after contributing to religious and charitable causes. The acting premier,
U Ba Swe, tried to remain neutral in the quarrel, but he generally
disapproved of Nu's purging tactics. The Nu-Nyein feud continued,
so that economic efforts were subordinated to politics during the remainder of 1956. Nu's return to power in February 1957 was certainly not welcomed by Kyaw Nyein, but it did afford opportunity
to review policies. Reciprocal promises were exchanged at the time
to prevent political controversy within the cabinet.

During the ensuing year the policy pendulum tended to swing
back and forth. Nu realized a clear gain in March 1957, when he
completed longterm negotiations for an American Export-Import
Bank loan of some $25 million, coupled with Washington's con-
tribution of $17.3 million in surplus agriculture commodities,
mainly cotton. A portion of the cotton was processed into thread
in Japan, so that Burma's new textile factory could finally get into
production. Confusion developed in June, when Nu proposed that
the entire economic development program be set aside until requisite
preparations were completed for its effective implementation. At the
same time, he accepted a Soviet offer to send to Burma a team of Russian advisers on agriculture and industrial development, a move
which caused the cancellation of a previously scheduled World Bank
mission. A reappraisal of economic policy, finally undertaken in
September, advocated greater emphasis on the private sector of the
economy and on additional joint-venture projects, combined with
efforts to improve management and tax revenue collections. Such

ideas could have had no observable correspondence with available Russian advice. British sources contributed a pharmaceutical plant requested by Nu, but its immediate output of a surfeit of yeast tablets added to the government's embarrassment. Meanwhile, Kyaw Nyein completed his own prestige project of a small steel mill, only to be faced with the problem that Burma lacked both requisite iron ore and coal needed for its operation.

Administrative problems beset the entire governmental structure. The top level economic and social board, headed by Premier Nu and including Kyaw Nyein and Ba Swe, was overburdened with trivial details because no effective secretariat existed which could implement assigned tasks. Specific government industrial projects, including joint-venture efforts, were not accorded the necessary autonomy for determining wages, prices, and labor-management policies generally. The most successful mills produced at less than 50 percent capacity, plagued as they were by problems of raw materials, machinery parts, excessive costs, and political graft. The best managed were cotton textile factories, sugar mills, and timber processing. Transportation and communication improvement plans ran aground as did irrigation projects and brick and tile manufacture. A new jute mill produced high quality gunny bags from imported hemp fibre, but at prohibitive cost.

Government efforts to encourage diversified agricultural production were equally ineffective. Peasants were not interested in experimenting with chemical fertilizers, new crops, and possible tractor usage. Government-sponsored lectures urging year-round effort and more efficient cultivation methods attracted only perfunctory attention. Peasants liked the familiar rhythm of the planting and harvest seasons, Lenten holiday celebrations, all-night pwe dramatic performances, and the acquisition of jewelry and Buddhist merit. Agricultural output improved gradually between 1956–1959, but it owed little to governmental planning.

Premier Nu's popularity was widely acknowledged but not well articulated or deeply rooted. He enjoyed the backing of many traditionalists and anti-communists, but commanded no mass worker or peasant or organized business support. His oratorical utterances and ethical exhortations often had little practical relevance to governmental efforts or problems. A perceptive Rangoon editor characterized his pronouncements as "mess and muddle . . . with a beautiful dream sitting incongruously on top of it all." It did little good for Nu to denounce administrative shortcomings for which he himself took no personal responsibility and offered no remedial measures.

Political fragmentation developed within the government itself. Under the direction of the Socialist Party home minister, the military police became heavily involved in politics along with local home guard elements under similar control. By comparison, the army commanded by the forthright but pleasure-seeking General Ne Win functioned under its own power, while demonstrating little evidence of governmental ambition. The politically-motivated home guard was challenged in the countryside by irregular partisan elements supporting the peasants organization (ABPO) led by Tin. Lacking any mass based popular support, the economic development minister, Kyaw Nyein, undertook to generate political backing from the plethora of uncoordinated economic boards and corporations (some four score), whose shortcomings became the principal target of Premier Nu's anti-corruption campaign. Thus, the apparent muting of political friction at the center during 1957 was largely illusory.

A concerted effort to resolve political differences was initiated in January, 1958, with the assembling of a comprehensive AFPFL convention at the Peace Pagoda site, composed of some 2,000 assembled delegates. As the unanimous choice of president of the convention, Premier Nu appeared to be in full control. In his opening address, he espoused anew the socialist objectives of the constitution while flatly rejecting the infallibility of Marxist dogma, particularly its advocacy of class violence and dictatorial control. Trouble developed because the voting strength of the several delegations was weighted in accordance with the relative size of the mass organizations represented, a policy which gave inordinate influence to Tin's ABPO peasant representatives. Factional rivalry came to focus in the selection of party secretary, a contest involving Tin's protégé Kyaw Dun (agriculture minister) and Kyaw Nyein's follower Tha Kin (home minister). U Ba Swe tried to preserve some measure of unity by proposing that both candidates be excluded from the executive committee sessions. The final compromise arrangement was that Kyaw Dun would continue for the time being as secretary of the AFPFL with Tha Kin designated as joint secretary. The understanding was that the latter would assume full control after several months, when

Kyaw Dun was expected to retire. The party rift was only papered over.

The quarrel erupted again a month after the convention disbanded. At the apparent instigation of home minister Tha Kin, Premier Nu began a purge of political corruptionists by authorizing the arrest of some 450 culprits drawn from both ABPO and Socialist Party ranks. This move was followed by Nu's abrupt announcement that approximately one-fourth of the total public service employees would be dismissed—a measure aimed particularly at the overstaffed economic corporations and commissions under Kyaw Nyein. When it became evident in late March that Kyaw Dun had no intention of sharing the duties of the party secretaryship with Tha Kin, the pro-socialist executive council of the AFPFL authorized Kyaw Nyein to start recruiting his own militant youth corps to counter the physical pressure being exerted by ABPO partisans. Premier Nu countered by himself assuming the post of home minister while the incumbent That Kin was absent in India. The change involved Nu's direct assumption of control over the military police and local militia.

In the face of the threat of armed conflict, a third political compromise was arranged in early May via a monk mediator. Under the new agreement, the premier would stop juggling the ministries and postpone for six months the proposed massive reduction of the civil service staff. The final resolution of governmental control would be settled in early June in accordance with the constitution by action of the reassembled chamber of deputies. Both sides agreed that the loser would accept the forthcoming verdict and pledge not to resort to violence or strikes.

By May 20 it became evident that the majority of the cabinet ministers, led by Ba Swe, was aligned with the Socialist Party faction. A rough tally of the deputies indicated that some two-thirds of the AFPFL members, plus a majority of Karen and Kachin delegates also favored the Swe-Nyein faction. Within the ensuing two weeks Premier Nu made correspondingly drastic efforts to maintain his control over the chamber. His first move was to enlist the support of the near fifty NUF members by promising to undertake a general program of rebel pacification and amnesty, including not only minority and PVO dissidents but the hardcore communists as well. The army became particularly unhappy over this prospect.

Nu then solicited the support of 18 of the 27 Shan and Kayah autonomy-conscious representatives in the chamber, and the conservative Arakan contingent, which was also demanding a separate Arakan state. At the last moment, he cancelled court charges pending against two imprisoned NUF delegates for treasonable communication with the communist rebels, so that they could be present and vote. After a perfunctory debate lasting for the better part of three days, the chamber of deputies on June 9 voted 127 to 119 in favor of the premier's ramshackle coalition. The session was conducted in good spirit, and Nu promised in view of his narrow margin of victory to submit the issue to the people in a general election to be arranged in October, at the end of the ensuing rainy season.

Political Crisis, June to September 1958

In an effort to make good his various promises to the disparate elements of his parliamentary majority of June 9, Premier Nu spent a busy three and one-half months preparing for the forthcoming elections. His first significant policy move was to replace socialist cabinet colleagues with a variety of moderate conservatives. In an overt move to prepare for future constitutional revision, he then convened a series of sixteen seminar groups representing a variety of interests well outside the circle of the AFPFL coalition, including conservative economic and non-Buddhist religious elements. Each seminar group was invited to submit at the close of its session specific reform proposals. The most common complaints focused on administrative abuses and governmental interference in areas of trade, education, and industry. Peasant spokesmen suggested a return to monarchy as a means of ending partisan strife and mob rule.

Premier Nu's principal response to the plethora of reform proposals was to restaff the public service commission with experienced non-political personnel. He would broaden the scope of the authority of the commission to determine the selection of members of governmental economic boards and corporations. He also proposed that uneconomic business ventures should revert to private control and that the government's economic development program be reexamined. Time was lacking for the translation of any of these reform proposals into reality, quite apart from the fact that many were rather contradictory in character. Political power continued to reside in large measure with the organized mass groups, still strongly anti-foreigner and pro-Marxist in orientation. If a comparable program of reexamination had been initiated in 1955–1956, when socialist policies were clearly on the defensive, it might have had a chance for careful consideration. It could hardly be done during the hectic rainy season of 1958, when Nu had important political problems to face.

The premier's efforts to fulfill promises made in June to the NUF contradicted many of his moderate proposals. The Indemnity Act which he promulgated on July 31, for example, offered total amnesty to surrendering insurgent groups as well as pardon to criminal offenders and army deserters. The move was coupled with promises of free participation for all such groups in the forthcoming elections. The response was far from unanimous. The minor leftist Mon Peoples Front surrendered on the understanding that its demand for an autonomous Mon state in the Tenasserim area would be sympathetically considered by Nu if popular support for it could be demonstrated. These same terms were offered to the conservative Arakanese. Some PVO rebels accepted Nu's amnesty terms, but they asserted their new political identity as the new Peoples Comrade Party, with headquarters in Rangoon. The Karen Revolutionary Council and the Red Flag (Thakin Soe) communists indicated no interest in accepting Nu's offer. Than Tun's communist group wanted to negotiate as a legal equal, retaining its own land reforms and identity both politically and as a separate military unit, terms which were completely unacceptable to Nu.

The most disturbing reaction to the amnesty program was the anger it generated among army officers and the increasing tendency of the military to become involved politically. General Ne Win's personal reluctance to participate in partisan controversy was not shared by many subordinate officers, especially when they saw their erstwhile rebel enemies permitted full political participation. They resented in particular the increasingly aggressive role assumed by the leftist Burma Workers and People's Party and the even more revolutionary Youth Front group and the People's Comrade Party, all of which talked about resuming the aborted "people's struggle." As early as June 1958, the conservative Democratic Party of Ba Sein had advocated that the army assume temporary control in alliance with a non-communist coalition government until new elections could be held. The idea of an army caretaker regime gained much wider support in September, when political controversy intensified.

A series of events contributed to the eventual abandonment of election plans. One involved Nu's decision in late August to forego the special budget session of the chamber of deputies scheduled to convene on August 28, in favor of promulgating an emergency budget by presidential decree. The constitution prescribed that such an ordinance, to be fully legal, must be approved by vote of the chamber within forty-five days of its issuance, which would carry over into the election period. Responding to Nu's action, Kyaw Nyein, at a mass political rally held at Rangoon, denounced the premier for violating the constitution and demanded that his government resign forthwith. Army opponents of the premier's amnesty program also took up the cry of reverence for the constitution. Ba Sein partisans chimed in to denounce Nu's continuing alliance with the NUF, while the Sangha Party argued for a Buddhist state and for abandonment of negotiations with all Marxist elements. On the extreme left, the People's Comrade group and the Youth Front challenged NUF participation in Nu's government as a betrayal of their common Marxist objectives.

During mid-September the atmosphere of political controversy shifted to one of physical violence. Strife erupted on the Rangoon docks between worker groups representing Ba Swe's TUC (B) and a rival organization loyal to Nu. In the provinces, Socialist Party home guard elements provoked similar clashes with ABPO cadres and with the army itself. Meanwhile NUF agitators spread fantastic propaganda alleging that factions opposed to Nu (Ba Sein, Ba Maw, and Kyaw Nyein) were collaborating with an American fleet reportedly present in the Indian Ocean in a violent plot to seize control of Burma.

A final and more provocative contribution to the atmosphere of violence was the threat to seize Rangoon made on September 23 by officers within the military police establishment, just one day following Premier Nu's return from a political campaign tour of upper Burma. When army colonels on September 26 abruptly challenged the proposed action of the military police, the authority of the civilian government virtually collapsed. At this critical juncture, Premier Nu asked General Ne Win and the army to take over control temporarily, the move being subject to legal ratification by the reassembled chamber of deputies after October 28. Preparations for holding elections would presumably be completed within the ensuing six months, which was the constitutional limit for emergency control. The Burmese public heaved a sigh of relief that chaotic strife had been avoided and that the constitutional system remained intact, even if precariously so. U Law Yone, editor of the *Nation,* summed up the general mood on October 21, 1958: "The AFPF has been in power . . . too long. . . . Something radical has to happen in the way of change. . . . We are perhaps fortunate that someone cast in the mould of General Ne Win is available. . . . In ten years of misrule by a single party, this country has run itself down, so that very few have the vision and the energy to strive for worthwhile things."

The Record of the Caretaker Regime

The most significant early accomplishment of the military care-taker government was to restore governmental authority by the un-inhibited exercise of physical power. Everybody learned fairly quickly, whether overt rebels, youthful agitators, or political op-ponents, not to take liberties with General Ne Win. He halted the brawling at the docks abruptly and eventually set up priorities for the guidance of rival unions. Youth corps leaders who organized student demonstrations in downtown Rangoon to bemoan the aborted "people's struggle" were forced to stop such nonsense. The local leaders of the Workers and People's Party and a contingent of revolution-bent Comrade Party followers enroute to join the Than Tun communists, were all brought sharply to account. The noisy National Unity Front protests against the army takeover gave way within less than two weeks to concurrence in a respectful statement of political grievances drafted by E Maung. By the time the chamber of deputies reassembled on October 28 to legalize the army takeover, all of the above-ground opposition groups had renounced the use of force. The first important action of the caretaker govern-ment was to cancel Nu's earlier offer of amnesty to all rebel ele-ments. The Than Tun communists were formally outlawed as were the Muslim malcontents in Arakan.

Somewhat less edifying was the army's arrest of hundreds of political figures, accused on a variety of counts. Repression tended to focus on the NUF leadership, of whom more than one hundred were jailed. The "clean" AFPFL faction of Nu found some sixty of its leading members arrested. Kyaw Dun, for example, the former secretary of the AFPFL, was imprisoned on kidnapping and extortionist charges. The entire politbureau of the Workers and People's Party was arrested along with leaders of the Youth Front and the People's Comrade Party. Criminal accusations were also levied against the officers of Tin's All Burma Peasants Organization and the Socialist Party's home guard units. Ba Swe's TUC (B) got away with only four members arrested. Such actions were more political than anti-criminal in motivation. Trials lagged far behind arrests, so that all the Rangoon jails were filled and a new prison complex was built on an island far offshore. On the night preceding Premier Ne Win's scheduled commencement address at the University of Rangoon on December 18, six potentially troublesome student communist leaders were arrested in their dormitory rooms. The general's address berated the students for their disrespect of authority, for neglect of their studies, and for participating in newly forbidden political activities.

The next disciplinary step involved economic offenders. Non-Burmese merchant violators of existing currency-control regulations were arbitrarily exiled. At the same time, 750 Burmese firms that had defaulted on repayment of government loans were debarred from doing business, and some 1,400 import licenses issued in the names of Burmese acting as fronts for alien merchants were abruptly cancelled. A raid on alien bazaar stalls ended in the confiscation of large quantities of illicit imports. Eight million kyats (worth 20 cents each) of overdue loans granted by the agricultural marketing board were recovered from delinquent rice milling firms. Finally, train schedules were revived; ticketless riders on both trains and river steamers were subjected to arrest. The caretaker government obviously meant business.

Starting in late November, a concerted drive to clean up Rangoon was inaugurated. With the aid of volunteers, who included ex-Premier Nu on one occasion, garbage collection operations were staged on successive Sundays. The debris collected on a given day amounted to an estimated 1,000 tons of refuse, previously left to rats, crows, and ownerless dogs to explore. A second move was to distribute poisoned meat overnight at numerous spots in the city, an action which cleared the street of hundreds of pariah dogs. (Theoretically, the dogs were not being killed in violation of Buddhist ethics, for no one forced the meat on them.) Finally, a concerted effort was made by the government to clear the city of many blocks of squatter hutments long recognized as major fire and health hazards. Under militarily imposed deadlines and with the assistance of army trucks, approximately one-eighth of Rangoon's population was moved to three new sites prepared for occupancy in the suburbs. House plots, building materials, well water and sanitary facilities, plus connecting roads and commuter transportation were provided at government cost. The huge task was virtually completed by March 1959.

In view of the difficulty and extent of such housekeeping chores, General Ne Win declared in early 1959 that preparations for elections would have to be postponed. Governmental services and the army were in no mood to halt essential policing and anti-rebel activities just to arrange for the political luxury of party activities and voting procedures for scheduled April elections. Nu tried in vain to hold Ne Win to the April election deadline, but the general simply threatened to resign. The only feasible alternative would be for Ba Swe to take over the premiership, since Nu's 1958 majority had disintegrated, and to forego elections entirely for the time being. Be Swe himself conceded that the caretaker authorities needed more time for preparations. Consequently, on February 28, the chamber voted to suspend the constitutional article limiting emergency rule to six months and granted a full year's extension to the tenure of the army regime. Detached observers conceded that most of General Ne Win's disciplinary actions had been salutary and necessary, but many of the persons directly affected resented being pushed around in arbitrary fashion, especially those in jail who still awaited trial.

The new cabinet was smaller and non-political, including several highly respected high court justices, a number of experienced professional and business leaders, and university lecturers. The ministers were responsible to Ne Win alone, who permitted them wide latitude. Since they had no political debts to pay, they were able to assume a bold and effective stance. The minority ethnic groups in the parliament were permitted to select their own ministerial representatives.

One of the first moves of the cabinet was to impose a 10 percent profit ceiling on all retail prices and a 5 percent limit on wholesalers. The result was that consumer prices fell by a welcome 12 percent within four months. Government economy measures included a 5 percent budget cut across the board, a reduction in the number of state scholarship grants from 200 to 50, and the cancellation of numerous fledgling industrial projects which called for foreign exchange now unavailable. The cabinet also brought in the distinguished economist, Dr. Hla Myint of Oxford University, to be the new rector of the University of Rangoon as of January 1959. He had long been *persona non grata* to the AFPFL politicians because he had refused as a student to participate in the famous 1936 strike, but no one could doubt his superior competence. The new minister of labor established priorities covering the dock-worker problem, abolished the troublesome Railway Workers Federation, and flatly prohibited all political activity by workers employed on state projects. When the annual independence day celebration rolled around on January 4, 1959, the previously favored mass political organizations of the AFPFL were barred from participation.

Most of the expensive foreign advisory personnel were dismissed as an economy measure. Twelve of the fifteen Russian agricultural advisers were sent home on December 20. The twenty-odd Nathan Associates group members, present since 1952, were given three months to wind up their affairs; before departing they prepared seventeen detailed memoranda of economic recommendations of a type previously avoided by the group. They underscored the need to encourage the private sector of the economy in selected areas by expanding capital depreciation allowances, giving guarantees to alien investors against nationalization and for repatriation of profits, and according three-year tax exemptions for new projects of high priority with free importation of needed capital equipment. They also recommended that cultivators and rice millers be offered price incentives to produce superior quality grains for the export market. Timber extraction activities were to be conducted on a business basis under private direction. Partly as a consequence of such constructive advice, Colonel Aung Gyi, head of the Economic Development Corporation, allowed free trade in low grade rice and also inaugurated a dozen or more joint-venture projects with foreign firms during the course of the ensuing year. Two of the efforts involved Japanese participation in explorations for oil and in the construction of a mammoth electric-generating plant in the south Shan states area, which was to be a part of Tokyo's war reparations. These moves were particularly welcome in circles where "state socialism" had come to suggest both inefficiency and corruption.

A somewhat more dubious aspect of the new economic program was the increasing involvement of inexperienced army personnel in a variety of administrative tasks. Many of the assignments made to army colonels extended far beyond routine security responsibilities and the operation of the defence services institute. Colonels took over the chairmanship of the budget committee, the direction of the port of Rangoon, the railways, and air services. Others headed the labor board, the housing authority, the rural development agency, and mining activities. The army also took over a fumbling cooperative agency concerned with the procurement and distribution of fish and prawn food products, with initially favorable results. To assist in economic administration assignments the government sponsored a number of training seminars in bookkeeping and accounting, intended for service personnel and others. One colonel was asked to initiate a long-overdue land survey program, which was to continue for seven years.

The principal political decisions made by the caretaker regime were conservative but constructive. One move was to discourage minority group expectations of possible secession from the Union. The Shan Chief Sawbwas were persuaded under some pressure to surrender their hereditary status at a Taunggyi meeting in late April 1959. This was done in return for a pledge that Shan officials would be left in general control and be spared political meddling from Rangoon in the future. Arakanese and Mon expectations for such autonomy were discouraged, but in return for promised construction of a much-needed jetty for the port of Akyab in Arakan.

In foreign relations, Peking enlisted Ne Win's favor by extending early recognition to his regime and by the revival of border negotiations, moves which proved politically helpful against communist rebel operations. But the Chinese *rapprochement* ran aground because Burman opinion reacted negatively to Peking's invasion of Tibet and the expulsion of the Lama in the spring of 1959. Burmese relations with Soviet embassy personnel deteriorated in early 1959, because of malicious charges by an embassy official that the editor of *The Nation* had accepted an American bribe, resulting in a libel suit which drove the Soviet accuser to hide away within the embassy compound. (The suit incidentally, covered the same amount as the alleged bribe, and the proceeds to be derived from a possible favorable court judgment were assigned by the editor to the Dalai Lama Fund.) In June 1959, an information officer at the Soviet embassy

defected and managed to escape from Rangoon to Manila in an
American plane, after exposing numerous instances of local Russian
political intrigue. The net result was a significant improvement in
Burma's relation with the United States. It led to the conclusion of
several additional loan agreements covering improvement of waterways, construction of a Rangoon-Mandalay highway, and the building of an intermediate college campus a short distance from the university proper.

The Elections of 1959–1960

In mid-August 1959, Ne Win announced that preparations for
the postponed elections could be completed by the end of the year.
The move was accompanied by a gesture of deference to constitutional forms in his convening of the parliament for approval of the
cabinet-prepared annual budget. The document was accepted with
little or no change following five days of debate, after which discussion was permitted regarding other matters of legislative concern.
Parliament set the date for the general election on February 6.
Partly responsible for the general's decision to honor his promises
to respect constitutional forms was his personal dislike of the
onerous burdens of governmental administration. He felt with some
justification that the task of his caretaker regime had been credit-
ably performed, and he entertained neither the wish nor the intention of using the army or its locally sponsored Solidarity
Associations to influence the elections. These were intended to promote patriotic self-reliance and civil responsibility, from fire-fighting
to providing anti-insurgency intelligence. Army spokesmen announced categorically on August 24 that officers would not offer
themselves as candidates in the elections. Most indications suggested
that the Ba Swe "stable" faction would probably win and would be
willing to cooperate in promoting a moderate program of socialistic
development. The army's agreement to cooperate in free elections
did not mean that it was surrendering its assumed autonomy or its
monopoly of armed power.

The reactions of informed and responsible Burmese observers
were ambivalent. The educated elite, in the British tradition,
valued constitutional forms as an essential guarantee against the
abuse of power, while the populace generally resented army dictation. The life of the 1956 parliament would expire in 1960, so that

an election must be held if the constitution was to survive. On the other hand, many of the same observers were disturbed over the prospect that a revival of political controversy would mean a return to the administrative corruption, inefficiency, and jobbery, which had characterized the decade of AFPFL rule. A cabinet whose continued tenure depended on the support of quarreling factions within the parliament had previously demonstrated serious limitations. Some expressed hope that a strongly sanctioned executive authority might be generated which would be willing to support for an indefinite period a capable nonpolitical cabinet, such as that of 1959. But proponents of this alternative were asking for a major constitutional adjustment, which was ill-defined at best and hardly feasible to realize within the time available. At the moment, it was encouraging that the army was prepared to accept the election results, but on two implied conditions: that rebel trouble makers must be curbed, and that the economic role currently performed by army personnel not be shifted back abruptly to party patronage incumbents. Many officers of the army were contemptuous of politicians generally, and had come to appreciate some of the perquisites of power.

Although all parties were invited to participate, the election campaign inevitably developed in a contest between the followers of Nu and Ba Swe. The ex-premier willingly divested himself of the troublesome NUF following of the previous year and made an outright bid for conservative support. He took full advantage of popular opposition to army rule. Nu gave mildly qualified approval to partisan demands for a Buddhist state, including a Buddhist university. He also agreed to consider anew the Shan demand for quasi-independence and similar expectations advanced by other minority groups and geographical regions. He exploited in particular the favorably omened arrival in Rangoon of a white elephant calf, born in upper Burma in 1958. The event stirred deeply rooted emotional chords which were hardly subject to rational evaluation, and when the orator Nu raised Buddhism over Marxism he evoked a response from the average man which neither the army nor the socialists could possibly match.

As a party group, the Ba Swe "stable" AFPFL was better organized and also committed to a more articulate policy of economic development, but it had little chance of victory in a popularity contest. Nu was respected as a sincere Buddhist, as a politician who had tried to operate above the morass of corruption, and as a masterful orator. In both the initial elections for local candidates, held in December, and in the parliamentary elections in February, Nu's traditionalist Union Party won out convincingly over the more modern socialists. His return to political power as premier in March was nevertheless qualified. It did nothing to alter the actual locus of physical authority still posited in Ne Win's army command. Nu's victorious party also had little to offer in the form of planned economic development or continued improvement of governmental administration. Finally, Nu was heavily compromised by the campaign promises he made to Buddhist partisans and to minority ethnic groups. The sixties would bear eloquent testimony to continuing political confusion.

XI The Nineteen Sixties

Initially, Nu's second premiership was welcomed by the public as a relief from rigid military control. But he soon encountered serious difficulties in trying to carry out promises made during the election campaign. He failed to deal with disorders accompanying his attempt to make Buddhism the official religion of the state, nor could he curb student unrest. The army leadership viewed his regime as drifting toward social and political disintegration, and became convinced of this when Nu started negotiations with ethnic minority groups seeking autonomy within the Burma Union. On March 1, 1962, the army political faction seized power during the course of negotiations between Nu and Shan leaders. Ne Win declared the constitution abolished, dismissing both the assembly and the high court. Premier Nu and his cabinet associates were imprisoned or subjected to house arrest, along with all others who dared criticize the new order.

Unable to enlist the services of experienced civilian administrators in the task of devising an alternative governmental structure, Ne Win ended by accepting the offered help of several doctrinaire communist advisers. The new order which took final form in 1963 was ideologically Marxist, but without a communist party or any people's revolution. It also lacked capacity for creative initiative. While the ruling revolutionary council was concerned primarily with the task of emasculating the political and capitalist opposition, it also acted to exclude all foreign visitors, whether missionaries, traders, entrepreneurs, or mere travelers, thus reverting to the xenophobic pattern which had long been a tradition of the Burmans.

The economy fell apart in 1963–1964. Peasants and workers demonstrated no enthusiasm for imposed price and wage regimentation; thus many ceased producing items for export purposes and failed to repay government crop loans or to respect the retail trade monopoly of the official people's stores. The government retaliated by curtailing consumer imports and by affirming that uncooperative people would have to learn how to provide for their own needs. When students and monks dared to protest openly against army coercion, they were simply shot down. In 1963 the university was closed down for an entire year, while the curriculum was altered along Marxist lines.

In foreign relations General Ne Win pursued a neutral policy with respect to the cold war. He accepted continued delivery of small arms from the United States until 1971, drawing on balances available from old loans, while enlisting major technological assistance from Israeli sources. He was cautiously friendly with both China and the USSR, his major concern being not to afford China any legitimate excuse to intervene. Soviet influence tended to balance off Peking's continued covert support for the communist rebels still operating in central Burma and across the Yunnan border. Trouble developed with the Chinese embassy in mid-1967 over its efforts to influence local Chinese opinion by exporting aspects of the cultural revolution, but this disagreement was resolved in 1968.

Internally the government was able to exercise effective control within Burma proper, but not over peripheral areas. These included the Kachin state in the north and eastern portions of the Shan states (especially KMT opium distributors), plus the borders of Thailand. Some signs of relaxation of police control appeared in 1968–1969, but little came of the effort to revive constitutional forms. Ne Win resigned his army command in 1972, but continued very much in control. The economy staggered along, but apologists could claim that few Burmese were hungry and the country escaped the ravages of warfare, which had scourged their neighbors to the east. Economics resources still awaited development.

Premier's Nu's Second Chance

Because Nu was unable in 1960 to enlist the services of previous associates who were now members of the opposition Socialist Party, and was unwilling to continue with the nonpolitical personnel of the caretaker government, his new cabinet was both inexperienced and lacking in self-confidence. In any case, his government's mood was now to play down the planned economic program. The Union

Party majority in the parliament was actually a coalition of heterogeneous political segments, each having its own favorite objectives to pursue.

The one constant element in Nu's political posture was his concern to exhort and persuade rather than to coerce, which contributed to his inability or unwillingness to assert governmental authority when vigorously challenged. The contrast between Ne Win's unihibited resort to arbitrary power and Nu's tolerant rule became particularly evident in the case of religious partisans, student protesters, and ethnic minority spokesmen. Nu also made no effort to assert his theoretical control, as head of government, over the army command itself. He permitted numerous military personnel to continue their previously assumed responsibilities in state-operated economic agencies. More or less symbolic of the lackadaisical mood of the restored civilian regime was the early reappearance on the streets of Rangoon of garbage heaps and pariah dogs.

Premier Nu's democratic philosophy was portrayed in winsome fashion in his address delivered in November 1960, before the Indian Council of World Affairs:

> The democratic system of government, though most desirable, is at the same time the most difficult . . . to operate . . . Democracy simply cannot be forced on a people, however enlightened the rulers may be. The basic principles of democracy have to be applied in such a way as to suit the local conditions, local beliefs, and local customs. This means a slow process of gradual growth and . . . education of the people. . . . Most of the countries of Asia have been independent for just over a decade. This fact makes doubly unfair the question "Are Asians fit for democracy?" I suppose the correct answer to this question is: "Ask in a few hundred years time, and I will tell you whether not only the Asians but all other peoples of the world are fit for democracy. . . ." Having come to power by democratic means, many of our leaders have fallen prey to . . . evils and have thereby forfeited the confidence of their peoples. In a long established democracy, such a government would be thrown out at the next election if not sooner. . . . These same corrupted leaders are . . . often tempted to evade the democratic consequences of their conduct by adopting unfair means to perpetuate themselves in power. . . . In Burma, we have a saying, "Only a gold cup is good enough to hold a lion's fat." Similarly, only good men can successfully operate a democratic system of government.

Nu's second premiership of two years' duration was not without its positive achievements. In the field of agriculture, his more relaxed policy produced favorable results in the form of increased production for export purposes. He continued to offer price incentives, as previously initiated by Colonel Aung Gyi during the caretaker period, for the delivery of top quality grain suitable for export purposes. Port facilities at Rangoon were expanded during the ensuing two years to accommodate twelve ships at a time, so that 85 percent of the country's seaborne trade was handled at the capital. Exports in 1961–1962 attained the level of 3.7 million tons per year compared with the prewar level of 5 million tons. Rice made up two-thirds of the export volume, with teakwood second at 10 percent. A substantial beginning was also made in the production of wheat in upper Burma, which was classified as a preferred incentive crop. Around 100,000 acres of wheat were under cultivation by 1961–1962, and annual increments continued up to a 400,000 acre total and a 900,000 ton output in 1966. The government was the sole purchaser of exportable grain, with inferior qualities left for free domestic sale and consumption. For a variety of reasons and in spite of the increase in wheat exports, Burma's export total declined steadily following the peak year of 1961–1962. But the country's potential for agricultural expansion was clearly demonstrated. Burmese later recalled with nostalgia the final year of Nu's regime.

Few if any productive gains were realized in the industrial sector of the economy from 1960 to 1962. Except for providing peasant incentives, Nu continued to espouse theoretical socialist ideals. For him as for other Thakins, capitalism still carried the connotation of being exploitive and alien. In the Buddhist context dear to Nu's heart the legitimacy of artificially stimulated "desire" and personal aggrandizement was suspect on religious grounds. He was convinced that socialism, by contrast, could more readily be accommodated with traditional ethical values.

The attention of Nu's government during the first six months centered on the initiation and passage of the State Religion Bill. It would establish Buddhism as the official cult and make the study of Buddhism compulsory in all schools and teacher-training agencies. Religious enthusiasm was generated in repeated monk-sponsored rallies, proclaiming the merit of such endeavors, coupled with prayer sessions and women's meetings. Minority religious groups were discreetly restrained from voicing their opposition and fears. A month after the approval of the State Religion Bill in August 1961, Premier Nu undertook to redeem his promise of guaranteeing continued religious freedom for minority communities, thereby releasing a torrent of fanatical pongyi criticism. He then resorted to the ruse of staging a secret predawn passage of the religious freedom constitutional amendment in order to escape threatened picketing. When the tactic was belatedly discovered, pongyi-led mobs attacked a number of Indian Muslim mosques within the city. Confronted with overt criminal violence, politically motivated, Nu could not bring himself to employ force to sustain the authority of his government. His repeated appeals for national unity and cooperation had no discernible effect in stemming the disorders.

At the end of his first year in office, the discouraged premier resigned his political post as president of the Union Party in favor of Thakin Tin. In January 1962, Tin succeeded in cornering all of the seats in the executive council of the party for his ABPO peasant union followers. This move offended many progressive observers as well as the increasingly restive army command.

Premier Nu's second major problem was to reach a political accommodation with minority groups who were asking for qualified freedom from majority Burman control. He selected a panel of jurists and lawyers to review the possibility of altering the constitutional framework in the direction of less centralized control. Groups inhabiting frontier regions would be guaranteed some kind of representation in a proposed national security council. Being committed by his campaign promises to consider the feasibility of decentralizing power. Nu was greatly concerned that minority groups should be encouraged to trust majority Burman elements, so that an all-pervading nationalist sentiment could be generated in time. For this reason, he accorded tolerance to the National Liberation Alliance which had been formed in 1960 by representatives of the Karens, Kachins, and Shans.

During 1961, two draft constitutional amendments were prepared which would grant qualified autonomy within the Burma Union to the Mon area of Tenasserim and to the province of Arakan. A conference was also held at Taunggyi, capital of the Shan state, to consider the more difficult problem of Shan demands for self-government. It included representatives of the several major ethnic groups inhabiting the region, but its principal leaders were Shan. A subsequent session for Shan representatives was scheduled for Rangoon in early 1962. It was on the latter occasion that the army intervened to seize control of the government.

A minor but significant incident was Nu's abrupt dismissal of Dr. Hla Myint, the university rector who had been brought in by Ne Win's caretaker cabinet. Prior to Hla Myint's dismissal Nu simply asked him to explain his uncooperative role during the 1936 university strike. This reference to the earlier student strike provided a signal for the revival of political agitation on the campus, in a complete reversal of Ne Win's requirement of proper student respect for authority. Such expressions of student unrest were regarded by the army leadership as additional evidence of social disintegration under Premier Nu's overpermissive regime. The premier on several counts was thus losing effective political control.

The Military Coup of March 1962

Impatient army observers, who had been waiting off stage since 1960 under restraint from Ne Win, while looking for some opportunity to reassert control, found an excuse in the convening of the Shan state conference at Rangoon on March 1, 1962. The distinguished Shan delegation included the former president of the Burma Union, Sao Shwe Thaike, who, like the others, had come in good faith hoping to formulate an acceptable pattern for the autonomy of the Shan state. Ne Win professed to see in the conference agenda the threat of complete disintegration of the Union. The army's intervention on March 2 was sweeping and abrupt. Premier Nu and most of the cabinet members were arrested immediately and held indefinitely without trial, along with all representatives of the Shan delegation. Also included among the fifty-three persons seized at the time were Chief Justice Myint Thein, Thakin Tin of the ABPO, and the Karen ex-president of the Union, Mahn Win Maung.

In explanation of his action, Ne Win declared flatly that the integrity of the Burma Union was in danger and that parliamentary democracy had proved to be unsuited for Burma. He therefore suspended the constitution and disbanded both the elected assembly and the chamber of nationalities. He also abolished the supreme court and the high court, substituting military tribunals in their

place. Six weeks later, he forced the representatives of the American
Ford and Asian foundations to depart the country and suspended
the operations of the Fulbright foundation. The same xenophobic
tendency was also reflected in Ne Win's curtailment of the English
language training program previously conducted by the USIS and
the British Council.

The army coup generated no effective protest, partly because
physical resistance was impossible in any case. The authority of the
civilian government was in such disarray that potential protesters
lacked both popular backing and self-confidence. The general mood
was one of reluctant acquiescence. The possibility of territorial
disintegration of the union was a valid concern, and Ne Win's
previous record as head of the caretaker regime had not been all
bad. The military command in general was rural rather than urban,
secularist rather than religiously committed, and seemed to be still
strongly anti-communist and anti-rebel. Some observers hoped that
a second limited exhibition of disciplined chauvinism by the army
might serve to restore Burma's lost sense of cohesion, bridging
political and racial rifts, and contributing to economic recovery.
The immediate evidence suggested that Ne Win's basic objectives
were political rather than ideological. He was determined to prevent
the prospective breakup of the Union of Burma, to eliminate alien
middlemen in the commercial sphere, and to establish state control
over the economy for nationalistic ends.

The Emerging Burmese Way to Socialism

The new regime's blueprint issued on April 30, 1962, was entitled
The Burmese Way to Socialism. The full implications of its political
pattern were unclear, and its authorship was not indicated. Several
suspected the pen of Thein Pe Myint. The word *Burmese* in the
title clearly had to be underscored. In an ostensible endeavor to
suppress exploitive capitalism, a system of social justice was designed
theoretically to free the people from all material anxieties including
food, shelter, clothing, and employment needs. The plan would
endeavor to achieve a balanced development of all available resources, including labor, raw materials, technical abilities, and the
instruments of production. The state itself or group cooperatives
functioning under national planning control would eventually
monopolize or direct the use of the means of production. The

profit motive would thus be eradicated, along with easy living, public freedom of criticism, and bureaucratic bottlenecks. Traditional educational objectives and religious sanctions to morality would be promoted, but bogus acts of charity and hypocritical piety would not be tolerated. All indigeneous ethnic groups, regardless of origin, religion, or language, would hopefully become united by a comprehensive patriotic bond. A monolithic political organization to be called the Burmese Socialist Programme Party would direct the new program, while the armed forces would support and defend the new order.

Executive leadership of the new regime was lodged in a revolutionary council, to which Ne Win at the outset hoped to recruit experienced personnel who would cooperate in directing the undertaking as outlined. But the response he received was largely negative. A few of the less skeptical AFPFL leftists and ABPO peasant group leaders came forward, but the original membership of the revolutionary council was almost entirely military. The council was supposed to extend its disciplinary control downward through successive lower levels of party cadres to the eventual peasant and workers councils (soviets), which would be created in due course. Army-controlled economic and governmental agencies, functioning under the council's direction but each one enjoying a considerable degree of operational autonomy, would take the place of the capitalist business community.

The Marxist character of the new regime was not easy to explain. Ne Win himself could not have been the author of *The Burmese Way to Socialism,* for he was not a doctrinaire Marxist nor a theoretical ideologist in any sense. The anti-democratic sentiment within the army command had apparently gained considerable momentum prior to the coup of March 2, and the term socialism was used to provide a cover for army dictatorship. The leftward drift of the army had begun in 1960–1961. For example, the intelligent and pro-western Colonel Maung Maung was ousted from the army leadership in late 1961. He was destined to return years later as an apologist for Ne Win. The democratic socialist Brigadier Aung Gyi who had served well during the caretaker period and now tried to oppose the full nationalization of the economy, did not last out his first year in the revolutionary council hierarchy. The relentless drift toward a communist pattern of economy, with the army rather than the usual party hierarchy acting in support, was probably due less to initial design than to the logic of events.

The only political group which eventually responded with some enthusiasm to Ne Win's appeal to collaborate with the revolutionary council was the National Unity Front and its associated Marxist theoreticians. The educated elite generally and most officials of previous governments stubbornly objected to the imposition of army dictatorship, however much they may have sympathized with declared socialist goals. Judges, minority leaders, bureaucracy, faculty and students, the press and the business community, and eventually the monks all refused to respond to invitations to support the Burma Socialist Programme Party. The army-sponsored national solidarity associations, carrying over from the caretaker period, enlisted even fewer recruits than in 1959. All of the minority groups distrusted army-imposed Burman domination and moved toward overt rebellion. Thus the NUF volunteers and the fractional communist-oriented army leadership led by Brigadier Tin Pe and Colonel Than Sein gained political ascendancy within the council largely by default, in the absence of any serious political competitors.

The Burma Socialist Programme Party was in fact a projection of the military government itself. In the absence of any means of independent financial support for the party, the revolutionary council decreed in October 1963 that party leaders should draw on the governmental budget to cover both party expenses and their personal needs. The reason given was that party workers dedicated to the improvement and well-being of the working class as a whole should not have to worry about providing their own food, clothing, and shelter. Burma's socialist utopia pattern was thus applied from the outset on a selective basis. From the start, the army program lacked the capacity to enlist popular cooperation, to improve governmental efficiency, or to achieve progressive economic development. The new order was also surprisingly puritanical in character. It denounced all bourgeois vices such as horse racing, public gambling, beauty contests, and westernized dancing performances. Golf and soccer football survived along with the traditional all-night dramatic pwe performances.

The program devised norms for educational accomplishment which stressed sciences and technology as contributing more directly to social and economic progress. Religion must also be made to serve the socialistic objectives espoused by the new government. National accomplishment as well as personal destiny were to be determined not by Karma but mainly by intelligence and industry, no matter how much Buddhism may have contributed historically to Burma's social and cultural values.

Problems of Pacification and Control

The first demonstration of General Ne Win's ruthlessness took place on the university of Rangoon campus shortly after the opening of the new school year in June 1962. A student protest against the so-called 3-F ruling (requiring dismissal of the student who had failed his examinations three consecutive times) turned into a riot on July 6, which threatened the campus residence of the rector. When the assembled police proved unable to establish control through the use of water hoses and tear gas, they requested active army support, which was initially denied. After one local magistrate had refused the request of the military unit to authorize the use of firearms, General Ne Win himself gave the fateful permission. The troops fired point blank into the student rioters and then pursued the fugitives into the dormitories nearby. It was a gruesome affair. Arriving army trucks hauled away several score corpses and picked up hundreds of the wounded.

When the still defiant students later placarded the premises of the university student union with insults levelled at Ne Win and his recently estranged wife, the general authorized the building's total destruction early the following morning. Thus on July 7 the symbol of student freedom since 1928 was destroyed. The university was closed for a month in the face of angry hostility against the military government. When trouble again developed at the opening of the second term of the following year, in November 1963, the university was again closed down, this time for an entire year. The government then implemented a complete reorganization of both curriculum and regulations, following patterns consonant with the socialist aims of the revolutionary council. It was divided into a number of autonomous institutes, to which student applicants were arbitrarily assigned corresponding to their aptitudes and to state needs.

Meanwhile, the several minority rebellion movements got increasingly out of hand. Much of the eastern portion of the Shan plateau fell from Rangoon's control. Shan hostility increased following the death in November 1962, of the imprisoned Sao Shwe Thaike. The Kachin rebellion had revived in the extreme north of Burma in late 1961, partly in response to Premier Nu's move to make Buddhism the state religion. Most of the educated Kachins were Christian rather than Buddhist, since Baptist and Catholic missionaries had won many converts among them. Ethnic distrust was thus buttressed by religious differences. Government forces could neither corner nor suppress the Kachin Independent Army. The most vigorous contingent was commanded by the charismatic Zaw Seng, who operated along the China border to the east of Myitkyina. Other Kachin rebel elements as well as Shan groups maintained limited contacts with the outside world via northern Thailand. The Karen peoples of lower Burma were equally distrustful of Burman rule, but they had pretty largely shot their bolt in the abortive rebellion of 1949–1951. They were incapable of mounting any unified effort to challenge the army dictatorship. Even so, Karen-inhabited border areas contiguous to Thailand ceased to be under effective control by Rangoon.

In June 1963 Ne Win set up the first of a series of conferences designed to pacify dissident elements through direct negotiations. Under promises of safe conduct, leaders of the various rebellious groups met with government spokesmen at Rangoon. Ne Win promised the Burman communists full amnesty, plus an opportunity to participate in his new revolutionary Marxist regime. The Than Tun White Flag groups still wanted recognition of their full administrative control over occupied areas, including the preservation of land reforms and other changes previously realized. The truce terms which were accepted by a conservative Christian Karen group in March 1964, promised in vague fashion that "at some opportune moment" in the future the government would assemble a convention of representatives of the minority peoples to draft a new constitution, although presumably still along socialistic lines. Ne Win also agreed to examine the possibility of extending the boundary of the existing Kawthulay state to include adjacent areas also occupied by Karens. The negotiating Karens hoped that such tentative promises might provide a possible basis for eventual peace. The government in turn hoped that the truce terms accepted by the Karens might provide a pattern which would prove a acceptable to

Kachin and Shan dissidents as well. The expectations of both sides proved to be ill founded.

Starting in late 1962, the revolutionary council began a persistent effort to exclude from Burma all alien business and professional personnel, particularly Indians and Pakistanis, including many who had long made their homes in Burma. Resident Indians were obliged to pay an annual foreign registration tax equivalent to $10 on pain of deportation. Applications for citizenship for such residents cost the prohibitive sum of $50, plus bribes to expedite the handling of their applications. Few aliens had the resources or the will to contest their individual rights in court, where the prospects for favorable decision were minimal in any case. It was estimated that within the ensuing four years (1963 to 1967) some 177,000 Indians and Pakistanis were excluded. Every precaution was taken to prevent the deportees from taking their savings, even to the point of X-raying their stomachs at the airport.

It was around August 1963, that the Ne Win dictatorship gave up its half-hearted attempt to negotiate with critics and rebels, and decided to suppress them. Among those arrested in that month were the socialist democratic leaders of the old AFPFL, U Ba Swe and U Kyaw Nyein, along with U Chan Tun, eminent Buddhist lay leader and former chief justice, and the leading newspaper critic and editor of *The Nation,* U Law Yone. Their main offense had been to criticize what the government was doing. Policy determination thereafter fell to several doctrinaire Marxists, sponsored by Brigadier Tin Pe, who had served briefly as minister of mines under the caretaker regime but had never achieved any personal distinction. His principal army supporter was Colonel Than Sein, and the leading theoretician was U Ba Nyein, a student of econometrics and a thoroughly committed follower of Mao Tse-tung's brand of communism.

The Drift Toward Communist Economic Policy

As long as Brigadier Aung Gyi continued influential in the revolutionary council in his role as minister of commerce, the program of nationalizing the Burma economy proceeded on a moderate pragmatic basis. He carried over into the 1962 growing season the policy of granting incentives for the delivery of exportable grain, so that cultivation expanded during the year by 84,000 acres. The year's crop permitted the export of 1.8 million tons of rice, a postwar peak. Aung Gyi's effort to obtain approval for continued offering of price incentives ran aground in the spring of 1963, when the seventeen-member revolutionary council vetoed the proposal. Protestations resulted in his abrupt exclusion from the cabinet and the council in March 1963. Special arrangements for exportable rice were ended in July, with no premium prices allowed thereafter.

The principal opponent of the incentive policy was the Marxist civilian economist U Ba Nyein. As an ardent Maoist, he stressed the need for an economy dedicated unreservedly to the welfare of the working class. He and his military supporters in the revolutionary council argued that Burma's aborted revolution under Premier Nu had run aground on political fragmentation, administrative corruption, and general confusion of goals. The gains which had seemed to be emerging in 1961–1963 were accruing not to the worker and peasant masses, but rather to a restricted urban elite, whose selfish objectives corresponded to those of the alien business community generally. A second revolution must therefore be fostered with determined zeal to replace the existing superficially socialistic and therefore fraudulent economic order. During 1962, the clique of Brigadier Tin Pe had managed the elevation of a number of democratically inclined and economically moderate officers; Aung Gyi was among the last of those to be forced from power, in 1963.

The new revolutionary goals were drastically thoroughgoing and doctrinaire. All "economic insurgents," especially the alien middlemen, must be eliminated from control of the market. In the absence of such experienced indigenous entrepreneurs, the state itself would have to direct and control both the productive and the distributive aspects of the economy. The plan was to enlist the participation of locally developed cooperatives and communal peasant and worker agencies to function under central direction to insure that market control by "insurgents" be prevented. The assumed gains realizable from a fully socialized order could eventually be devoted to meet the educational and health needs of the people and to provide additional capital improvements and transportation facilities. The consumer demands of the urban elite would have to be sharply curbed in order to give priority to production within Burma of the essential needs of all the people. Only in such fashion could Burma hope to achieve independence of both foreign capital and overseas sources of supply. Ba Nyein's scheme had little relevance to economic reality.

Ba Nyein and Brigadier Tin Pe inaugurated in 1963 a persistent program of governmental and newspaper indoctrination in support of their goals, but without a little red book to circulate or any credentials of personal sacrifice on their own part to display. They convened a series of annual seminars attended by selected representatives of either peasants or workers for the purpose of explaining governmental objectives and soliciting cooperation in realizing socialist goals. Ba Nyein held out the promise that as soon as a satisfactory level of cooperation could be achieved, he would sponsor the creation of two nationwide councils (soviets), one for peasants and the other for workers, to share in policy determination and economic control. Pending such time, he would continue to oppose all "working class enemies," especially the alien money-lenders and traders. Such exhortations failed to arouse any affirmative response. Workers complained about wages, peasants about grain prices, and both about the shortages of consumer goods. In actuality, a new privileged elite appeared in time in the Socialist Programme Party itself, numbering at its early peak only 9,000 members. All officials at the higher echelons of government and army command had to be either full members or persons acceptable to the party. Probationary candidates for membership as of 1967 numbered around 185,000, including 54,000 army officers, but few of them down to 1971 were ever adjudged worthy of full membership The ruling revolutionary council was itself impervious to public opinion.

The imposition of state control over the economy accelerated in 1963–1964. The government took over with minimal compensation all private banks and trading companies, plus the surviving remnants of large British corporations. The latter included approximately two score joint-project operations previously sponsored by Aung Gyi for the Burma Economic Development Corporation under the caretaker regime and by Premier Nu himself. The facilities thus acquired were now assigned to a variety of governmental agencies, despite the absence of competent personnel to manage most of them. Among the foreign banks which were forced to liquidate were two operated by the People's Republic of China. The action may have been intended to reduce Peking's control over the credit resources available to the Chinese business community of Rangoon. Starting with the growing season of 1963, government lending agencies undertook to provide the funds needed by peasants to finance the year's rice crop. The results were largely negative. In the industrial and mining sectors of the economy and in transportation services, an estimated one thousand firms closed down during 1963, leaving some two million workers without employment.

Inefficiency and bungling appeared everywhere in the burgeoning public sector of the economy. Management and technological experts were simply not available to replace previous operators. Required fuel and raw materials were not supplied where and when needed. Spare parts for broken machinery could not be found. The state agricultural marketing board, which assumed a complete monopoly of the rice trade, was notoriously inefficient, keeping no adequate accounts, not even a careful inventory of goods on hand. When the amount of rice available for export began to decline progressively from year to year, the volume of imports was arbitrarily cut proportionately, at the expense of acquisition of needed machinery, replacement parts, motor vehicles, raw materials, and consumer goods generally. The decline of business was also reflected in the 70 percent fall in newspaper advertising within a few months during 1963.

More of the same came in 1964. The government assumed not only a complete monopoly of foreign trade but also control over the sale of essential consumer commodities, including salt, rice, cloth, cooking oil, and electrical supplies. Governmental distribution facilities for such necessities proved highly deficient. Meanwhile, the persistently conservative fiscal policy left around 10 percent of available foreign credits unused, so that foreign currency reserves actually increased in 1964 because imports were so heavily curtailed. Since private investment opportunities were nil and purchasable goods in short supply, savings deposits also increased and internal debt, both public and private, declined. But such apparent gains were deceptively temporary.

In May 1964 the revolutionary council declared that all circulating currency notes of 50 kyat denomination and above were no longer legal tender and must therefore be exchanged for newly printed currency. The move was designed to expose wealthy "class enemies" and to place wealthy hoarders under governmental control. Large holders obtained only a portion of their new currency immediately, the balance being held back as a means to facilitate tax collections. Those who dragged their feet or who were suspected of trying to evade the decree were liable to arrests and fines. Actually, the regulation was widely evaded, although government tax collections were facilitated by the move. Ba Nyein took advantage of the event to explain again to his favorite mass audience the beneficent aspects of governmental policy and to solicit more active cooperation from favored peasant and worker classes. During the ensuing year, the nationalization of retail sale operations started in Rangoon and proceeded northward in its implementation.

In the same year of 1964, General Ne Win moved to restrict the entry of foreign visitors and reporters. He said he did not want outsiders looking on while "housecleaning" was in progress. Travelers who did gain entrance were usually deterred from venturing outside Rangoon, and journalists who wrote stories critical of the regime were forbidden reentry. Ordinary visas were limited to 24 hours. Burmese who corresponded with foreigners were regarded by the authorities as suspect. Resident diplomats had to request permission from the Rangoon foreign office for travel outside Rangoon and to submit a preliminary agenda covering whom they intended to see and the topics to be discussed. All Burmese officials and party members had to seek permission before issuing or accepting invitations to social events, and they were required to report subsequently the substance of all conversations with foreigners. Wiretapping was widely used as a means of espionage. When classes were resumed at the university in November 1964, after a year's suspension, all political activity was strictly forbidden. Ne Win may have had little to do with formulating economic policy, but he made it clear that he would permit no expression of dissent.

Continued Economic Decline

Private business and industrial establishments which were not nationalized gradually died out because of imposed regulations which denied them raw materials and machinery parts. Former employers known to have property and savings were obliged to keep their workers on the pay rolls, even though business operations were completely discontinued. The sixteen banking institutions (down from 32) became virtually indistinguishable from the treasury units of the several administrative districts. Selected banks were assigned to meet the functional needs of private industry, agriculture, and foreign trade. The Union Bank supplied the government with needed cash by buying its bonds. Meanwhile, tax revenues and the receipts of the expanding people's stores were put into the same till. The principal economic decline sustained in 1965–1966 was due to a 40 percent cut in the volume of imports. This negative development was due in part to governmental inefficiency in ordering items which were urgently needed for production. The total domestic output suffered a 3 percent loss for the year, especially evident in the virtual collapse of the once-profitable teakwood industry. A few gains were registered in 1967–1968 by the government-operated People's Oil Company, as a result of successful drilling operations conducted by Rumanian technicians along the lower Arakan coast and in adjacent areas offshore. The achievement was qualified by the threat of seasonal typhoons in the region.

The decline of agricultural output was far less drastic in volume than that of industry, but the results affected more people and were therefore politically more important. The complete ineffectiveness of the government's agricultural credit program and its associated policy of monopoly purchase of the rice crop was amply demonstrated. Cultivators had little incentive to produce efficiently, since in the absence of effective oversight the per-acre credit loans which were advanced by installments during the course of the crop season could be used for other purposes. Many cultivators resorted to broadcast planting instead of the laborious transplanting procedures essential for a normal crop. Credits thus came too easily; supervision of the utilization of the loans was casual at best; the government's monopoly purchase price for rice was very low. Loans advanced to the cultivators, often not repaid, put more money into circulation than could be absorbed by the limited volume of consumer goods available from legal sources of supply. Black market prices soared.

The average cultivator had several options open to him. He could sell his entire rice surplus to the government for 350 kyats per one hundred baskets, realizing little profit and risking being shot by insurgents. Alternatively, he could sell to the insurgents or black marketeers for 480 kyats per one hundred baskets, incurring official abuse and the denial of cloth and salt rations for the year. A third alternative was to sell minimal quantities to the government, sufficient to procure rationed items, and to hoard for barter purposes the rest of the surplus over family consumption needs. The net result of the latter tactic was to deny to the government an expanding volume of exportable rice needed to provide foreign exchange for the purchase of essential imports. The rice export figure dropped progressively from the high of 1.8 million tons in 1963, to 1.3 million in 1965, to 1.1 million tons in 1966, to .6 million tons in 1967 and only .3 million tons in 1968.

U Ba Nyein continued to stage his futile annual seminars. The one held in the spring of 1966 was typical. It included some 2,000 peasant representatives. Government spokesmen extoled their proletarian policy: cultivator credits, some 4,000 tractors available at 78 stations, the provision of fertilizers and pesticides, and favored peasant access to rationed consumer supplies. The landlord and moneylender enemies of the masses were being denied any share of the crops and interest collections, and family plots were being enlarged. The spokesmen then bemoaned the fact that the cultivators' response to such favored treatment had been disappointingly negative, so that disciplinary measures would have to be enforced. Peasants must repay their crop loans and would have to stop transferring paddy land to banana and pineapple production; they must also maintain water control systems and make more adequate use of the tractor station services. Peasant spokesmen replied that the rental cost of tractors was too high, that the deep Russian plows cut through the soil pan and caused the water to drain away, that the price paid for their paddy was too low, and that consumer goods were costly and not adequate for their needs. Others denounced the arrogant attitude displayed by both civilian officials and army officers. Burmese peasants thus made poor Maoist enthusiasts.

An opportunity to reconsider the completely ineffective economic control system came in late 1967, when a serious consumer rice shortage developed prior to the harvesting of the new crop. Rice riots developed in some twenty towns. For a limited period the government relaxed its controls over a number of consumer items in short supply, permitting the urban population to buy food directly from peasant suppliers at open market prices. Private traders were also permitted temporarily to handle important staple items at prices above those legally enforced at the people's stores, but considerably below the black market rate. But former restrictions were reimposed as soon as the new crop was harvested in early 1968. Peasants thereafter began systematically to withhold rice for barter use, from government purchasing agencies, up to an estimated 70 percent of total production in 1966–1968. Meanwhile rice available for export purposes fell from 30 percent to a mere 6 percent of total production during the same years. Despite accompanying cutbacks of 50 percent in consumer imports, Burma's international currency reserves fell in 1969 to one-half of their previous total.

Distribution Problems: the People's Stores

The imposition of state control over virtually all essential aspects of retail trade in 1964–1965 contributed much to the situation of economic shock manifested during the ensuing years. Adding to the total scarcity of consumer goods was the government's inability to move available supplies expeditiously. The net result was a thriving black market. At the local level, the government operators of the people's stores had little or no incentive to do an efficient and conscientious job. They got the same 82 kyats per month wage ($17) regardless of their performance. Unable to live on their salaries, most of them augmented their incomes by disposing of portions of their supplies to the black market operators. Distribution to remote areas was particularly bad, so that travelers leaving Rangoon by whatever conveyance included soap, cloth, and salt in their luggage. Light bulbs and other electrical appliances were distributed whenever available only to persons who deposited the burned out item which had to be replaced. Moth balls and dry cell batteries were unobtainable. The person at the head of the textile queue took only the item of cloth which happened to be on top of the pile.

Playing the people's stores became an exasperating game. For the less industrious, queuing up at the stores developed into a kind of new vocation. Participants could realize a quick 10 percent profit on whatever the stores had to offer by disposing of the goods to private dealers operating around the corner. This was far more than paddy farmers could earn and much less arduous work. Sometimes goods in short supply were distributed on a lottery basis, to

be exchanged later in the black market for whatever the lucky
winners might happen to need. The Burmese kept their sense of
humor just the same. The pwe performance comedian, in reply to
the clown's persistent questioning, explained that the bandits
featured in the previous act had all found jobs of late in the
people's stores. A typical complaint in the *Guardian* of May 30,
1968, ran in part as follows:

> It is glaring as daylight that our parasites get their stuff through
> links and connections with the respective branches of the govern-
> ment. . . . Many individuals are making a great deal of money,
> while others are . . . worrying for tomorrow's food. . . . We
> Burmans have the habit of making a lot of noise over something
> from the start and gradually forgetting the whole thing the next
> day.

The failure of the government's production and distribution policy
was freely admitted even by General Ne Win himself, who declared
that economic conditions were indeed "in a mess." It was quite
another thing for him to do something about it. U Ba Nyein continued to berate the annual workers' and peasants' seminars for
lack of popular cooperation, implying that the accompanying
privations were part of the discipline needed to obtain their com-
pliance.

The growing dissatisfaction with "the Burmese way to socialism"
was reflected obliquely in the occasional column which Ne Win
allowed to appear in the controlled press of Rangoon. Three such
items can be cited for 1967 and 1968. In November 1967, an officer
on special duty in the ministry of national planning, U Chan Aye,
was permitted to comment freely on the inadequacies of the budget
recently submitted by the revolutionary council. He denounced the
budget report as self-deceptive in refusing to recognize the serious-
ness of the economic crisis and in treating it as merely a temporary
problem. Burma's agriculture could survive only if minimal incentives were restored by permitting free internal trade in grain, and
by removal of governmental controls over all consumer items except
the most critical raw materials, especially the complete decontrol
of salt, *ngapi* (fish paste), and prawns. Available investment funds
should be allocated as interest-bearing loans wherever they would
be most productive, and public enterprise must be reorganized into
manageable autonomous units. Continued budget balancing by
curtailing the import of essential productive facilities was folly.

The author concluded by calling for the convening of a high level conference to consider basic reform problems.

A second critical column appeared in the *Working People's Daily* of January 1968. It was contributed by Thakin Ba Thoung, one of the venerable founders of the Thakin Party and the author of Burma's national anthem. His attack was levelled primarily at the revolutionary council's security and administrative committee, in charge of supervising local government and conducting police surveillance. Thakin Ba Thoung likened Ne Win himself to a Roman dictator and challenged the security control system as "unnecessary, uncalled-for, and amateurish." What was needed was not the release of more political prisoners but permission for ordinary citizens to be free to earn a livelihood by trading, and the abolition of police threats to cancel ration cards unless ward committees kept security officials informed of every move made by persons within their assigned areas. No emergency existed to justify such punitive measures; socialism must not be equated with the denial of normal and necessary personal freedoms. Police interference in penalizing the efforts of citizens to make a living was allegedly compounded by official "inefficiency, highhandedness, and bureaucratic corruption." A third complaint in the form of a letter to the editor in May 1968 argued that "power intoxication and its complications, haughtiness and conceitedness, are now the worst obstacles in our march toward our cherished goal." Conceit was preventing the government from facing the facts in the serious crisis enveloping the agricultural sector of the economy.

The following editorial comment in the May 30, 1968, *Guardian* newspaper reflected the reasons for popular discontent with the people's stores system and offered a feeble rejoinder:

There are many people who grumble and grouse these days. . . . Prices have soared and the daily 'bazaaring' has become most annoying. . . . Many of the queuers do not need what they queue up for, except for the profit they can get out of it in the black market. It is surprising to come upon people standing in a long queue without the slightest idea of what is being issued at the other end. . . . [But] we have abundant food. . . . Nobody need starve. The climate is equable. . . . Our life and limb are in no unusual danger. . . . The soil is fertile and we have timber for our houses. Come what may we will always have our food, our clothes, and our shelter. That is a blessing not many countries in the world can boast of.

Educational and Social Adjustments

When the university campuses at Rangoon and Mandalay reopened for classes in November 1964, following the year-long hiatus,
the regulations and curriculum were considerably altered. The new
educational reorganization plan divided the university into semi-
autonomous institutes, stressing various aspects of science and technology. The students were placed under strict discipline, forbidden
to concern themselves with politics, and assigned to respective curricula according to ability and public need, with minimal freedom
of choice. In the social studies, primary attention was accorded
superficially to Marxist interpretations. Political science courses
stressed the study of the official *Burmese Way to Socialism* document, the constitution of the Socialist Programme Party, and an
associated tract entitled *Correlation of Man and His Environment.*
Premedical training was assigned at the upper level to a special
faculty staffed by Polish and Czech lecturers. The technical institute
at Insein that was donated by the USSR was run by reputedly competent Russian instructors, who were obliged to lecture to their
select student groups in faltering English. Months passed before
most students could begin to understand what the Russians were
trying to communicate. English instruction and literature generally
were sharply downgraded, with no courses offered in Western
literature. History retained a bit more of its integrity as a discipline,
with emphasis at the honors level on modern Burma.

Despite the restricted nature of the imposed regimen, attendance
at the several university centers grew rapidly. The total enrollment
for 1964–1965 of 20,600 students swelled to 33,700 in 1967–1968.
Even though entrance requirements were lowered, only some 12
percent of the candidates for entry into the university regularly
qualified as matriculants. The level of instruction in the preparatory schools, already dismally low in the fifties, deteriorated still
more after Ne Win nationalized all mission high schools in 1962
and finally excluded all missionary personnel in late 1965. The
situation for the students became extremely frustrating. Higher
education appeared to be the only available avenue for enhancement of social status, and yet no jobs were available for graduates
in a prostrate economy and a government bureaucracy dominated
by army personnel. The price of educational success for many

Burmese youth, was measured in social alienation and personal tragedy.

Socialist propaganda emanating from government sources had little relevance to accepted ethical values. Propaganda efforts of the dominant revolutionary council did nothing to disprove Burma's age-old adage that governments were one of the major scourges which people must learn to endure. The exhortations of U Ba Nyein fitted not at all into the Burmese tradition. His concepts of modernized national goals "for Burmese as Burmese" were only vaguely formulated and traditions survived. Attendance at traditional pagoda festivals increased, and both sexes from necessity reverted to the traditional *longyi* wraparound skirt and jacket garb, abandoning previously used western types of clothing. Eastern European residents in Rangoon reportedly commented: "It would not be so discouraging if the Burma government did not call what is happening socialism."

Religious Response to the Revolutionary Council

The Burmese religious tradition was far more resistant to the proposed changes introduced by the revolutionary council than was the partly westernized educational system. Ne Win inherited from Premier Nu the problem of dealing with monastic political involvement despite all of the rules against it in the Vinaya scriptures. Nu's persistent efforts during the 1950s to promote the study of Buddhist scriptures by professing monks had prompted an orgy of cheating on the examinations. Subsequent efforts to register the genuine monks, so that the spurious wearers of the robe could be disciplined ran firmly aground. General Ne Win's response to pongyi agitation was brutally direct. When monk demonstrators in 1962 took to the streets of Mandalay to protest the government's abandonment of Buddhism as the official state religion, Ne Win simply ordered troops to fire on the mob. Several were killed, and such overt resistance came abruptly to an end. But the general had no more success than Nu in his efforts to impose discipline within the Sangha by registering its membership.

Even though in a sad state of decline, Burmese religion was too deeply rooted to be eradicated. Calendrical religious celebrations, such as planting and harvest rites, Lenten and New Year holidays, and the veneration of sacred objects and taboos continued to be honored. The initiatory ceremonies for youthful neophyte monks were regularly performed as were the corresponding ear-boring ceremonies for girls. In addition, a medley of nat spirits had to be propitiated to take care of more immediate needs. The Buddhist faith and associated indigenous animistic cults still provided the most meaningful symbols of Burmese national identity, serving as a kind of foil against cultural and political threats from the outside. These threats for many included not only the liberal concepts of democracy, but mainly the imposed socialism of the revolutionary council, which by 1965 had become the principal agency of popular oppression.

The Marxist dichotomy of class struggle, once it was divorced from hatred of foreign economic domination, became largely artificial and alien to the Burmese scene. Within the hierarchy of traditional Burmese values, thrift and cumulative savings were not commendable practices unless associated with acts worthy of Buddhist merit. Meritorious contributions to one's own Karma composite was a more effective sanction for ethical conduct than solicited dedication to Ba Nyein's unrealistic goals for Burmese socialism. Monks continued to command respect as custodians of religious and moral verities, but they could not become an effective agency to promote the achievement of modernized economic development.

Actually the late sixties witnessed a resurgence of Buddhist sentiment, partly as a foil to anti-traditional governmental pressures. Denied political expression, Burman youth became increasingly active in religious celebrations, particularly in protesting alleged communist plundering of lower Burma shrines. General Ne Win himself eventually adapted to the pro-Buddhist trend, hoping thereby to generate a modicum of support. He visited the Buddhist shrine of Gaya in India and brought back a sapling allegedly derived from the original Bodhi tree which had sheltered Gautama during his experience of enlightenment. The pendulum started an inevitable swing back to more traditional values, which had little to do with the Burmese way to socialism or with economic development generally.

Foreign Policy of the Revolutionary Government

Burmese opinion at all political levels agreed on the necessity of avoiding involvement in another world war, and particularly on the importance of maintaining friendly relations with neighboring China. Both Premier Nu and Ne Win made persistent and eventually successful efforts from 1956 to 1960 to settle the 1360-mile China boundary dispute. The extravagant territorial claims advanced by the nationalist Chinese regime prior to 1949 were very substantially reduced by the communist negotiators in early 1960. Final signatures to the border settlement were appended in Peking on the occasion of Premier Nu's visit in October 1960 following the completion of extensive surveying operations. Overtones of the traditional vassal-suzerain relationship were present in China's stipulation that Burma must not permit its territory to be used by a third party for any aggressive purpose against China or become a party to any such hostile alignment. A supplementary treaty of friendship and mutual non-aggression was ratified on January 4, 1961, the anniversary of Burma's independence. The Ne Win regime after 1962 never became cordial toward China but continued nevertheless to be carefully neutral. Ba Nyein's pro-communist exhortations and tactics did establish a kind of ideological rapport with Maoism, which was buttressed by frequent exchanges of visits.

Burma's neutralist (but left-leaning) stance carried important implications with respect to foreign aid. The revolutionary council decided to decline all forms of foreign aid except when accorded on a government-to-government basis or when following some kind of established international pattern. This eliminated U.S. missionary and foundation support and other alleged forms of western propaganda. China responded by extending to Burma an $84 million loan in return for Rangoon's agreement to provide rice to China on a barter basis. The loan was intended for irrigation works and factory installations to be built with the aid of Chinese technicians. For a variety of reasons, only one-third of the loan was utilized by 1967, when a temporary break occurred. Although officials of the United States embassy and consulate enjoyed very little contact with Burma government personnel and with civilians generally, Washington continued to honor an agreement signed previously with Nu, in 1961, to provide small-caliber military equipment for

Burma's army at reduced prices. Around two score million dollars were involved, and unpublicized American arms shipments continued to reach Rangoon over the ensuing decade. Another earlier American grant of some $30 million to help finance the construction of an improved trunk road running from Rangoon to Mandalay was cancelled by Rangoon, presumably at Peking's insistence.

Ne Win's relations with the USSR which had been far from friendly during the caretaker regime, improved noticeably after 1963. Russian technicians were permitted to complete several of the contributions pledged by Chairman Khrushchev in 1956–1957, including a luxury hotel, the Rangoon technical institute, and the sports stadium. Six other promised Soviet gifts were cancelled. Growing friendship for Burma on the part of the Soviet Union was based only partly on Marxist ideological considerations. Moscow's primary interest appears to have been twofold: to maintain via Burma an open door into Southeast Asia for future Soviet influence and trade, and to counterbalance the prospect of growing Chinese importance in Southeast Asia. Moscow's alignment with Rangoon meant Soviet abandonment of the Burma Communist Party, which tended thereafter to fall under Chinese influence.

Burma's improved relations with Eastern Europe generally, especially Poland and Czechoslovakia, had no counterpart in relations with the West except for a cooperative agreement made with the government of Canada dating from the caretaker period of 1959. Counterpart kyats derived from the local sale of Canadian wheat were used to help finance the new Pazundaung Creek bridge connecting Rangoon with two new satellite cities. The services of Canadian engineers and the cost of materials sent from North America were financed later from scarce foreign exchange resources in order to complete the project. In 1966 Brigadier Tin Pe accepted a Canadian invitation to attend the Montreal trade fair, and shortly thereafter students were permitted to go to Canada for scientific and technical training.

Rangoon continued to be cautiously wary of accepting substantial help from any outside source. Self-sufficiency was the espoused long-range goal, which must not be compromised. Economic difficulties were rationalized as the necessary price which Burmans must pay to stay clear of great power rivalries and to learn how to run their own affairs. The policy was vulnerable since excessive concern for neutralism actually impoverished and weakened the country both

militarily and economically, thus rendering it more exposed to outside pressures. It was this apparent weakness which Peking attempted to exploit in the controversial situation which developed
in 1967.

During the course of the mid-sixties General Ne Win and advisors
became increasingly concerned with political developments in
neighboring countries of Southeast Asia. The rapid expansion of
American military intervention in South Vietnam, the entry of
South Korean forces into that war, and the permission granted by
the Thai government for American establishment of airfield bases
for intensified bombing raids against North Vietnamese forces constituted for Rangoon ominous warnings of the approach of another
world war. The Burma government consequently avoided ties with
even the most innocuous regional groupings developing within
Southeast Asia. Burma refused, for example, to send a delegation
to an Asian agricultural conference, which was completely non-
political in character. Rangoon insisted that its strictly neutral
stance implied no enmity toward the United States or toward its
immediate neighbors, provided however that they leave Burma out
of their plans. Unwillingness to become involved was reflected in
Ne Win's refusal to utilize a $3 million interest-free agricultural
loan offered by communist China, because it called for the entry of
Chinese experts to implement the project. This action prompted a
special protest visit from Chou En-lai.

Partly to maintain a semblance of balance of relations with cold
war rivals, General Ne Win accepted an invitation to visit Washington in September 1966, presumably to match his repeated visits
to Peking and Moscow. No elaborate reception program was prepared in Washington in deference to the expressed preferences of
the visitor, and no serious economic or political talks were
scheduled. Elaborate precautions were taken to maintain surveillance over Bo Let Ya, one of the founders of the national liberation
council, who was resident at the time in the United States. At his
dinner reception President Johnson praised Burma's efforts to
follow an independent foreign policy for nationalist reasons and
attempted to reconcile that policy with America's efforts to help
other peoples of Southeast Asia to live and prosper free from the
threat of outside interference or aggression. Ne Win's response was
minimal. He expressed the hope that his visit would contribute to
better understanding; he shunned all contacts with the press; he

enjoyed his specially arranged golf game with Gene Sarazen, an old acquaintance. Tentative contacts were subsequently renewed with World Bank and International Monetary Fund officials, and the United States renewed its modest program of arms assistance. Immediate results were otherwise virtually nil.

The Trouble with China, 1967–1968

The rift which developed between Peking and Rangoon in June 1967 was related to events of the previous year. China's Liu Shao-chi and Foreign Minister Chen Yi failed during the course of their formal visits to Burma in the spring of 1966 to influence Ne Win to denounce openly the American presence in South Vietnam and to abandon plans for the Washington visit. Thereafter, Liu's influence at Peking began sharply to wane. Red Guard activities started in August 1966. Burmese press notices in early 1967 indicated that Chinese agents appeared to be preparing to extend aspects of the youth-led cultural revolution within China to countrymen resident in Burma. The government countered by subjecting the several hundred Chinese technical experts then present in Burma to travel and other restrictions.

Formal relations remained polite and friendly into May 1967, when Burmese authorities surrendered to Chinese custody a number of KMT refugees recently captured along the frontier, but the storm broke in June. It began with the distribution of Mao badges in the Chinese schools of Rangoon, in an effort to force all resident Chinese students in line. Several school buildings were barricaded; protesting teachers were abused as were news photographers; police orders were openly defied. The pro-Maoist activists who manned barricades received food from the Chinese embassy, whence came also the badges. The popular Burmese reaction to Chinese-instigated violence, involving embassy support, was to invade and sack the Chinese business quarter of Rangoon. The mobs attacked particularly the rice-hoarding black marketeers and killed an unknown number. A shot fired later from the Chinese embassy into a protesting mob outside led to the premises being completely overrun, with one embassy person killed. Effective police action to stop the mob rioting was taken belatedly, since the army was obviously not in favor of encouraging revolutionary violence. Foreign Minister

Chin Yi in Peking similarly restrained a Red Guard mob threatening the Burmese embassy.

It seems clear that, once begun, the violence exceeded the wishes and intentions of both governments. Peking could hardly have been so badly informed about Burma to expect that this type of agitation would seriously challenge Ne Win's authority, but China apparently needed to win some kind of prestige increment to compensate for the growing Soviet influence in Southeast Asia. For a brief time, the Peking radio openly praised the cause of Burma's communist "liberators" on the Yunnan border. In Burma, the incident only enhanced the status of the regime among the population, diverting attention from governmental deficiencies.

From the official Burmese point of view, the China authorities had acted both contemptuously and with gratuitous insult. A press spokesman cited Ne Win's four visits to Peking, his studiously neutralist stance, and his demonstrated cooperation in restraining border KMT refugees. Particularly resented were Peking's unrestrained denunciation of the revolutionary council government as "fascist, racist, and reactionary," and as directly responsible for fomenting the rioting at Rangoon. Peking's threatening language left scant room for any immediate reconciliation with Ne Win: "The Burmese people will . . . rise up in rebellion against you, seize your power . . . strike you to the ground, stamp on you, and keep you down forever."

Ne Win replied by arresting some 200 Peking sympathizers and by closing the Chinese language newspaper, *People's Daily*. He also expelled more than 500 Chinese technicians along with the correspondent of the *New China News* Agency, and then recalled the Burmese ambassador from Peking. Chinese embassy officials were challenged openly for political interference and for fomenting activities which led to the mob rioting. Ne Win's next move was to solicit aid from both the Soviet Union and the United States. A seven-man economic mission from the Soviet Union made an extended visit to Burma in August-September 1967. The limited flow of arms from America was resumed after a Burmese defense team was invited to visit a Tokyo military exhibit to select what they wanted. A number of American pilot instructors were enlisted to train crews to operate several new F-86 fighter aircraft.

The net foreign policy effect of Rangoon's quarrel with China in

1967 was to diversify its outside connections. The Soviet Union was the principal gainer, along with Poland, Czechoslovakia, and Rumania. Overseas students previously sent to China to study were now sent to Eastern Europe. Balancing relations were also developed with West Germany and Japan, neither of which could be accused of harboring anti-Chinese or pro-Russian designs. Germany's Chancellor Keisinger visited Burma in November 1967, at which time tentative agreements were worked out for increased German purchase of Burmese exports of rubber and timber. In return, Germany agreed to help supply needed machinery for the production of fertilizers, bricks, glassware, and electrical appliances, along with equipment for fishing operations, all at the cost of some $20 million. Partly to show that Burma was not assuming a partisan position in the cold war, newspaper press coverage was broadened to include items from North Korea, both Vietnams, and Czechoslovakia. The Burma government declared that it would not oppose a Viet Cong victory, so long as Chinese influence and control were not enhanced thereby. Burma's changing international orientation was designed to please neither Peking nor the United States.

The folly of the gratuitous Chinese quarrel with Burma became increasingly obvious to Peking during 1968, as the Red Guard excesses waned. Cooler heads gained a hearing, and efforts at a rapprochement were begun. The Chinese embassy at Rangoon halted the profitless pro-Mao agitation in the schools, along with Peking's previous insistence that Chinese youth must go to China for advanced educational training. Meanwhile, Rangoon's revolutionary council also concluded that further deterioration of relations with China would be unwise. In early 1969, Ne Win, while in West Pakistan, conferred with Chinese spokesmen over terms of a possible reconciliation. His primary demand that China cease supporting the Burma communist rebellion was not immediately accepted, but the conversations continued. No settlement of differences was realized until 1970, but tensions eased and Burma maintained a generally neutral stance. One political result within Burma was to enhance public respect for Ne Win for his refusal to be intimidated by Peking.

After the events of 1967, Burma attained high rank within the orbit of Soviet-favored third world states (alongside Syria, Egypt, and Algeria), partly because of its compatible governmental structure, ideological commitments, and strategic location with respect to China. Moscow tried to exploit China's gratuitous support of Burma's border communists. But whereas Soviet visitors were welcomed by Rangoon, General Ne Win refused to antagonize China unnecessarily, and gave it support during the course of the East Pakistan crisis of 1972. Rangoon continued to regard China's limited support of border insurgents as essentially a local matter, objectionable but not posing any serious threat to Burma.

Domestic Opposition to the Military Regime

Domestic political unrest became widespread in Burma after 1963, but it was far from united and not capable of challenging army control. Ethnic differentiation contributed to the confusion, coupled with mixed minority reactions to rebel communist efforts to exploit general dissatisfaction. Burman resistance efforts centering in the National Liberation Council (NCL) initiated secretly back in 1963 by Bo Let Ya, Bo Kya Doe, and Dr. Ba Maw's son-in-law, Bo Yan Naing. The group assembled a small rebel force in May 1965, but it failed to reach agreement with Shan and Kachin dissidents. Leaders of the NLC finally took refuge in a jungle headquarters located along the Thai border behind Moulmein and Tavoy, where they cooperated with local Karen rebels. The two groups conducted desultory raids into the Tenasserim region of Burma, continuing into the 1970s.

The Karen rebels eventually split four ways. The older and more conservative Christian-led group had come to terms with the government in 1966. A more radical younger group collaborated with the White Flag communists as long as the latter were active in the middle Sittang valley. Bo Mya's group in Tenasserim was courted by the communists, but with no success. The same was true of the fourth group of Irrawaddy delta Karens, whose principal activity was to raid periodically various nearly people's stores, Robin Hood fashion, to obtain and distribute essential supplies to needy villagers.

The Shan dissidents were comparably split. The more conservative Shan unity preparatory committee shunned communist collaboration, and eventually offered in the spring of 1969 to enter into a ceasefire arrangement preliminary to peace negotiations with the Ne Win regime. Some 1,500 Shan rebels eventually turned in their guns. But no acceptable peace terms were formulated, and some dissident elements drifted back toward a communist alignment.

Along the Shan state–China borders further north, a small band of Peking-supported Burman communists invaded Burma in 1967 as far as Kutkai in an effort to join hands with Kachin rebels, only to be repulsed by government forces. Other Kachin insurgents still further north continued defiant, refusing to trust the Burman communist elements any more than they did the Ne Win regime. Meanwhile, the main Burman communist group split into pro-Chinese and anti-Chinese factions, the first headed by Than Tun and the second by Ba Tin (Goshal). The feuding climaxed in the assassination of Than Tun on September 24, 1968. Government troops thereupon overran the old Pegu Yoma communist headquarters, so that the principal directing center shifted to the China border above Kutkai. Contributing to the White Flag communist debacle in central Burma was Ne Win's friction with China developing after June 1967.

Prospects for Improved Relations with the People

General Ne Win's popular standing improved slightly after 1967 on grounds other than his defiance of Chinese intervention. He ordered the release of some 750 political prisoners, including former high officials and cabinet members. He also removed some 34 consumer goods items (in a total of 426) from the government controlled list. He pointed to gains in government housing construction and in providing health and security benefits. He visited a number of Burman localities in the delta and central valley area to listen to popular complaints. The response was superficially favorable, although little was done to satisfy the multiple grievances.

In May of 1968, the government convened the first central people's workers' council of 1,400 selected delegates in a gesture widely proclaimed as a major step toward realizing the long-promised popular participation in the government. The week-long session proved to be something other than a love fest. Angry delegates proposed that the annual seminars be discontinued unless the government was prepared to make constructive corrective decisions concerning the complaints raised. Others declared that the principal obstacle to the exercise of the workers' rights and privileges derived mainly from policies pursued by the state enterprises themselves, including the people's stores. Nothing was being done to correct rising food prices and unemployment resulting from the closing of factories, public and private, as a result of the government's failure to provide machinery replacements and raw materials.

The angry replies of government spokesmen did nothing to calm the atmosphere. General Ne Win's address to the delegates blamed both the organizing committee and the participants for their resort to pressure tactics. He flatly reserved to himself any decision to transfer leadership from the existing Socialist Programme Party to the contemplated council structure until actual performance of the latter justified such a move. U Ba Nyein's exhortation to the delegates followed the familiar self-righteous pattern, running in part as follows:

> Workers and peasants . . . can make or mar the Socialist Revolution. . . . The new order will collapse if the basis is not strong enough. . . . All means of production, transportation and distribution have been nationalized. The workers today work for themselves and for the country . . . , not for the benefit of any employers. They must show a greater sense of responsibility and discipline in their work . . . , not so much slackening on the job, so much malingering. . . . They are late in coming, early in leaving, slovenly in work. . . . The time has come for workers to put more heart in their work. . . . The old antagonistic stance against administrators, managers, supervisors, and superintendents must be replaced by a spirit of cooperation, comradery, and . . . venture for the common good.

XII Problems and Prospects in the Seventies

While it was obvious by the late sixties that the Burmese Way to Socialism had failed to achieve its idealized goals of social welfare and freedom from want, the prospects for change of government or policy were not encouraging. Few informed persons wanted Ne Win to leave the scene abruptly. Such an event would have left Brigadier Tin Pe and his self-serving army followers in full control, or it would have precipitated a struggle for power within the armed forces, which could benefit no one. Many hoped that the hardcore Marxist leadership within the revolutionary council might somehow be phased out, leaving Ne Win in control but in a position to espouse a more pragmatic and less doctrinaire policy. As an early associate of Aung San and as a nationalist champion, General Ne Win still possessed sufficient authority to control the army and to awe rebellious civilian elements. It would be difficult under any circumstances, however, for anyone to deny the army leadership the perquisites of power which they had come to enjoy—from houses and cars to golfing equipment—plus innumerable opportunities for marginal income.

Renewed Political Challenge from Nu

Among the several hundred political prisoners who were liberated in 1967, former Premier Nu emerged as the most likely political challenger of the revolutionary council government. His political appeal was surprisingly widespread. In the context of the dismal record of the existing army regime, Nu's own faltering administrative and economic performance as premier was remembered as the high point of the postwar period. He was widely respected as a sincere Buddhist and was probably trusted by minority peoples more than any other Burman leader. Nu and his friends achieved initial prominence in May of 1968, as leaders of a group of former detainees who canvassed Rangoon city to solicit relief funds for victims of a savage typhoon which had devastated the lower Arakan coast. At the time, the government was highly displeased, but it hardly dared intervene to stop such an obviously meritorious activity. Later in the same year, Nu toured Moulmein, Mandalay, and other urban centers as a lecturer on Buddhism. He attracted large crowds everywhere. Drivers of buses and pony carts reportedly cut their fares to transport the eager public to attend the meetings.

In November 1968, the released detainees moved into further prominence when Ne Win designated thirty-three "elder statesmen" to serve on an ad hoc internal unity advisory board to explore ways to promote national cooperation. As commissioned on December 4, the board included former Union President Mahn Win Maung, a Karen, as chairman, and such leading former cabinet members as Ba Swe, Kyaw Nyein, and Raschid, plus Nu himself. The board was authorized to propose policy changes, desirable provisions for a prospective new constitution, and other considerations calculated to promote national unity.

The move was not popular within the revolutionary council. Brigadier Tin Pe and Ba Nyein chose the moment to escalate the government's nationalization program. They took over the remaining half dozen Rangoon cinemas, two score private saw mills, and 160 small industries, representing a selected residuum of surviving private enterprise. The differences within the revolutionary council were reflected in the *Guardian* newspaper's comment that further nationalization moves might well have been postponed until previous efforts in the same direction had proved themselves useful. The editor also suggested that personal vanity provided no valid grounds for aggravating at so late a date the admitted failure of excessive socialization.

The internal unity advisory board delivered its final report some five months later in May 1969. The document received full publicity and an initial indication of qualified approval by General Ne Win himself. The majority version, supported by 18 of the 33 members of the board and attributed to U Nu, proposed, as a first step, the restoration of the façade of constitutional government. At the outset, Nu would resume the post of premier from which he had been expelled in 1962, after which all available members of the 1962 parliament would reassemble to legalize the selection of General Ne Win as the new president of the Burma union. Nu would eventually resign the premiership, but not until after the independent authority of both the legislative and judicial branches of the government was recognized and the rights of the people, both political and economic, were constitutionally restored. Once legally installed as president, Ne Win would be empowered to choose a new cabinet. Members of the advisory board who were not selected to become officials of the new government should continue to be available, as a kind of unofficial advisory group. One of the first functions of the new president would be to call a national convention representing all parties and minority groups, including the armed forces, to draft a new constitution. It was also suggested that an Arakan and a Mon state should be added to the Burma Union membership.

A more conservative alternative version of the report, sponsored by eleven members, recommended as the principal change the broader functional representation of workers, peasants, political intelligentsia, and technicians as part of the socialist single-party system. Democracy was rejected, but by implication so was army rule. This minority group proposed a policy of progressive relaxation of the monopoly of economic activities currently being exercised by the government. Foreign capital investment should nevertheless be rejected, and the state should continue its control over large-scale industry. In the field of medium-size industry, however, cooperative agencies and joint state-private enterprise should be afforded opportunity to function, and no impediment should be placed in the way of small-scale private business. A group of three members, headed by U Kyaw Nyein, diverged from the other two reports by giving greater emphasis to centralized socialistic planning, while limiting the powers of the several constituent states of the union to matters affecting religion, culture, and local custom.

The activities of the advisory board became the object of bitterly hostile criticism from the official press, both Burmese language and English papers, before the final reports were actually released. The editors denounced the ex-premier personally for seeking to return to power through an appeal to Buddhist partisanship, which was not evident in the report at all. He was accused in this connection of having accepted "bribe" donations from Indian and Chinese businessmen in the early 1950s. General Ne Win's initially open-minded if not favorable reaction to portions of the unity board's report was not shared by his revolutionary council colleagues, who obviously had much to lose. In the end, the general was either disinclined or unable to break with his military associates by permitting a revival of constitutional government, which he himself had denounced so unequivocally in 1962.

The unity board report had no immediate chance of adoption, but it did provide a possible opportunity for public consideration of alternative patterns for future governmental organization and policy. It was deficient principally in not taking adequate account of the grievances and distrust of ethnic minority groups. These might trust Nu, but not a future cabinet appointed by President Ne Win, especially in view of their limited role in the prospective constitutional convention. They wanted a substantial measure of political autonomy, including control over mining, timber, and other economic resources found within their respective boundaries. It was unfortunate that adequate opportunity was not provided for serious consideration and emendation of the alternative constitutional proposals. The report was actually ignored in its entirety. In a less tense atmosphere, it is conceivable that discussions might have proceeded under Ne Win's supervision until some compromise conclusion was reached.

Nu's early departure from Burma made him share some of the blame for this failure of accommodation. He sought and received, in June 1969, Ne Win's permission to go to India on a Buddhist pilgrimage. From India he proceeded to Thailand, invited by Premier Thanom Kittikachorn to inspect the canopy erected over the giant Buddha statue at Ayuthia, to the construction of which he had contributed substantially in 1956. Nu failed to return to Burma from this trip and later supported dissident Burman elements operating in Bangkok and elsewhere, thus ending any possibility that may have existed to work out a compromise with Ne Win.

Challenge to Ne Win's Dictatorship from the Outside

Nu's public denunciation of Rangoon's revolutionary council as oppressive and fascist began during the course of his residence at Bangkok. He declared that the council had disrupted Burma's economy, provoked minority rebellions, and violated the rights of the people by staging arbitrary arrest and detention without trial. The nationalization program, as pursued, was "false socialism," involving the robbery of citizens' property by army men for their personal aggrandizement. From Bangkok Nu traveled to London, where he met the rebel army leader, Bo Let Ya, who had served as his defense minister in the late forties. They declared that overseas Burmese could no longer sit idly by and see their country ruined. All dissident groups must unite to expel the usurpers, since the ruling military clique would respond only to force. Proceeding to New York in early September 1970, Nu conferred briefly with his longtime friend, U Thant, at the United Nations headquarters, and addressed representatives of that body informally. He indicated to the press that the first revolutionary step would be to broaden the "liberated area" along the Thai border, where a rival government could be installed, raising a standard to which all dissident elements could rally. He also anticipated that the eventual popular rising would include elements within the government and the army.

Progress in preparations for insurrection was discouragingly slow. Nu's endeavors to solicit official aid were rebuffed by both the United Kingdom and the United States governments. Private support was very limited, coming presumably from sympathetic individuals and from firms interested in possible future economic operations within the country. Meanwhile, communist resistance in central Burma faltered after Than Tun's assassination in late 1968, and collapsed after the capture of the Red Flag Communist leader Thakin Soe in the delta area in November 1970; events which substantially strengthened Rangoon's control in Burma proper. Preliminary efforts of non-communist rebels in Thailand to infiltrate the Tenasserim coastal regions behind Moulmein and Tavoy in 1971, coupled with appeals for dissident Mon and Karen support, evoked only a limited response. Karen insurgency actually faded in early 1971, with mass surrenders occurring along the Salween frontier and in the Henzada district of the western delta region.

More serious rebel initiatives began in late 1971 and early 1972. Formal proclamations by Premier Nu's alleged "de jure government" on December 15 and January 1 appealed for patriotic support of the impending invasion. The prospective new provisional government promised to establish the full enjoyment of all civil rights. These included political representation of party and minority groups, democratic elections, the pragmatic application of economic incentives, an actively neutral foreign policy, and control of local productive resources by the several states of the union. The military proclamation of January 1 by Bo Let Ya made a deliberate effort to suborn army units sent against the liberation army. Officers who elected to avoid contact with the invading patriotic forces were guaranteed full retirement rights under the new government, and those who decided to join the resistance were promised substantial honors and rewards for their assistance. Civilian sympathizers were warned not to provoke the vengeance of the desperate army ruling clique, since the country had already endured more than enough of bloodshed. The two proclamations carried the obvious implication that the anti-Ne Win rebels did not expect to succeed without substantial aid from sympathizers within the regular army.

The immediate outlook for the success of the provisional government was discouraging. Defections from the army were few, and coordination of disparate opposition elements was difficult. Press reports as of late April indicated that Nu was considering withdrawing his connections with the provisional government, because the proposed offers for autonomy for the Shans in particular went beyond permissible limits, in his opinion. Battle reports as of mid-May 1972 indicated only minor contact with regular army forces along the Thailand frontier with claims of only limited success. The overthrow of Ne Win's regime obviously had a long way to go.

Foreign Policy Developments After 1969

In the field of foreign policy, Ne Win continued his efforts to cultivate cordial relations with both the Soviet Union and the People's Republic of China. Burma restored diplomatic relations with China in October 1970, with the appointment of a new Burmese ambassador to Peking. The Chinese embassy at Rangoon was restaffed in April 1971. Ne Win visited Peking as the guest of Chou En-lai in August 1971. Shortly thereafter, in October, a new Sino-Burmese economic and technical cooperation agreement reactivated the unused two-thirds of the $84 million aid loan of 1961, which had been suspended since 1967. Interest on the previously utilized one-third of the loan was made immediately payable, but China granted a ten-year interest moratorium for the remaining two-thirds. Continued cordial relations with the USSR included renewed cultural as well as economic ties. The year 1971 was highlighted by the visit to Rangoon of President Nikolai Podgorny en route back from Hanoi in June. Russian economic assistance was solicited in connection with a newly scheduled Sittang River development project. At the same time, Burma rejected a United States offer to renew its modest aid program in military equipment,

including the proffered sale at bargain rates of surplus trucks and
other transport facilities from South Vietnam. The American military equipment delivery team departed Rangoon at long last in
June 1971.

Burma's relations with its more immediate south Asian neighbors,
India and Thailand, continued formally friendly. The demarcation
of Burma's western boundary with India proceeded on schedule,
completing some 225 miles of the total of 900. Rangoon's prompt
recognition of the independence of neighboring Bangladesh in early
1972 improved Burma's relations with India as well. It provided a
more acceptable context for Burma's continuing program of repatriation of Indian and ex-Pakistani residents who lacked citizenship
status.

Tensions with Thailand were eased somewhat in October 1971,
following the visit to Rangoon of the brother of Marshal Thanom
Kittikachorn, Sa-Nga Kittikachorn, then deputy foreign minister at
Bangkok. Negotiations apparently involved Thailand's assurances
that it would police more effectively the border areas from which
Burmese insurgent elements drew their supplies, in return for
Rangoon's relaxation of restrictions previously imposed on Thai
fishermen operating off Burma's southernmost port of Mergui. The
unanswered question was the actual extent of Thailand's support of
anti-Burman insurgency along the border.

A minor international incident occurred in connection with the
Asian Youth Festival held at Rangoon in March 1971. Angered
youth groups staged a riot outside the stadium, when they were
denied entry to a popular football match because scalpers had
bought up all the available tickets. The army had to intervene.
Proficiency in soccer football became a significant mark of Burmese
identity and prestige, following successive victories in 1970–1971 in
five international match competitions.

Economic Prospects

Following 1967–1968, agricultural production improved substantially, but mainly for the domestic market. A major problem
was the collapse of export prices for rice to a level some 20 percent
below that of 1962. Only 11 percent of the large 1970–1971 rice
crop was marketed overseas at a meager profit, compared to the 37
percent export sale in the early 1960s. Burma's per unit output in

rice production continued to be one of the lowest in the world, due in part to poor cultivation methods and lack of incentive. Miracle rice cultivation, which was partly responsible for the world price decline, was limited in Burma to a mere 2,500 acres. Other agricultural gains were registered by wheat and sugar cane; cotton production held its own, while the output of jute and tobacco declined. The total value of exports in 1970–1971 was only half that of 1963, with rice accounting for 50 percent and teakwood for another 25 percent. A deliberate policy was adopted in 1970 to diversify agriculture with less emphasis on rice.

State finances also showed a steady decline. Loss of revenues from diminished sales overseas was matched by a decline in tax receipts, especially in the income tax category. State-owned enterprises failed to meet target expectations by some 23 percent. Not only did new capital investment needs remain unmet, but replacement parts for older machinery continued to be unavailable. The private mills suffered most, but publicly operated river transport facilities reached a post-independence low due to cumulative mechanical breakdown. The state-subsidized coastal service Five Star Line steamers suffered heavy operational losses. The Burma Airways dwindled to 18 operable planes in 1970–1971. Meanwhile, foreign currency reserves fell to less than 40 percent of the 1962 level, with adverse balance of payments continuing despite drastic cuts in consumer imports. The value of total imports in 1970 was only three-fourths that of 1962. Within the same decade, the total debt of the government had doubled.

Meanwhile, the system of consumer goods distribution via the people's stores ran almost completely aground. In 1970 the task was reassigned to local consumer-run cooperatives sponsored by the government. The first year saw only 29 percent of the targeted cooperatives established, and these were seriously hampered by the mountain of paper work required of the management in an effort to curb corruption. Much available inventory was not distributed. Most of the surviving people's stores were reported half deserted. When a number of legalized "free sale" shops were permitted to open in Mandalay and Rangoon (no ration books required), the registered prices for staple wares, although below the black market level, were five to eight times more expensive than were identical goods in Thailand.

The beginning of significant changes in economic policy came with the prospect of offshore oil and gas exploration. Limited early explorations were begun by Rumanian and Japanese experts. The diminished output of older oil fields of Chauk and Minbu (some 20,000 barrels a day) was to be supplemented by new sources found to the west of the lower Chindwin river, in the lower Arakan Yoma behind Bassein, with deposits of gas known to be off the Martaban and Arakan coasts. A $10 million Tokyo loan was offered to finance additional prospecting off the upper Tenasserim coasts, with high expectations. American oil interests also became involved.

A new phase was reached in 1973, following Ne Win's visit to Java, when the state-owned Myanma Oil Corporation, fashioned on the pattern of Pertamina in Indonesia, assumed title to all of Burma's gas and oil resources. Foreign companies (38 all told) were invited to submit competitive bids for exploration rights within the twenty-five designated offshore areas covering Burma's coastal frontage. The proposal required that contract winners would bear the full cost of exploration with no return unless discoveries were made, these costs being recoverable from eventual sale proceeds, with the companies taking a seventy percent share. By May 1974, three such contracts were let and nineteen others were under consideration. Exploration rights were limited to three years' duration and exploitation to twenty years only. The prospect of oil riches thus overcame Burma's long-standing official opposition to foreign investment. At the same time, the aid of West German mining experts was solicited for developmental activities in the Shan plateau region, despite the threat of rebel operations and local demands for control over such resources. The Germans complained as had the Japanese that they could act with more confidence if the existing provisional government were replaced by one based on a formal constitution.

Reform Gestures of 1971–1972

The governmental and political pattern also began to change in the early seventies. One move in November 1970 was the forced retirement of Brigadier Tin Pe. The reasons were not given, but Tin Pe had long outlived his usefulness. Another change was the abandonment of the futile annual seminars of peasants' and workers' delegates. Tin Pe's successor as General Ne Win's chief lieutenant was Brigadier San Yu, a part-Chinese army officer completely devoted to the ruling general. San Yu became secretary general of the Burma Socialist Programme Party (BSPP) and head of an ad hoc election supervision commission, which was authorized the call the first congress of the BSPP. He was later named chief of state.

The first assembly of the party congress convened for a brief two weeks' session on June 28, 1971, at the Mingaladon cantonment outside Rangoon. The meeting was officially described as the first step toward the eventual goal of transferring political control to representatives of the people. The initial item on the agenda was to promote to full membership in the new People's Party approximately one-third of the 185,000 long-time probationary candidates of the older BSPP. This action increased party membership from around 9,000 to 73,000 persons, who would thereafter constitute collectively the ruling People's Party. The army leadership retained control of the party's central committee, in which civilian representation numbered only 31 of 150 members. Four civilians were included in the fifteen-member revolutionary council, still headed by General Ne Win, while the central executive committee included only one civilian. Ne Win assumed the post of premier in the new eleven-member cabinet (exclusively military), while the newly elevated General San Yu became the deputy premier.

One major policy action of the congress involved the appointment of a 97-member commission headed by General San Yu to draft a formal constitution for the Union of Burma. The document was scheduled for implementation in 1972, but was actually delayed for another year. The congress imposed strict guidelines on the commission, calling for the preservation of the socialist state system and requiring the direct collaborative participation of all minority peoples. The only carryover from the aborted unity board of 1969 was an advisory consultative committee of thirty members, predominantly civilian and lacking authority. Government spokesmen also presented a new four-year plan of economic development (covering 1971–1975) designed to increase production, coupled with the usual denunciations of continuing poor cooperative performance on the part of peasant cultivators and workers. Sponsors of the new plan contributed the grim reminder that full realization of the socialist development program might extend over another twenty years unless proper public participation was forthcoming. The brief congress session probably contributed more discouragement than hope.

Little happened during the ensuing year to provide any substance to the reforms promised by the 1971 congress. The work of the cumbersome constitutional commission ran aground on repeated revisions of successive draft proposals. In late 1971, General Ne Win was obliged to enter an English hospital to care for his chronic liver ailment and other health problems. Meanwhile, the several subversive moves made by the rebel provisional government from near the Thailand border, headed by Bo Let Ya and U Nu, attracted little support from dissident minority groups within Burma and no positive response from the economically restive worker and peasant elements. The government had all the guns. The early months of 1972 witnessed the familiar spectacle of the government's closing down a substantial number of small family-sized industries devoted to the production of consumer goods. The operators were accused of utilizing black market connections to obtain raw materials and to dispose of the finished products.

When Ne Win returned from England, he began to take a somewhat more active role in domestic affairs. On the occasion of the Peasants' Day celebration on March 2, 1972, the tenth anniversary of his army coup, Ne Win exhorted the assembled audience to look forward to the new constitution, which was intended to restore some semblance of democratic rule. This was followed on April 22 by his well-advertised resignation of his personal army rank and command, while continuing in his role as premier and head of the new People's Party. Several other army members of the cabinet followed his example by surrendering their officer status and associated perquisites. General San Yu took over the ministry of defense assignment and became head of the army, in addition to his continuing role as deputy premier. The door was thus opened, however slightly, for ending direct army control of the government, although the personnel involved remained unchanged and the same basic policies persisted.

It would take more than a new constitution to solve a number of troublesome commercial problems. Among them was the fact that border smuggling operations had become an established Burmese enterprise because of the curtailment of official imports. Black market rice was regularly bartered in India for such items as soap, cosmetics, razor blades, transistor radios, and other industrial goods. Relief medicines and oversized clothing intended for devastated Bangladesh found their way to the Burma market in return for food. From Thailand came radios, fans, and other electrical supplies, plus good quality cloth, in return for Burma's rubies, jade, antiques, cattle, tin, and opium. Tenasserim coast's rice, fish, and lentils were traded illegally in Penang for all kinds of consumer goods. Because of low pay and declining morale, army customs officers were themselves widely involved in the smuggling traffic.

The Upheaval of 1973–1974

The crisis foreseeable in Burma's continuing economic decline came to a head in 1973–1974. The urban food shortage and lack of consumer goods took a turn for the worse even though the rice crop of the 1972 season was somewhat better than normal. Because many farmers refused to deliver their newly harvested paddy to government purchasing centers at established low prices, official people's stores ran out of rice and the shortages again attained the high point of 1967–1968. Panic consumer buying of food and cooking oil began in January 1973. The government countered by seizing supplies found in some five hundred black market centers in Rangoon and Mandalay. By March, the authorities were obliged to suspend all rice exports and to decontrol domestic prices temporarily. Prices in upper Burma reached such fantastic levels that the hungry urban poor resorted to maize and root substitutes. A hastily convened emergency party council produced majority rejection of Ba Nyein's customary insistence on adherence to Marxist discipline, the new policy favored encouraging production in an expanding number of private industrial activities, plus the offer of price incentives to promote rice production, and the active encouragement of foreign investments in strategically important sectors of the economy. The four-year development plan of 1971 was abruptly terminated.

The new trend became more substantive later in 1973. In July, Ne Win announced that privately owned rubber plantations would be guaranteed against nationalization over a period of thirty years, as an essential means of encouraging much needed replanting operations. To facilitate foreign investments, the government also repealed the existing confiscatory tax on all corporate earnings above the level of 100,000 kyats ($21,000) annually, and granted such firms permission to apply current profits to cover developmental costs and dividend obligations. Several hundred designated minor areas of industrial activity were opened to private economic development. These and other moves were clearly associated with Ne Win's negotiation of a World Bank loan of $33 million to rehabilitate Burma's railway and water transportation, to expand storage facilities for rice and vegetable oils, and to buy refrigerator trucks for the nearly prostrate fishing industry. It was followed by a 1974 loan of $24 million to provide facilities to move the vast backlog of girdled teak logs to market. The solicitation of a smaller Asian Development Bank loan of $6 million was followed by the advance of Japanese and German credits to expand oil, gas, and mineral exploration. New customs regulations reduced tariff duties on equipment imports needed for economic development projects. Burma thus began to reenter the modern world economy, even though it still refused to participate in ASEAN activities.

In curious contrast to the revisionist trend in economic policy was the stodgy new constitution implemented in early 1973. The People's Party continued to monopolize political control, including the approval of all election candidates from village and district levels up to the national people's assembly. Local constituencies were permitted theoretically to reject government-proposed candidates, but all nominees of their own selection must be approved by the party. An adaptation of Soviet-type democratic centralism was the general pattern. The total administrative structure was elaborately reorganized into general and specialized departments and committees, but with expanded authority accorded to local workers and peasants council agencies covering both judicial and administrative aspects of control and the implementation of economic plans. Not surprisingly, Ne Win was elected president of the Union of Burma by the supreme council of the party, of which he was also head. General San Yu continued as minister of defense and became secretary of the new state cabinet council, with a former police officer, U Sein Win, named premier of the fifteen-member cabinet, composed for the most part of ex-army officers. People's inspectors would check reported abuses of power by local officials, who could be removed for demonstrated misconduct. Two former cabinet ministers were temporarily convicted by peoples courts in 1975 for abuse of power. No overt move was made to encourage accommodation with dissident minority segments of the population. An early action of the new government was to boost official salaries and to issue new currency notes.

The government's projected budget for 1974–1975 contemplated a deficit of some $240 million, which it hoped to reduce by foreign loans, but involving a substantial trade imbalance even if scheduled exports were made. A major fiscal innovation provided incentives for rice cultivation and sale by approving a 45 percent price increase (to 600 kyats for 100 baskets) for delivery of initial procurement quotas and another 25 percent increase for amounts above the assessed quotas. Despite the increase in prices, many cultivators still preferred to deal with the black market, ignoring both quota allocations and dubious consumer goods allotments. When the March 31, 1974, deadline for delivery of paddy quotas came around, the government was obliged to cut rice rations by half, whereupon the black market price rose to five times the official rate. Urban wage employees, unlike the hoarding cultivators, had no way to meet the spiraling prices. At the annual sessions of the workers' council in April 1974, the protests reached explosive dimensions.

May and early June witnessed a rash of worker strikes in more than two score national industries in the Mandalay and Rangoon areas. State-owned textile mills, a match factory, and the railway corporation workshop were shut down in Mandalay, along with the locomotive yards at Insein (near Rangoon), and the principal port facilities at Rangoon. When police intervened to arrest spokesmen of the unions and to seize laborer hostages, mob violence ensued, accompanied by large scale destruction of property. The casualties were listed as twenty-two killed and seventy-three wounded, including thirteen policemen. After order was restored on June 8, the authorities banned all public assemblies and closed the university and all high schools for an indefinite period. The deteriorating situation was aggravated in August by excessive monsoon rains, which produced the most extensive Irrawaddy flooding in half a century, reducing paddy production by a full one million acres. In the absence of foreign currency reserves, the government tapped loan funds to purchase such essential items as soap, cloth, medicines, tires, cart rims, and metal roofing. Meanwhile, the September press revealed the widescale spoilage and wastage of undistributed food, medicines, footwear, and textiles, all found in stockpiles.

It was within this troubled context that returning university students rioted on December 6, protesting Ne Win's niggardly burial plans in a remote racecourse cemetery for the body of the deceased United Nations Secretary General U Thant, who had been a life-long friend of U Nu. Interrupting the actual funeral proceedings, hundreds of students seized the body and transported it to the university campus for their own interment on the site of the destroyed student union building. The move was triggered by genuine resentment over the government's denial of respect and courtesy to Burma's most distinguished postwar personality, but it was also symbolic of popular hostility which ran much deeper. Even after Ne Win shifted the burial site to the slopes of the sacred Shwe Dagon pagoda, the students refused to cooperate.

Serious trouble developed on December 11, when the army intervened in a predawn raid to recover Thant's body and to bury it in a hastily prepared grave near the Shwe Dagon hill. An estimated 20,000 students, supported by monks and cheering observers, moved into downtown Rangoon, where they eventually attacked police stations, burned unguarded government buildings (road transport and housing board headquarters) and a twenty-five-car train. The authorities imposed martial law, arrested some 1,500 or more rioters, and sentenced several score of them to three to five years in prison. A dusk to dawn curfew closed all shops and cinemas, and quiet returned by December 16. For weeks thereafter, the marble-paved platform of the Shwe Dagon pagoda was crowded daily with worshipers, who could look down the slope of pagoda hill on the unmarked but symbolic grave of U Thant.

Even though the army was still in unquestioned control and Ne Win resumed his weekly golfing routine, several changes of significant scope were in the making. One was the demotion of the troublesome doctrinaire Marxist, U Ba Nyein, from head of the cooperatives ministry and from his long-time membership in the central committee of the People's Party. Probably associated with Ba Nyein's removal from power was the party's decision to adopt a more generous paddy purchase policy for the currently harvested 1974 rice crop. Quota paddy prices were raised by 50 percent over the previous year, and above-quota deliveries were priced up 100 percent. The government also promised to provide basic consumer and cultivater needs at half the prevailing black market prices. Whether such belated actions could restore some measure of popular confidence that Burma's military rulers were genuinely interested in meeting the needs of the people was doubtful. But even if such were not the case, the alternatives to going along with Ne Win's continuing domination were limited. The army was commanded by his personal followers, and they still had all the guns. Furthermore, the exodus from Burma over the previous thirteen years of many able public figures, including experienced administrators and politicians, technologists and economists, educators, and professionally trained persons generally had drained the country of needed leadership. The country and its resources would outlast the aging dictator (who again visited a British hospital in 1974), but the shape of Burma's future was hard to predict.

Summary of the Postwar Experience

The course of Burma's postwar history and its hardships have much in common with other newly independent colonies, and much that is peculiar to that country. In the realm of politics, alien democratic institutions proved particularly difficult to operate, not only because they were alien but because the country was ravaged by war and riven by economic and ethnic antagonisms. Constitutional government faltered and fell, unable to cope with political and economic problems and to bridge chasms of distrust separating articulate minority peoples. Yet the alternative of army rule along Marxist lines had no greater success. Power proved corrupting, and no mechanism existed to protect human rights and provide means for redress of legitimate grievances.

In the field of economics, native and historically rooted xenophobia combined with Marxist principles to the detriment of growth and development. Vindictive and arbitrary discrimination against alien residents, whether workers, traders, moneylenders, or former colonial investors, brought about loss of productivity, lack of consumer goods, and consequently suffering for the public. Traditional Burman hostility to foreigners betrayed national interests and provided no valid expression of national ideals. On the other hand, repeated political exhortations to pursue utopian ideals of a state devoid of exploitation, whether U Nu's Pyidawatha or Ne Win's Burmese Way to Socialism, proved futile in the absence of realistic development policies and essential administrative competence. Doctrinaire concern to end worker and peasant exploitation, even if sincere, ignored the need for realistic efforts to elicit the cooperation of indigenous leadership for achieving feasible objectives. Finally, the need to offer incentives for honesty and efficient performance on the part of employers and laborers, cultivators, people's stores operators, directors of cooperatives, and government officials generally, could hardly be dismissed as a nefarious creation of capitalism. It had to be taken into account as an essential aspect of human nature.

In the international context, Burma's isolationism and mistrust yielded positive consequences in view of the disasters that befell other parts of Southeast Asia. The country managed to maintain a measure of identity and self-respect as a sovereign nation. It refused to be used or bullied by outside powers and refrained from hostile actions against its neighbors, nor did it become involved in the great powers' struggle which took such a heavy toll in Indochina. Burma's leaders wanted no repetition of the dire experiences of World War II. They accepted assistance at times from various sources without becoming the puppet or dependency of any donor, and this despite Burma's critical geographical position.

As part of this effort to preserve the country's independence and identity, successive governments also tried to promote self-sufficiency in producing essential needs, and in adjusting patterns of consumption to fit available resources. Both men and women, and youth also, wear their old-fashioned cotton longyis without complaint, while hoping that some friendly visitor would provide the moth balls to preserve what modern woolen clothing they still possess. Buddhism still continues to be very much alive, even though the partisanship of the depleted ranks of the monks has largely subsided. Religion has provided a focus of reverence, an undergirding sanction of ethical and social values, the capacity to endure the fumbling efforts of successive governments, and above all a rational explanation of events based on the impermanence and relative insignificance of mundane affairs. The indigenously operated Christian churches of the Karen, Chin, and Kachin minorities also continue to thrive. Burma's valuable resources of soil and water, oil, minerals, timber, and transportation facilities remain largely intact, while its assets of intelligence and manpower would also be adequate if some measure of political and economic freedom could assure their availability. The people of the countryside continue to await the coming of that wise and righteous ruler, who would command the appropriate Karma credentials to restore an atmosphere of creativity and peace.

Glossary

Adipadi, leader (Fuehrer), head of state

Ahmudan, royal status service group

Anashin Mingyi, lit. "dictator prince," Ba Maw's wartime title

Asu, royal service unit

Athi, non-royal service group

Athin, synonym for *asu*

Baho, central or headquarters; early Burmese wartime authority

Bhikku, learned Buddhist monk

Bo or *Boh,* colonel rank in the Burmese army; title appropriated by any leader of an armed band

Bogyoke, army general officer

Bu athin, secret village organization of 1920s

Byedaik, office of the assistant interior palace officials; lit., bachelor quarters

Dacoit, armed brigand

Dhamma, fundamental Buddhist law

Dobama Asiayone, We Burmans Society

Einshemin, heir-apparent to the throne; lit. "Lord of the Eastern House"

Gaing-gyok, top officer of the district monastic hierarchy, a kind of bishop

Gaung, head person, village constable

Gyi, big or great, widely used as a suffix

Hlutdaw, royal council chamber; lit. "place of release" of royal decrees

Karma, the Buddhist law of deeds

Kempetai, Japanese military police

Konbaung, Burma's last royal dynasty

Ko-yin, novice Buddhist monk

Kutho, Buddhist merit

Kyat, Burmese coin, theoretically worth 21 cents

Kyaung, monastery

Kyaungtha, monastery students

Kyedangyi, village official, largest taxpayer

Ludu, the mass population

Maha, great

Mahadan-wun, royally appointed ecclesiastical censor

Mahathera, Buddhist teacher of 20 years standing; lit., "great teacher"

Maung, Mr., used in referring to oneself, or for younger males

Min, prince or royal official

Mingyi, great prince

Minami Kikan, Japanese-sponsored youthful rebel group

Myo, town or township domain

Myochit, "love of country" party, organized by U Saw

Myook, township officer under colonial rule

Myosa, princely fief holder; lit., "eater of the town"

Myosade, sacrificial dedication of a city gate or wall

Myothugyi, township headman, royally approved

Myowun, royal provincial governor or burden bearer

Nat, spirit being

Pon, glory or prestige; a respected village elder possessed *pon*

Pongyi, possessor of great glory, used for senior Buddhist monk

Pwe, popular dramatic performance

Pyidawtha, lit. "pleasant or happy country," or welfare state

Sangha, order or assembly of monks

Sangha Sametggi, monks' political council

Sasana (Pali), religious teachings

Sawbwa, Shan chief or prince

Saya, respected teacher

Sayadaw, royal title for abbot of monastery

Shin pyu, initiatory ceremony for Buddhist *Ko-yin*

Shwe, gold

Shwedaik, gold house or treasury archives at court

Sinyetha Party, "poor man's party," sponsored by Ba Maw in 1936 election

Swaraj, name of Hindu freedom party, freedom

Taikthugyi, circle headman, alternative to *myothugyi*

Taung, hill

Taungtha, hill people

Taungya, hillside cultivation

Thakin, master or lord; title assumed by youthful nationalists in
   1930s

Thathameda, tax on non-agricultural income, upper Burma

Thathanbaing, court-appointed head of the Buddhist Sangha

Thanat, rifle or firearm

Thanat Wun, defense Minister

Thugyi, village headman

U, term used in reference to respected elders, never for oneself; lit.,
   "uncle"

Vinaya, (Pali) , monastic discipline

Wun, burden, or burden bearer; high government official

Wundauk, assistant (or prop) to the *Wungyi* Ministers of the
   Hlutdaw

Wungyi, royal Minister of state; "great burden bearer"

Wunsa, family food reserve retained after harvest

Wunthanu athin, organization for protection of the national interest, 1920s

Yoma, mountain range

Bibliographical Essay

Among the accessible reference materials on the early history of Burma the most useful are the Chronicles. The last and the most authentic nineteenth-century royal Chronicle, the *Hmannan Yaza-win,* was based on a classic literary account of the early eighteenth century, which carried the story to 1721. It was repeatedly updated and revised in 1832, 1867, and 1885. Selected portions of the final draft (Burmese edition, Mandalay, 1908) were translated into English by Gordon C. Luce and Pe Maung Tin in 1923 (London, Oxford Press) under the title, *The Glass Palace Chronicle of the Kings of Burma.* The first comprehensive British accounts of Burma's history by Phayre and Harvey owed much to their access to the Burmese versions of the *Hmannan Yazawin* and its *Konbaungset* supplement.

The Chronicles were invariably court-sponsored, and they therefore reflected the objectives and viewpoints of the rulers rather than portraying a critically accurate historical record. They dealt primarily with political considerations, such as royal succession, warfare or rebellion, the meritorious (kutho) deeds of royalty, lineage claims, and adaptations from legendary and fictional prehistorical accounts calculated to enhance the prestige of the sponsoring dynasty. The royal scribes, following the Buddhist tradition, usually suggested that their accounts illustrated the principle of the impermanence of mere earthly existence, but might provide moral guidance drawn from the stories of legendary or actual activities of the rulers considered. History under the Chronicles was thus as much a literary exercise as a description of events, and was designed to denigrate the role of dynastic enemies and to enhance the prestige of favored rulers.

The first British historian who undertook to reconstruct Burma's history on the basis of the royal Chronicles was Arthur P. Phayre, a career military and civilian official of the Indian service from 1828–1867. Phayre's *History of Burma,* was completed after his retirement and was finally published in London in 1883. It was based on the *Hmannan* Chronicle but it did not presume to carry the story past 1837, the date of his arrival in Arakan. A number of earlier portions of the *History* appeared previously in various issues of the *Journal of the Asiatic Society of Bengal.* Like the authors of his Chronicle sources, Phayre evinced little interest in describing governmental operations and even less in social, economic, and cultural developments. His was a history of the Burma kingdom itself; he relegated modern European contacts to a final appendix chapter. The classic monograph of his associate in the India civil service, Henry Yule, entitled *A Narrative of the Mission Sent by the Governor-General of India to the Court of Ava in 1855* (London, 1858), owed much to Phayre's own notes and to his generous collaboration. Phayre's communications with India's governor-general during the early period of his service in lower Burma were later edited by D. G. E. Hall in *The Dalhousie-Phayre Correspondence* (London, 1932). Despite the facts that Phayre lacked formal academic training and that his concept of history was narrowly chronological and political, he contributed significantly to the portrayal of Burma's history.

The preparation of the more detailed standard history of Burma to 1824 was the work of another British official of a later generation, G. E. Harvey. His *History of Burma from the Earliest Times to the Beginning of the English Conquest* was eventually published in London in 1925. Although Harvey's standard account was both informative and interestingly written, later scholars such as Furnivall discounted a number of his interpretations on the ground that he was not fully competent in written and spoken Burmese. Harvey's subsequent effort to continue the story down to World War II, in *British Rule in Burma, 1824–1942* (London, 1946) demonstrated little acquaintance with the enormous accumulation of British colonial sources then available and was therefore far less satisfactory than his early work. Meanwhile, John Nisbet's detailed two-volume *Burmah Under British Rule and Before* had appeared in London in 1901, but it also left much to be desired.

Other studies on nineteenth century Burma were contributed by foreign visitors, mainly British diplomatic agents and missionaries who added materially to the more traditional sources. The diplomatic emissary sent twice by the government of India, Michael Symes, wrote revealing accounts of his successive visits to the Burma court in 1794 and 1802. His *Account of an Embassy to the Kingdom of Ava* (London, 1800) was promptly published, but the journal of his second visit was long denied publication, possibly because it was too sympathetically favorable to the Burmese court. It was finally published in London in 1955 under the able editorship of D. G. E. Hall as *Michael Symes: Journal of His Second Embassy to the Court of Ava in 1802*. Hall's eighty-page introduction is particularly valuable. Also interesting, although somewhat less dependable was John Crawfurd's *Journal of an Embassy from the Governor General of India in the Year 1827* (London, 1834).

Father Vincentius Sangermano, a long-time Italian resident in Burma (before and after 1800) contributed his *A Description of the Burmese Empire* which was translated into English and published in Rome in 1833 and in Rangoon in 1885. Perhaps the most useful American missionary commentary on the early British colonial period was Howard Malcom's story of his visit to Burma in 1837, entitled *Travels in Southeastern Asia, Embracing Hindustan, Siam, and China, and a Full Account of the Burman Empire*, 2 volumes (Boston, 1839). Malcom's visit was short, but he apparently drew heavily on information provided by Adoniram Judson and other resident American missionaries. Somewhat less useful was the later contribution of Father Bigandet, *An Outline of the History of the Catholic Mission from the Year 1720 to 1887* (Rangoon, 1887).

Immediately prior to and following the British annexation of upper Burma in 1885, a number of historical and descriptive monographs appeared, written by articulate British officials with first hand experience in the country. Prominent among them were the writings of Sir James George Scott, long an official resident of upper Burma and the Shan states. His earliest and classic study was entitled *The Burman: His Life and Notions*, which appeared under the pseudonym Shway Yoe (Golden Honest) in London in 1882, 1896, and 1910 and was reissued in New York in 1963. A few years later Scott contributed *Burma as It Was, as It Is, and as It Will Be* (London, 1886), and subsequently *Burma From the Earliest to the Present* (London, 1924 and 1925). Scott introduced a new pattern of paying major attention to the Burmese people themselves rather than to their rulers and the invading foreigners. The same pattern was continued by H. Fielding Hall in his mildly patronizing *The Soul of a People* (London, 1899) and *A People at School* (London, 1906 and 1913).

The political aspects of the British colonial conquest during the mid-1880s were covered in a moving first hand account by Geary Grattan entitled *Burma, after the Conquest, Viewed in its Political, Social, and Commercial Aspects, from Mandalay* (London, 1886). Governor Sir Charles Crosthwaite described later aspects of the same story from 1887 in his *The Pacification of Burma* (London, 1912). A later Governor, Sir Herbert Thirkell White, wrote more modestly of his incumbency immediately following retirement in *A Civil Servant in Burma* (London, 1913). White's *Burma* appeared in London in 1923. Historical contributions were few during the period of World War I and the political turbulence of the 1920s.

Two retiring civil service officials, John S. Furnivall and Maurice Collis, opened a new chapter in the evaluation of colonial rule in the early thirties. Furnivall was a long time member of the land settlement administration. More than any other individual spokesman, he shattered the ban previously imposed on the open discussion of prevailing political and economic problems by such groups as the Burma Research Society. Furnivall's first contribution was *An Introduction to the Political Economy of Burma* (Rangoon, 1931), which was substantially revised by Professor J. Russell Andrus in 1938 and 1957. It was followed by his *Progress and Welfare in Southeast Asia* (New York, 1941), *Education and Social Progress in Southeast Asia* (New York, 1943), and the classic *Colonial Policy and Practice: A Comparative Study of Burma and Netherlands Indies,* written during the war and published in 1948 and 1956 in New York. Furnivall's *Governance of Modern Burma* appeared in New York, 1958. Illustrative of his historical interests was "The Fashioning of the Leviathan: the Beginnings of British Rule in Burma" in the *Journal of the Burma Research Society* (1939), pp. 1–137. For a full listing of Furnivall's writings, see Frank Trager's, *Furnivall of Burma, an Annotated Bibliography* (New York, 1963).

Maurice Collis was a more accomplished writer than either Harvey or Furnivall and was the author of eight or more books about Burma and its people. He served in various Burma civil service capacities during the twenties and thirties. His *Siamese White,* which appeared in London in 1935 and 1936, covered an interesting historical episode dating from the 1680s. His more significant *Trials in Burma* (London, 1938, 1945, and 1953) concerned the difficulties attending his judicial experience at Rangoon and qualified as required reading for all serious students of the period. His later books included *The Land of the Great Image* (London, 1943) concerning Arakan, *The Lords of the Sunset* (London, 1938) related to the Shans, along with others which he discusses so engagingly in *The Journey Up, Reminiscences, 1934–1968* (London, 1970).

Other significant historical contributions from the civil service ranks included numerous settlement department reports by Furnivall and others, particularly U Tin Gyi's *Report on the Original Settlement Operations in Labutta Township 1924–1925*. James Baxter's *The Report on Indian Immigration* and B. W. Swithinbank's *Report of the Bribery and Corruption Enquiry Committee, 1940* (both 1941) also merit special mention.

Another dimension was added to the study of the history of Burma with the establishment of the independent University of Rangoon in 1922. The two most distinguished British historians associated with the university were Professors Gordon H. Luce and D. G. E. Hall. Luce was essentially a philologist and epigrapher, a linguist, and a poet. His principal area of historical interest related to medieval China and Burma's Pagan dynasty. His year-long course in East Asian history usually ended around the close of the Ming dynasty. Luce mastered not only Old Mon and Old Burmese, but also Sanskrit, Pali, and Chinese languages plus a number of the minority people tongues. He was interested in inscriptions and episodes rather than in narrative history, and a number of his early contributions were published in the *Journal of the Burma Research Society* from 1923 to 1941. Luce's magnum opus, entitled *Old Burma-Early Pagán* (Locust Valley, N.Y., 1970), was a massive three-volume work, only a portion of the first volume being historical text. The rest portrayed a complete photographic reproduction of the hundreds of inscriptions and carved plaques associated with the principal monuments of Pagan, together with translations and commentary, sometimes presented in poetry. Associated with the preparation of the book was U Ba Shin, a Burmese Muslim scholar and once my own student in Judson College. His other prominent Burmese student collaborator was U Than Tun, who earned a Ph.D. at the University of London in 1955 with a thesis on

Buddhism in the Pagan period. Than Tun became the author of a number of journal articles in 1959 and three studies covering the history of Burma from 1000 to 1400. Luce's dedicated contribution to early Burmese history was beyond calculation.

Professor D. G. E. Hall was a more orthodox political historian, concerned primarily with the modern period of Burma's history following the arrival of the Europeans. His advanced lecture course at the university was in the field of modern European history. In addition to his two previously mentioned monographs on the Phayre-Dalhousie correspondence and the second mission of Michael Symes, Hall contributed a number of significant historical items to the *Journal of the Burma Research Society* while teaching at the university. His one monograph of the period was entitled *Early English Intercourse with Burma, 1587–1743* (London, 1928 and 1968). As Professor of History at the School of Oriental and African Studies at London after 1933, Hall expanded the scope of his earlier study under the title *Europe and Burma: A Study of European Relations with Burma from the Earliest Times to the Annexation of Thibaw's Kingdom* (London, 1945). He also published a brief monograph entitled *Burma* for the Hutchinson University Library series (London, 1950 and 1956). Hall's comprehensive *History of South-East Asia* appeared in London in 1955 and went through several later revisions and numerous reprintings down to 1968. Professor Hall, unlike Luce, was a professionally trained narrative historian, scholarly and meticulously accurate. His approach nevertheless was essentially politically oriented with emphasis on the role of Europeans in the modern history. He tended at times to be defensively apologetic with respect to Britain's colonial role, although highly critical of both the Dutch and the French roles in Southeast Asia.

Also on the staff of the University of Rangoon was Lecturer W. S. Desai, a native of Bombay, who taught Indian history. Desai contributed two books: *History of the British Residency in Burma, 1826–1840* (Rangoon, 1939) and later *India and Burma* (Calcutta, 1954). On the Judson College side of the campus, Professor J. Russell Andrus was engaged during the 1930s in writing his *Burmese Economic Life*, published by Stanford University Press in 1947. Professor B. R Pearn of University College was also exploring sources on various aspects of nineteenth century Burmese history and published his useful *History of Rangoon* (Rangoon, 1939).

It was into this moderately active scholarly milieu of Rangoon

University of 1935 to 1938 that I moved as head of the history department of Judson College and as Hall's successor as lecturer for the honours course in modern European history. The principal difficulty was that most advanced history courses were designed to prepare candidates for the civil service examinations, which were laden with a surfeit of political minutia. Although asked repeatedly to assist Luce in the completion of the modern aspects of his China history course (three centuries in four weeks), I was flatly refused permission to teach modern Far Eastern history on my own. Since I lack training in Oriental languages, being limited to English and Western European sources, my first research venture at Rangoon and enroute home in 1938 focused on the role which the French had played in Southeast Asia and the Far East in modern times. The study was suspended during World War II. My serious study of Burmese history began in 1943, when I went to Washington as Burma analyst in the research and analysis branch of the wartime Office of Strategic Services. In April 1945, I moved over to the State Department as the first Burma desk officer, then became a member of staff of the reopened consulate-general at Rangoon in early 1946, and subsequently head of intelligence research for Southern Asia, including Burma. I managed to contribute to a substantial I.P.R. publication in 1948 on *The Development of Self-Rule and Independence in Burma,* utilizing two research studies, declassified, which I had previously prepared for the O.S.S. I also wrote the Burma chapter for Lennox Mills, *The New World of Southeast Asia* (1949). Returning to academic life in 1949, I completed my *Roots of French Imperialism in Eastern Asia* (1954) while at Cornell in 1952, and then embarked on *The History of Modern Burma.* In the process, I spent ten months on the Rangoon campus, 1955–1956, where I enjoyed limited contacts with both Luce and Furnivall, and the generous help of several Burmese associates, particularly Daw Mya Sein of the university history staff. The Burma history was published by Cornell in 1958, with Ford Foundation support. A supplement was added in 1960.

John L. Christian's *Modern Burma. A Study of Political and Economic Development* (Berkeley) appeared in 1942 and 1943 (London). It was expanded later under the title of *Burma and the Japanese Invader* (Bombay, 1945). Christian had taught in a mission high school in Central Burma in the 1930s, and the book had been intended initially as a Ph.D. dissertation at California. Captain

Christian was killed in mid-1945 by a bomb explosion in the
Rangoon River as his boat approached the dock. As objective history, Christian's book was weak in its handling of economic and
trade matters, and reflected throughout the author's strongly pro-
colonialist convictions. He discounted virtually all expressions of
Burmese nationalism and deprecated particularly the rising tide of
anti-Indian sentiment. Professor Andrus in his informal review of
the book in October 1942, cited some four score mistakes of fact or
interpretation, some of them of major import. The book contained
a useful bibliography.

What I undertook to do additionally in my *History of Modern
Burma* was to explore not only the available monographic references
which Christian had used, but also the Burma government's
voluminous series of published *Reports* covering all aspects of administrative, legislative, and constitutional problems, dating mainly
from 1911 to 1941. These materials were supplemented by the
equally significant but less extensive British government publica-
tions regarding Burma, including many items in the Sessional
Papers of successive Parliaments from 1917 to 1948. Even so, my
research on the *History of Modern Burma* was far from definitive. I
was able to do little more than sample on my way home from
Burma in 1956 the thousands of manuscript volumes relating to
Burma, especially from 1885, deposited in the India (or Commonwealth) Office library in London. The unfinished task can command
the attention of English-speaking scholars over the next generation.

Research in postwar Burmese history has been seriously handicapped because the flow of British governmental documents stopped
abruptly at the end of 1941, and London's interest tended to fade.
Hugh Tinker published two significant studies, one on *Foundations
of Local Self-Government in India, Pakistan, and Burma* (London,
1954) and his illuminating survey of *The Union of Burma, A Study
of the First Years of Independence* (London, 1957, 1959, 1961),
displayed a valiant effort to be objective. Edmund Ronald Leach
described the upper Burma Kachins in his *Political Systems of
Highland Burma* (London, 1954). Maurice Collis did a disappointing study of the role of Governor Sir Reginald Dorman-Smith entitled *Last and First in Burma, 1914–1948* (London, 1956).

One of the most active American students of Burma covering the
last two decades has been Frank N. Trager, who saw duty at
Rangoon in the early fifties during the closing years of the aborted

American Aid Program. He edited the initial draft of the three-volume Human Relations Area Files study of *Burma* (New Haven, 1956) and supervised the preparation of an *Annotated Bibliography of Burma* (New Haven), also in 1956. Trager then directed a study covering *Burma's Role in the United Nations, 1948–1955* (New York, 1956) and edited a monograph on *Marxism in Southeast Asia* (Stanford, 1959), including a Burma chapter by John Seabury Thompson. Trager's *Toward a Welfare State in Burma* (New York, 1958) proved to be vastly over-optimistic. His more ambitious *Burma: From Kingdom to Republic. A Historical and Political Analysis* (New York and London, 1966) was informed on the post-1948 period but demonstrated no substantial scholarly commitment to the colonial period, where his Anglophobic predilections were in evidence. More recently he has edited *Burma: Japanese Military Administration: Selected Documents, 1941–1945* (Philadelphia, 1971), which really extend only to 1943.

Most other American studies about Burma have related to the postwar scene. Josef Silverstein edited and contributed to *Southeast Asia in World War II: Four Essays* (New Haven, 1966), in which Dorothy Guyot presented a useful chapter on "The Burma Independence Army." James F. Guyot contributed an extended and perceptive article on "Bureaucratic Transformation in Burma" in Ralph Brabanti's *Asian Bureaucratic Systems Emergent from the British Imperial Tradition* (Durham, 1966). Lucian Pye's *Politics, Personality, and Nation Building: Burma's Search for Identity* (New Haven, 1962, 1963) was followed by William C. Johnstone's *A Study in Neutralism. Burma's Foreign Policy* (Cambridge, 1963). Richard Butwell produced the standard biography of *U Nu of Burma* (Stanford, 1963). Religion as a factor in Burmese politics has been the subject of several monographs, one by Donald Eugene Smith, *Religion and Politics in Burma* (Princeton, 1965), and another by Fred R. Von der Mehden in *Religion and Nationalism in Southeast Asia; Burma, Indonesia, the Philippines* (Madison, 1963, 1968), E. Sarkisyanz's *Buddhist Backgrounds of the Burmese Revolution* (The Hague, 1965) was a contorted attempt to reconcile Theravada Buddhism with the Marxist objectives of the "Burmese Way to Socialism." Manning Nash contributed his *The Golden Road to Modernity* (New York, 1965) based on a careful study of two upper Burma communities. John Badgley's *Politics Among Burmans; A Study of Intermediate Leaders* (Athens, Ohio, 1970) was added to his succession of informed articles in *The Asian Survey*. He also contributed a chapter to Robert Scalapino's *The Communist Revolution in Asia* (Englewood Cliffs, N.J., 1965). Melford E. Spiro has recently contributed two valuable interpretations of Burmese religion, based on research in 1960–1961: *Burmese Supernaturalism* (New York, 1967), and *Buddhism and Society* (New York, 1970). After 1962, Burma was closed to such research efforts.

Recent progress in the examination of British and New Delhi sources relating to Burma's history includes a number of scholarly monographs. The first one is Cheng Siok Hwa's study on *The Rice Industry of Burma, 1852–1940* (Kuala Lumpur, 1968). Then comes Aparno Banerjee's impressive University of Calcutta dissertation entitled *Anglo-Burmese Relations (1840–1885)*, completed in 1972 but not published. Michael Adas' *The Burma Delta: Economic Development and Social Change on an Asian Rice Frontier* (Wisconsin, 1974) adds a significant dimension to Mrs. Cheng's study. C. L. Keeton's *King Thebaw and the Ecological Rape of Burma* (New Delhi, 1974) covers events prior to the third Anglo-Burman war of 1885. Albert D. Moscotti's *British Policy and the Nationalist Movement in Burma, 1917–1937* (Honolulu, 1974) contributes many details to the generally accepted account. Finally, a particularly valuable study of the Kachin peoples of north Burma has been contributed by Herman G. Tegenfeldt, entitled *A Century of Growth: The Kachin Baptist Church of Burma* (South Pasadena, California, 1974).

It remains to indicate several significant contributions to Burma's history by a number of Western-trained Burmese scholars. Daw Mya Sein, the daughter of U May Aung, completed before the war her *Administration in Burma: Sir Charles Crosthwaite and the Consolidation of Burma* (Rangoon, 1938). Another scholar, Mi Mi Khaing, contributed a delightful study of *The Burmese Family* (Bombay, 1946). U Nu, with some outside help, produced his *Burma Under the Japanese Occupation* (London and New York, 1954); and *Saturday's Son: Memoirs of the Former Prime Minister of Bruma* (tr. by U Law Yone, New Haven, 1975). Burma's postwar President U Ba U published his rather disappointing *My Burma, the Autobiography of a President* (New York, 1959). More significant was Dr. Ba Maw's *Breakthrough in Burma: Memoirs of a Revolution, 1939–1946* (New Haven, 1968), even though his presentation was marred by personal bias and selection of evidence.

The manuscript had to be smuggled out of Ne Win's Burma. U Hla Myint, Economics Professor at Cambridge, has written on the *Economics of Developing Countries* (London, 1964) with special attention to his native Burma, while U Mya Maung of Boston College has provided an incisive critical analysis of the "Burmese Way to Socialism" in *The Asian Survey* for June 1970.

Unfortunately, some evidence has developed suggesting a reversion to traditional concepts of Burmese history. The trend is apparent in the writings of U Htin Aung, a folklore specialist, former rector of the University of Rangoon, and onetime head of the Burma Historical Commission. He is currently an exile resident in the United States. He revived the spirit of the royal Chronicles in *The Stricken Peacock, Anglo-Burman Relations, 1752–1948* (The Hague, 1965) and later in his *History of Burma* (New York, 1967). Patriotic concern is understandable, but hardly his discounting of the valid findings of Western scholarship and his gloating over the forced recanting of U Than Tun, the leading Burman protégé of Gordon Luce. Htin Aung cautiously limits his account to the pre-1948 period, praising all postwar leaders as national heroes. The same reversionist tendency is also apparent in the nationally oriented writing of U Maung Maung, Western law-trained scholar and Burma's Chief Justice under Ne Win. He wrote *Burma in the Family of Nations* (Amsterdam, 1956), *Burma's Constitution* (The Hague, 1959), and *A Trial in Burma, The Assassination of Aung San* (The Hague, 1962). Particularly disturbing was his *Burma and General Ne Win* (New York, 1969), a political biography portraying his subject as a national hero and political paragon.

Index

World Bank, role of, 212, 258, 276
World Federation of Trade Unions, 203
World Health Organization, 209
wundauk officials, 47
wungyi officials, 47
Wunthanu athins, 110, 112, 116, 119, 131, 152

Yan Naing, Bo, 261
Yandabo, treaty of, 62–64
Young Men's Buddhist Association, 101
Young Pongyis' Association, 148
Youth Front, 221
Yung-li in Yunnan, 50

Zaw Seng, 241

The American Foreign Policy Library

The United States and the Arab World   THIRD EDITION
William R. Polk

The Balkans in Our Time   REVISED EDITION   Robert Lee Wolff

The United States and Burma   John F. Cady

The United States and Canada   Gerald M. Craig

The United States and the Caribbean   REVISED EDITION
Dexter Perkins

The United States and China   THIRD EDITION
John King Fairbank

The Americans and the French   Crane Brinton

The United States and India, Pakistan, Bangladesh
W. Norman Brown

The United States and Ireland   Donald Harman Akenson

The United States and Israel   Nadav Safran

The United States and Italy   REVISED EDITION   H. Stuart Hughes

The United States and Japan   THIRD EDITION
Edwin O. Reischauer

The United States and Malaysia   James W. Gould

The United States and Mexico   REVISED EDITION, ENLARGED
Howard F. Cline

The United States and North Africa: Morocco, Algeria, and Tunisia
Charles F. Gallagher

Scandinavia   REVISED EDITION, ENLARGED   Franklin D. Scott

The American Foreign Policy Library